Literary Silences in Pascal, Rousseau, and Beckett

ELISABETH MARIE LOEVLIE

CLARENDON PRESS · OXFORD

OXFORD
UNIVERSITY PRESS

Great Clarendon Street, Oxford OX2 6DP

Oxford University Press is a department of the University of Oxford.
It furthers the University's objective of excellence in research, scholarship,
and education by publishing worldwide in

Oxford New York

Auckland Bangkok Buenos Aires Cape Town Chennai
Dar es Salaam Delhi Hong Kong Istanbul Karachi Kolkata
Kuala Lumpur Madrid Melbourne Mexico City Mumbai Nairobi
São Paulo Shanghai Taipei Tokyo Toronto

Oxford is a registered trade mark of Oxford University Press
in the UK and in certain other countries

Published in the United States
by Oxford University Press Inc., New York

British Library Cataloguing in Publication Data

Data available

Library of Congress Cataloging in Publication Data

Data available

ISBN 0-19-926636-0

1 3 5 7 9 10 8 6 4 2

Typeset by Hope Services (Abingdon) Ltd.
Printed in Great Britain
on acid-free paper by
Biddles Ltd,
Guildford and King's Lynn

ACKNOWLEDGEMENTS

THIS book has emerged through various dialogues, silent and otherwise. I would especially like to thank my thesis supervisor Dr Mike Holland for his invaluable inspiration and Professor Terence Cave and Professor Arne Melberg for their support and comments. Thanks also to my thesis examiners Professor Geoffrey Bennington and Dr Wes Williams for their useful evaluation. Finally warm thanks to Dr Anne-Lise Schibbye, who has carefully read and commented on many versions of the work in progress.

The Research Council of Norway and the ORS scheme have generously provided funding for the completion of this work. Thanks also to Jesus College for financial and academic support.

CONTENTS

INTRODUCTION

> Whether it was the voice of a boy or a girl I cannot say, but again
> and again it repeated the refrain 'Take it and read, take it and
> read'. At this I looked up, thinking hard whether there was any
> game in which children used to chant words like these, but I
> could not remember ever hearing them before. I stemmed my
> flood of tears and stood up, telling myself that this could only be
> a divine command to open my book of Scripture and read the
> first passage on which my eyes should fall. . . . in an instant, as I
> came to the end of the sentence, it was as though the light of
> confidence flooded into my heart and all the darkness of doubt
> was dispelled.
>
> St Augustine, Confessions (1991: 177–8)

> les mots sont là, quelque part, sans faire le moindre bruit, je ne
> sais pas ça non plus, les mots qui tombent, on ne sait pas où, on
> ne sait pas d'où, gouttes de silence à travers le silence
>
> Beckett, L'Innommable (1953: 159)

St Augustine's confession regarding his famous conversion was written at the turn of the fourth century. Beckett's *L'Innommable* was
written in 1953. Surprisingly, perhaps, the two quotations can be read
in dialogue. In their different eras' modes of expression the two
authors address a similar problem, or rather, they celebrate a similar
phenomenon. At stake is the ability of reading and text to give rise to
a mode of language that is irreducible to our normal, everyday
conception of language. Augustine finds the solace of his ultimate conversion through reading. Conversion, however, challenges articulation. I cannot tell someone to believe and expect conversion.
Conversion requires a non-linguistic, non-symbolic experience. Yet
the example suggests that reading can cause conversion, and hence
that text might transcend the limits of the language we rely on for
everyday communication. The quotation from *L'Innommable* echoes
this suggestion by portraying words in terms of silence, 'gouttes de
silence à travers le silence'. Again, everyday, symbolic language cannot become silence. Silence is the absence of symbols, whereas language is always a symbolic mode. Silence starts where language ends.
Or does it? Beckett, by depicting words as drops of silence, indicates

the text as a privileged, different mode of language that might actu-ally become silence. This underlying view of language in text and reading emerges through the two quotations. We are invited to think a language that can become silence, that can convert, that can say the unsayable.

It is this paradox, this seeming impossibility, this ability of texts to say the unsayable that I shall explore as a potential literary silence. More precisely I shall be looking at the relationship between texts and the unsayable, or, as I shall call it, the *non-symbolic*. There are texts that state the specific aim of expressing a truth or meaning that is simultaneously defined as unsayable. These are texts that present a claim to a truth that is non-linguistic. They are texts that insist on writing, on producing text, as a means of disclosing a truth that, and this they also insist, will always slip away from language. In other words, these are texts that approach the silence of the unsayable and that introduce a more or less constant relationship with this silence. My intention is to study this rela-tionship between the text and the silence it strives to express. Interesting are those texts that both posit the impossible silence of the truth in ques-tion, and still profess the aim to express this silence. In other words, the text both conditions and undermines silence. It is this relationship, this dynamic of back and forth that I intend to approach. Because this rela-tionship arises between a literary text and a silence, I have chosen to develop the notion of a *literary silence* which in turn suggests that this silence is a specifically literary dynamic.

If we return to the two quotations above, we are dealing with a view of text that supports the possibility of such a literary silence. Text can behave differently from normal, everyday language, it can become these weird drops of silence that again can create non-rational con-version. The example of Augustine's conversion introduces the ques-tion whether reading can change us in manners that are irreducible to rational explanation: can reading give rise to experiences, insights, meanings that are non-rational, non-linguistic and immediate in nature? Can a text produce dynamics that in turn move the text towards becoming its own silence? It is this question, this paradox, that inspires this book. My overarching aim is to explore how and if a text can become the privileged mode of (silent) experiences that every-day language cannot contain, and how reading texts can change us by giving us (silent) immediate insights.

In order to explore further these indications, I shall focus on two questions that have produced two hypotheses. First, how does the text become literary silence? My hypothesis is that there are dynamics in the text that indicate the ability of text to become the unsayable, to witness the non-symbolic and continue where everyday language would fall silent. My intention is to be able to recognize and identify these dynamics and thereby show how text can become the dynamic of the unsayable. By studying texts that range from the seventeenth to the twentieth century it will also be possible to determine how literary silence behaves as a historic dynamic, if indeed it does behave as a historical dynamic. The second question concerns the reading of literary silence: how does one read literary silence? My second hypothesis is that to read literary silence, or to read the unsayable, is to be willing to enter into a relationship with the text that permits alternative experiences of text and language. I shall delineate, as far as possible, how this reading will take place, and what theoretical and methodological frameworks are required.

The study is divided into two sections. The first section I have called 'Describing Literary Silence', and it includes Chapters 1–3. I have here chosen to underscore the descriptive rather then the explicative aspect, a choice that is linked to the nature of literary silence. As will become clear, this is a concept that escapes objective analysis and empirical description. To pretend to explain it is therefore not only misleading, but also reductive. It is a dynamic that can be described, pointed towards, circled around and indicated, but never fully analysed. The aim of Part I is to approach the concept itself, delineate its dynamics, and provide theoretical associations and nuances. Whereas Part I is more theoretical and descriptive, Part II, called 'Exploring Literary Silence', is a textual exploration of the concept (Chapters 4–6). I shall be discussing Pascal's *Pensées*, Rousseau's *Rêveries*, and Beckett's trilogy of novels. I shall also refer to Mallarmé and some of his observations regarding the role of silence. The choice of the main texts is motivated by two main factors. First of all the texts actively relate to and explore the limits and borders of language as they all seek to 'say the unsayable'. In other words, they actively relate to the silent non-symbolic, and it is my hypothesis that through such an active relation the text will stage the different dynamics whereby reading can emerge as an experience of literary silence. Second, the choice of texts represents what can be seen as three different versions of the non-symbolic: Pascal's non-symbolic God, Rousseau's non-symbolic Self, and Beckett's, what we might for the time being call, non-symbolic 'nothing'. The choice of texts is of course based on a decision to exclude other texts that would also lend themselves to readings of silence. Flaubert's work is one such omission that is worth mentioning. A consideration of his work might in turn have led to a slightly different understanding of silence and of the non-symbolic. Without going into detail, we can say that a reading of Flaubert might have steered the direction of this exploration towards considering a *silencing* of characters and of their immediate surroundings, whereas the choice of reading Mallarmé (and especially Blanchot's reading of Mallarmé) rather emphasizes a silencing of language itself that is central to my understanding of literary silence. I underscore this merely to indicate the possibility of exploring different histories, or 'stories', of the role of silence in literature.

Part I has been divided into three chapters. The first chapter, 'Moving towards Literary Silence', is an attempt to delineate the relationship between silence and text. The chapter is largely a bibliographic overview of other approaches to silence and text, but also indicates the first move towards literary silence. Central are Maurice Blanchot's observations on silence and literature as articulated in 'Mort du dernier écrivain' (1959). The first chapter also introduces some of the major concepts and the three different authors. The second chapter is a theoretical exploration of literary silence. The concept requires a theoretical context, a theoretical 'make-up'. I will develop these by associating the concept in relation to Gadamer's hermeneutics and French post-structuralist thought. I shall experiment with words such as play, force, and dialogue and see what aspects of literary silence they highlight. The notion of the literary will also be discussed in more detail. As mentioned above, literary silence cannot be empirically exhausted, and the intention is therefore to provide theoretical *descriptions*, not explanations. The same delimited aim characterizes Chapter 3. This can be called a methodological chapter, although it is not a traditional declaration of method. My intention is to identify and name the dynamics of literary silence in the text. Whereas Chapter 2 describes the concept itself, Chapter 3 describes what can be called the 'behaviour' of literary silence in the text. I shall focus on three dynamics: repetition, aporia, and what I define as implosion. Again, these do not systematically exhaust literary silence. Rather they are pointers or indicators that permit a focusing on the dynamics of literary silence in the actual text and the experience of reading these dynamics. As such these notions are methodological tools; they inform my approach to the text.

Part II consists of three main chapters, each one focusing on one author. Although the order is historical, I should forewarn that my intention is not primarily to provide a historical analysis of literary silence. Because literary silence is a dynamic that arises in the moment of reading, it is intrinsic to my contemporary historical horizon. As it is not my aim to provide a history of readings, any attempts at reviewing how literary silence changes, or does not change, throughout the centuries, would be limited to speculation. Within the scope of this exploration, it is therefore more interesting to consider how literary silence behaves as a temporal dynamic in the moment of reading. Despite this reservation, some readers might still question the lack of any nineteenth-century text. However, the choice of Rousseau and Beckett partly make up for this. Rousseau's project is so clearly pre-romantic, thereby foreshadowing the nineteenth century. In a similar manner, Beckett's texts are a result of the transition into the thought of modernism that also took place in the late nineteenth century. In other words, both authors can be traced to the nineteenth century. Having said this, literary critical thought undergoes some important changes in the time that elapses between the pre-romantics and the late modernists. This transition can best be summed up as a renewed reflection regarding the literary text's awareness of itself as literature. This new willingness to investigate and probe the realm of the literary can perhaps best be traced in the works of Stéphane Mallarmé. In order to account for this transition and its influence on literary silence, I have included an 'Interlude' between Chapters 5 and 6. The intention is to show how this period, represented here by Mallarmé, witnessed certain innovative thoughts regarding the relationship between text and silence, and how this in turn affected the status of the unsayable. I shall focus primarily on Blanchot's reading of Mallarmé and specifically on the idea of a *langue poétique*. This prepares the scene for my reading of Beckett as it indicates how the innovations in question also affect the dynamic of literary silence.

The first section of the book provides the theoretical apparatus that allows us to think literary silence as a concept. Part II provides three close readings that will explore how this dynamic is manifest in the texts and how we read it. Ultimately the aim is to trace a concept, both theoretically and in texts, that can provide further insight into the experience of reading as a unique and singular experience. By singular experience, I mean an experience that is irreducible to ordinary language, that cannot be summarized, that is singular to reading text.

Furthermore I shall view this experience in the light of the immediately unsayable—exactly that which escapes our everyday language. The text will therefore be explored as a unique 'playground' where language reaches for new, unheard-of horizons. Literature, as the art of words, is the place where language itself can reveal its own difference from everyday language. To study how this happens is to study how the text can become a privileged place that can give rise to different relationships to the world and to ourselves, articulated through language.

I

Describing Literary Silence

MOVING TOWARDS LITERARY SILENCE

INTRODUCTION

For the critic to approach and define a concept of silence is to approach a seductive concept. To seduce, from *seducere*, means to lead astray or to separate from, and my suggestion is that a critical approach to silence can easily be led astray, separated from its original intention. First of all, silence resists empirical observation and description. It cannot be analysed as a thing or an object, it cannot be pointed to or defined. Silence slips away from description: to talk of it is to lose it, or at least to defer it. As such, silence is always just ahead of our critical discourse, seducing us to follow it just one step further in the attempt to catch it, but never there to be caught. Critical discourse about silence lags behind its object of study. The seductive impact of silence is also linked to what might be called its flexibility. Silence, precisely because it is not a definable, graspable thing, is subject to numerous different understandings and can be used in a sufficiently vague manner to make it serve many purposes. It is available for various projections of meaning because no meaning or definition can 'match' the notion of silence; it is always already somewhere else.

Writing about silence, I have necessarily, and willingly, been seduced in the sense that I have not attempted to approach silence as an empirical object. Rather I suggest that the seductive impact of silence reveals more about silence than most analysis by showing that silence cannot be approached *objectively*. Therefore my intention is not first and foremost to overcome this seductive impact by pretending to approach silence *objectively*. Rather my intention is to show that the seductive appeal of silence has led to a topos of silence that presupposes and reproduces a limited understanding of silence.

In this chapter I hope to understand more about the seductive appeal of silence by tracing this topos through what I shall call the Dream of Silence and see how this colours critical approaches to silence. Having traced the seductive appeal of silence, I will ask whether it is possible to move towards a different understanding of silence and its relationship to the literary text. I will turn to the author and critic Maurice Blanchot and his essay 'Mort du dernier écrivain' (1959) and see how it delineates a radical departure from the topos of silence. Based on my reading of Blanchot's essay, I shall suggest a first understanding of literary silence and the textual dynamics it describes. Finally I shall present some of the project's main terms, including the notion of the literary, and introduce the three authors that I will be reading.

THE DREAM OF SILENCE: A SEDUCTIVE TOPOS

As suggested above, silence owes its flexibility and seductive appeal to the difficulty we experience in providing a positive definition of silence. What is silence? Where is it? John Cage, in his collection of lectures and essays entitled *Silence*, observes:

In fact, try as we may to make silence, we cannot. For certain engineering purposes, it is desirable to have as silent a situation as possible. Such a room is called an anechoic chamber, its six walls made of special material, a room without echoes. I entered one at Harvard University several years ago and heard two sounds, one high and one low. When I described them to the engineer in charge, he informed me that the high one was my nervous system in operation, the low one my blood in circulation. Until I die there will be sounds. (Cage 1999: 8)

Even in a silent chamber there are sounds. Cage's observation reveals two things. First of all it presupposes silence as the absence of noise. The quest for silence leads one to a silent chamber, thereby excluding any noise. This is in accordance with a common-sense approach to silence, namely to see it as the dualistic opposite of noise.[1] Secondly Cage's observation claims that silence, as such, is impossible. There will always be noise.[2] Silence, then, is impossible according to its most basic definition. But rather than lead to a rejection of the concept, this impossibility is inherent in the *mystique* of silence. Although scientifically unfeasible, silence is poetically still a possible reality, still an ideal to be sought. It is still talked of, still dreamt of, still largely a romanticised notion. Precisely because it cannot be fixed, because it cannot be

---

[1] *The Oxford English Dictionary* defines silence as 'The state of condition when nothing is audible; absence of all sound or noise, complete quietness or stillness; noiselessness'.

[2] Vladimir Jankélévitch's work *La Musique et l'ineffable* makes a similar point by claiming that 'ce silence lui-même n'est jamais complet' and 'le silence n'est donc pas non-être' (Jankélévitch 1961: 171).

pointed to as a positive state or reality, silence is a notion dominated largely by imagination.

Seeking silence in a silent chamber is to seek silence as the dualistic opposite of noise. However, the dualistic understanding of silence also has another aspect. Silence is also the opposite of language. This is arguably the second most universal understanding of silence.[3] When there is talk of silence, Wittgenstein's famous sentence from *Tractatus Logico-Philosophicus* is regularly alluded to: 'Whereof one cannot speak, thereof one must be silent.' Wittgenstein here famously affirms silence as the opposite of language. Silence is posited as congruent with a sense of a 'beyond' of language, a realm that is free from discourse and linguistic ordering. Wittgenstein implies that silence can give meaning to all those experiences, insights, intuitions, feelings, states 'whereof one cannot speak'. Indirectly, Wittgenstein's observation suggests that silence can 'contain' or support that which language cannot explain. It follows that silence can accept that which the verbal expression must dismiss as irrational or illogical. Silence affirms the existence of a realm of experience that escapes language.

Of course, the positive existence of this silence cannot be scientifically tested. Compared to the silence that remained absent in the silence chamber, this is an unscientific silence. Whether it exists or not is largely a concern of private, theoretical or philosophical opinion.[4] However, it is clear that this less scientific view of silence is central to the notion's seductive allure. Where language fragments, disperses, and transforms the immediate experience, silence remains its designated haven. In short, silence becomes the potential solution to general dissatisfaction with language; it becomes an alternative. And it is as such an alternative that it becomes most seductive. That which is experienced as beyond language can be approached in terms of silence.

---

[3] Cf. the definition of silence in *The Oxford English Dictionary*: 'The fact of abstaining or forbearing from speech or utterance (sometimes with reference to a particular matter); the state or condition resulting from this; muteness, reticence, taciturnity'.

[4] This view of silence does rely upon a specific theory of language, namely one that recognizes that language is limited and that there is something beyond language. As we know, Wittgenstein adopted a different view regarding language in his later work, *Philosophical Investigations* written between 1945 and 1949. At the risk of simplification, we can say that the *Tractatus* offers a view of language as a limited reflection of given reality. The later work, however, considers reality as a reflection or product of language, hence questioning to what extent there is a reality beyond language. Clearly the latter view brings a radical challenge to the more traditional concept of silence as the beyond of language.

It is clear that the value of silence is tied to the shortcomings of language. The sense of shortcomings gives rise to a discontent or distrust in language that repeatedly appears in every culture. Susan Sontag, in what has become one of the classic texts on silence, 'The Aesthetics of Silence', indicates the existence of 'a perennial discontent with language that has been formulated in each of the major civilisations of the Orient and the Occident' (Sontag 1983: 195). In other words, the essence of the discontent barely changes. Language fragments and distorts the Origin and cannot attain the Absolute.[5] Language is blamed for the dispersion of the sense of presence and plenitude that is equated with the mythical, pre-verbal or non-linguistic state. Language, too tainted with the material world, is of course also a poor companion to spiritual enlightenment. Without going into detail, we can see how general distrust in language would spark the dream of a silence that can embrace all that which is not language.

The discontent with language seems to increase in proportion with a certain impoverishment of language that has characterized the second half of the twentieth century. If we consider the accelerated evolution of the information- and image-centred society, we can trace what George Steiner, in 1961, observes as 'the retreat of the word' in the essay with the same title (see Steiner 1985). The 'retreat of the word' is the paradoxical result of the fact that language is everywhere. The broadcasted word, the televised word, and the electronic word literally permeate the atmosphere. But rather than make language richer, this proliferation of words points towards an impoverished and simplified language. Politics, advertisement, media, Internet—all seem to gravitate towards an increasing simplification and devaluation of language accompanied by an increasing valuation of the image and the screen (see Sontag 1983; Steiner 1985). In the wake of this dissatisfaction, silence, as the opposite of language, also takes on increasing value as bearer of truth, before and after language. Max Picard's comment in the classic *The World of Silence* is symptomatic: 'The silence out of which language came is now transformed into the mystery surrounding truth' (Picard 1952: 31).

Silence, we can conclude, is seductive because it is seen as an alternative to what is increasingly experienced as an impoverished state of language. Language proliferates yet its value diminishes, and a

---

[5] We are of course reminded of Rousseau's *Essai sur l'origine des langues*, where the ideal state of nature is largely defined as non-linguistic.

general longing for silence arises. But the high value placed on silence can also be traced historically as it relies on any given era's tendency to devalue language and dream of a beyond. It follows that silence can become an important alternative within a linguistic discourse, a historical discourse, a political discourse, a socio-critical discourse, a literary discourse, a religious discourse, an aesthetic discourse—in short, any discourse that is concerned with the dynamics of language, truth, and the beyond. Silence can always be posited as an antidote to the dissatisfaction with language.

The tendency to posit silence as an immediate alternative to fragmenting discourse I shall call the Dream of Silence. By it I designate the tendency exactly to evoke silence as a beyond that is the realm of the unsayable, and to rely on silence as an unverifiable conclusion that leaves nothing more to be said. By calling it a Dream I hope to indicate that this silence cannot be verified or measured, but rather adheres to different categories of experience. The Dream of Silence transcends the silence sought in the silent chamber as it transcends a silence that can be positively indicated. More than anything it is a myth that enables us to accept the insufficiencies of language.

The Dream of Silence has two 'sources' that are crucial to its predominance and seductive impact. A first source is related to the Christian story of the creation of man.[6] The Fall into sin was also the fall into language.[7] In other words, man is forever doomed to speak in fallen language, a language that can never grasp God or the Absolute and that constantly distorts any immediate reality.[8] This story consequently defines silence as congruent with the sense of plenitude, peace, and a continuous relationship with God that existed before the Fall. There can be little doubt about the influence of this narrative on the collective Christian world's attempt to understand the existence of

---

[6] Needless to say, the value of silence first and foremost figures in Oriental religions, such as Taoism and Buddhism. Here enlightenment is achieved by a progressive abandonment of speech and language. Only in silence can truth be released from the claims of logic and reason that characterize language. (See Steiner 1985: 30–1; Dauenhauer 1980: 111.)

[7] The seventeenth-century mystic Jacob Böhme says that Adam, before the Fall, spoke a so-called natural language or sensual speech. This designates a language that is free from the distortion and alienation that characterizes fallen discourse. The original language is thought as one that knew no difference and that coincided perfectly with the world in a relation of similitude. Foucault, of course, tells the same story in *Les Mots et les choses* as he remarks: 'Sous sa forme première, quand il fut donné aux hommes par Dieu lui-même, le langage était un signe des choses absolument certain et transparent . . . Les noms étaient déposés sur ce qu'ils désignaient' (Foucault 1966*b*: 51).

[8] I will develop the notion of fallen discourse in relation to Pascal and Port-Royal in Ch. 4.

man. Both directly and indirectly it validates and fuels the Dream of Silence as the prelapsarian state of blissful knowledge of God and nature.

A second powerful narrative that has shaped our relationship to the Dream of Silence stems from psychoanalysis. Although this is the 'talking cure', it has brought attention to the importance of the pre-linguistic state of the infant. Lacan especially develops the notion of the Imaginary as the stage that precedes the Symbolic.[9] In the Imaginary the infant experiences a continuous relationship with the surroundings. Its reality is immediate, not organized, fragmented, or separated by means of symbols. The entry into language is experienced as a major loss and rupture (though of course also a gain!) in that it fragments and discontinues the continuous sense of being. Silence is identified with the pleasure of immediacy, of wholeness that precedes reflexivity and language. As such psychoanalysis invests the Dream of Silence with the unconscious wish of a possible release from language and return to infancy.

The Dream of Silence elucidates two basic aspects of silence. First of all it can help explain the impact and universality of the seductive impact of silence. As the other of language, silence can represent all our dreams and yearnings for a beyond not ruled by language.[10] Secondly, the Dream of Silence reveals how much is invested in the dualistic understanding of silence as the other of language. Not only is this the dominant, universal access to silence, it is also the one that can sustain the impact of the Dream of Silence. In other words, the Dream of Silence presupposes a dualistic view of silence and language. Consequently the seductive appeal of silence relies upon such a dualistic view.

As I said in the Introduction, my aim is not to overcome the seductive aspect of silence by pretending to an objective approach. However, I do suggest that there might be a different manner of thinking silence that again will challenge the dualistic view of silence that dominates the Dream of Silence. To foreshadow this I intend now to explore possible moves towards an alternative understanding of silence.

[9] See e.g. 'Le stade du miroir comme formateur de la fonction du Je' (Lacan 1966: 89–97); 'Fonction et champ de la parole et du langage en psychanalyse' (ibid.: 111–208).

[10] Brice Parain, in his book *Petite Métaphysique de la parole* (1969), argues that our yearning for freedom is intrinsically linked to our longing for silence. As long as we are in language, he argues, we are necessarily linked to the other and therefore not free in the sense of being solitary (see Parain 1969: 25). The observation underscores the power of our longing for silence.

OTHER CRITICAL APPROACHES TO SILENCE

The overall bibliography of silence is overwhelming and very varied. My intention is therefore not to exhaust it in detail. Such a task seems pointless as well as almost impossible. The more fruitful approach is to delineate the major areas within literary thought that have focused on silence and used it as a tool or concept. I shall consider five such areas that each deals more or less critically with a concept of silence: mystical literature, critical approaches to the Holocaust, feminist criticism, criticism of drama, and linguistic and phenomenological studies. Of course, many approaches overlap and do not distinctly adhere to any one category. However, by subscribing to and discussing these general tendencies, I believe it is possible to draw a sufficiently complete and in-depth picture of the role of silence within both the literary tradition and its criticism.

Mystical literature has a long tradition evoking a privileged silence.[11] It is a silence that signals the shortcomings of language in face of the mystical union with the Absolute. The importance of silence in Christianity can be traced back to frequent mentions of the word in the Bible.[12] However, throughout the tradition of Christian writing, it is mystical writing specifically that has been most concerned with the limits of language. Repeatedly silence arises as a privileged topos that alone can 'contain' the immediate and immaterial spirit (see e.g. Smith 1998). Numerous mystical thinkers are noteworthy in this context, some of the most classic being Pseudo-Dionysius, Hildegard von Bingen, Meister Eckhart, Jacob Böhme, Teresa of Avila, and St John of the Cross.

Typical of the mystical tradition is the quotation from St John of the Cross's *Spiritual Sentences and Maxims*: 'One word spake the Father, which Word was His son, and this Word He speaks ever in eternal silence, and in silence must it be heard by the soul' (St John of the Cross 1974: 228). God's words, as well as any understanding of these

---

[11] Some useful anthologies of mystical literature are *A Dazzling Darkness: An Anthology of Western Mysticism*, ed. Patrick Grant (1985), *Mysticism: A Study and an Anthology*, ed. F. C. Happold (1970), and *An Anthology of Mysticism and Mystical Philosophy*, ed. William Kingsland (1927).

[12] See André Neher, *L'Exil de la parole: du silence biblique au silence d'Auschwitz*. Neher aims to 'pénétrer dans ce chantier où s'élaborent successivement une *morphologie*, une *syntaxe* et une *sémantique* du silence dans la Bible' (Neher 1970: 9).

words, are irreducible to material, symbolic language and hence resound only in silence. Furthermore, to presume to speak of God is sinful in that it reduces God to a symbolic being subject to man's understanding. The anonymous author of *The Cloud of Unknowing* proclaims: 'For I dare not take upon myself with my blundering, earthly tongue to speak of what belongs solely to God' (Anonymous 1978: 95). Teresa of Avila in *Interior Castle*, known in Spanish as *Las Moradas*, writes: 'I am so fearful as I write this that, when it comes to my mind, as is very often the case, I hardly know how to get the words down, or how to go on living' (Teresa of Avila 1974: 20). Mystical literature, perhaps more than any other literary tradition, operates with a devalued notion of language as material, flawed, and ultimately fallen (see Sontag 1983: 195). Against this dissatisfaction, silence arises as the only perfect medium for any understanding of God. Needless to say, the Dream of Silence dominates the mystical view of silence.

The mystical tradition is the most obvious place to look for a coherent view of silence. However, there are other areas of literary tradition that also seek silence when faced with experiences of the unsayable. Silence, for example, reappears as an important topos in literature dealing with the Holocaust and the Nazi concentration camps. It here designates the opposite spectre of the unspeakable, namely that which is inhuman or an unspeakable atrocity.[13] Hannah Arendt, in her book *On Revolution*, remarks: 'Where violence rules absolutely, as for instance in the concentration camps of totalitarian regimes . . . everything and everybody must remain silent' (Arendt 1963: 9). Faced with the cruelties of the Nazi regime it is as if human discourse falls silent, unable to grasp that which has trespassed its explanatory abilities. Elie Wiesel is perhaps the one author that most explicitly testifies to this distrust of language and its accompanying call for silence (see Sibelman 1995). His authorship represents a general wariness of the disparity and incongruence between language and the event itself. Symbolic language cannot do it justice. We recall the famous words of Adorno: 'No poetry after Auschwitz'. To translate into language the experiences of Auschwitz can be seen as invariably reductive of the evil that took place. To suggest that it is possible to talk of the events

---

[13] Some critical approaches dealing with silence and the Holocaust in different manners are Deborah Lefkowitz (1999), 'On Silence and Other Disruptions'; Ernestine Schlant (1999), *The Language of Silence: West German Literature and the Holocaust*; Roger S. Gottlieb (1990), *Thinking the Unthinkable: Meanings of the Holocaust*; and André Neher (1970) *L'Exil de la parole: du silence biblique au silence d'Auschwitz*.

of the Holocaust is often seen to imply that these events are explicable and that they can be made meaningful.

However, the literary criticism addressing issues concerning the Holocaust also talks of dynamics of repression, denial, and shame in terms of silence. This is a negative silencing. Therefore the value placed on silence is paralleled with a repeated call for testimony against and through the silence; Auschwitz must not be forgotten. It is possible perhaps to distinguish between a silence *of* the Holocaust and the silence *about* the Holocaust (ses Schlant 1999: 1–20). The challenge then is to guard the former silence while repeatedly breaking the latter.

The silence that arises through the events of the Holocaust underscores both the degree of evil of the Holocaust and the impotence of discourse. It is a silence that bears witness to the unthinkable—the dissolution of what language can tolerate. Although it seems inappropriate to talk about the Dream of Silence, the silence in question still signals the unsayable and thereby fuels a dualistic understanding.

Recently the silence associated with the Holocaust has also triggered feminist accounts, concentrating specifically on the fates of Jewish women during the Second World War.[14] In many ways the silence surrounding the Holocaust is seen as especially relevant to women. This is connected to the role of silence in feminist discourse. Adrienne Rich states: 'The entire history of women's struggle for self-determination has been muffled in silence over and over' (Rich 1979: 11). Jewish women who survived the Holocaust have then arguably experienced a double silencing due to their gender.[15]

From the feminist perspective silence is not so much (although it can be) a mark of the unspeakable or unthinkable, but of repression and silencing of women within the patriarchal society. In their introduction to feminist theory, 'Introduction: "Feminist Paradigms" ',

[14] See Deborah Lefkowitz (1999). Lefkowitz also lists the following studies: Joan Ringelheim (1990), 'Thoughts about Women and the Holocaust'; Myrna Goldberg (1990), 'Different Horrors, Same Hell: Women Remembering the Holocaust'; Carol Rittner and John K. Roth (1993), *Different Voices: Women and the Holocaust*; Marlene E. Heinemann (1986), *Gender and Destiny: Women Writers and the Holocaust*; Claudia Koonz (1987), *Mothers in the Fatherland: Women, the Family and Nazi Politics*; and R. Ruth Linden (1993), *Making Stories, Making Selves: Feminist Reflections on the Holocaust*.

[15] It should be mentioned that this view has been rejected by those who object to the distinction between genders as far as the Holocaust is concerned. The fear has been that to talk about Jewish women would weaken the identification of the Jewish fate in the Holocaust. Joan Ringelheim reports that she has been met with such objections. (See J. Ringelheim 1990: 141–9.)

Julie Rivkin and Michael Ryan define the development of feminist literary criticism as an exploration of the 'conditions as well as the limits of its own possibility in language and in literacy' (Rivkin and Ryan 1998: 532). Feminism has largely developed as an exploration of repressed and muffled voices.[16] It has led to an increased awareness and concern regarding who speaks, who holds the word, and the power of naming in patriarchal society. Not surprisingly, the notion of silence has risen as a central topos and an important critical concept for understanding the position and status of women.[17] Silence has the power of testifying both to women's presence (there is an almost audible silence) and absence (there are no voices). Consequently the idea of silenced voices has become a powerful image within feminist rhetoric. In the words of Rivkin and Ryan, feminist discourse 'discovers a field or work that takes it back beyond its own beginning in the emergence from silence into language—to undo the silence of those who still do not speak' (ibid.).

Furthermore, there has been an increasing focus within feminist theory on silences that operate in the literary text such as omissions, self-censorship, gaps, disruptions and discontinuity. These silences reveal the more subtle dynamics of repression. However, they can also be interpreted as operations of resistance to dominant discourse. To choose silence is then viewed as a dynamic of power rather than powerlessness (see Laurence 1994). However, it should be noted that both these forms of silence are largely characterized by being the absence of speech and hence reproduce the largely dominating dualistic view of silence that I have considered so far. Again, it might not be accurate to talk here of the Dream of Silence, as silence again is not a romantic sense of a beyond. But even as a mark of repression and marginal, silenced voices, the feminist notion of silence reproduces and presupposes the more traditional definition of silence as the opposite of discourse and language.

---

[16] Worthy of mention is the study *The Madwoman in the Attic: 19th Century Literature* by Sandra Gilbert and Susan Gubar (1980). Gilbert and Gubar show how women, in literature, are largely silent or silenced. Those who speak up against this silence are stereotyped as mad, unfeminine, and monstrous.

[17] The first study to develop the notion of silence in relation to feminist thought was Tillie Olsen's *Silences* written in 1978. Olsen's book focused largely on the silence of unpublished female authors and on the circumstances that caused this silencing. For a collection of more recent essays that develop the theme of silence in feminist thought see Elaine Hedges and Shelley Fisher Fishkin (1994), *Listening to Silences: New Essays in Feminist Criticism*.

Studies of drama can highlight the use of silence in a different manner. Stage productions, because they produce noise, can also produce a silence that is the literal absence of noise and the opposite of the spoken word. Similarly, written drama can include silence in the stage directions as pauses. Critics of modern French drama identify silence as an important 'tool' of expression.[18] Leslie Kane, in his study *The Language of Silence: On the Unspoken and the Unspeakable in Modern Drama*, observes how 'the drama of the fin-de-siècle turned more and more to the mode of silence to convey that which was not understood and could not be articulated: the invisible, the inexpressible, the unintelligible' (Kane 1984: 23). There is a tendency towards a productive exploitation of silence at the cost of the spoken word. May Daniels's work *The French Drama of the Unspoken* (1953) identifies this tendency in the work of, among others, Maeterlinck and Bernard.[19] Daniels adheres to the term the 'theatre of the Unexpressed', or the 'Théâtre du Silence', to trace the privileging of silence in theatre. Needless to say, the tendency in criticism of drama is to produce a dualistic understanding of silence. Silence arises against the spoken word on stage and is the dramatic pause.

Finally there is the linguistic or phenomenological approach to silence. This includes studies that attempt to advance a more systematic understanding of silence itself. The tendency is to develop the notion of a discourse not reducible to a transparent code of signs that expresses thought. Rather discourse is a complex matrix of communication; to speak is to presuppose the other: 'la parole, par vocation naturelle, est parole pour autrui' (Ducrot 1972). This view in turn introduces the complexities of the unsaid. Ducrot, in his linguistic study *Dire et ne pas dire*, talks about the *implicite* and the *présupposition* that surrounds, accompanies, and complicates the literal sense.[20] Discourse is consequently seen as a reservoir of silent lacunae that the listener is invited to bridge and interpret (ibid.: 8). Predominant is a dualistic view of silence as corresponding to the unsaid.

---

[18] For a discussion of the role of silence in French classical drama see Arnaud Rykner (1996), *L'Envers du théâtre*. Rykner identifies silence as a threat to this period's drama. He argues that silence is unacceptable to the classical doctrine of a transparent language.

[19] Harold Pinter is of course another dramatist whose work has been approached in terms of silence. See Alan Bold (1984), *Harold Pinter: You never Heard such Silence*.

[20] The title of Ducrot's study repeats the title of a chapter in Pierre Macherey's book *Pour une théorie de la production littéraire* (Macherey 1966: ch. 15), which deals with the same issues. For a similar but less linguistic and systematic argument for this view of language see Brice Parain, *Petite Métaphysique de la parole*. Parain argues that 'Il faut accepter de vivre sans la garantie d'exactitude que nous exigeons des mots' (Parain 1969: 80).

Select studies focus more specifically on silence itself as a phenomenon. The common intention here seems to be to offer a more comprehensive approach to silence, often from a philosophical and ontological point of view (see Picard 1952; Dauenhauer 1980; Rassam 1980; Van Den Heuvel 1985). A general tendency is to provide a systematic, almost scientific, presentation of the ontology of silence. Although these studies deal with relatively traditional notions of silence, their aim is to see silence as a positive principle rather than a negative one. Rassam, in his *Le Silence comme introduction à la métaphysique*, underlines that it is as a positive phenomenon that silence is central to philosophical and ontological study, whereas psychology, for example, relies on a negative view of silence (Rassam 1980: 14). Generally all these studies approach silence in informative, careful, and innovative manners, thereby contributing to a raised awareness regarding the complexities and importance of silence. Again Rassam's study is noteworthy in that he suggests that silence is the only unifying principle to all metaphysical discourse: 'la source et le fondement de la réflexion philosophique se trouve dans un au-delà du langage . . . [qui] est le seul point de référence objectif susceptible de porter la vérité qu'aucun discours ne peut prétendre constituer' (ibid.: 145). This original silence is the only truth that characterizes all metaphysical discourse.

To sum up, these studies invariably view silence as a positive force worth studying in itself. In this regard these studies are closer to my project and have informed my thoughts regarding silence. However, the risk still remains that silence at times seems reduced to an empirical object of study. And furthermore, that silence is limited to the dualistic other of discourse. This latter limitation is revealed by Dauenhauer, who in his study *Silence: The Phenomenon and its Ontological Significance* (1980) operates with definitions such as 'fore-and-after silence' and 'intervening' silence, thereby focusing on silence through its dualistic relation to language. In a similar manner Van Den Heuvel says in *Parole, mot, silence*: 'le langage s'organise à partir du vide autour d'un silence qui est le commencement et la fin de tout discours' (Van Den Heuvel 1985: 68). Again silence is before and after discourse, discourse arises against silence, it is surrounded by silence. Spatial metaphors underscore the dualistic view. Indicative is Van Den Heuvel's analysis of silence in Camus' *L'Étranger*. He suggests that the text is built around a silence, around unsaid presuppositions and implications: 'De la même manière que le silence, dans la communication orale, n'existe que par les paroles qui l'entourent . . . , le vide du texte n'apparaît que par les mots qui sont réellement inscrits dans le text' (ibid.: 166). Silence, in a dialectical manner, depends upon words and can only appear with them. Although a valuable comment, we see that silence still remains the opposite of the words *qui l'entourent*. The dualistic approach to silence prevails.

So far we have observed that the general approach to silence adheres to a traditional view that remains largely dualistic: silence arises either where language or discourse ceases or is missing, or in the gaps and interstices of language and discourse. So far, none of the mentioned approaches, although informative and interesting, provides an alternative framework for thinking silence. In different forms the Dream of Silence therefore prevails and silence risks becoming a thing, an object to be studied, observed, measured. The question still remains whether there have been any studies challenging this approach to silence.

In the next section I shall consider two almost classic texts on silence that deal explicitly with the relationship between silence and literary or poetic expression.

POETRY AND SILENCE

I have chosen Steiner's and Sontag's essays because they represent approaches to silence that are not predominantly linguistic or philosophical, but more literary. Although Sontag's essay focuses on art in general, she is most concerned with literary arts. Steiner mainly addresses poetry and silence.

Both essays recognize a longing in art for silence. Steiner specifically relates this longing to both a mythical and a contemporary disenchantment with language: 'We live in a culture that is increasingly a wind-tunnel of gossip . . . an unprecedented noising of private concerns' (Steiner 1985: 73). Steiner warns against a proliferation of words that in turn causes an emptiness at the core of language: 'In how much of what is now pouring forth do words become words' (ibid.). From the mythical point of view, Steiner argues that language represents risk as it replicates the original act of naming that was the *Logos*, the origin of creation. And the poet, more than anyone, risks this presumption or sin of pride as his activity is primarily to name and create through language. It follows that, both from the mythical and the contemporary points of view, silence becomes the object of a long-ing. Silence can redeem the contemporary development, and make words words again. And the mythical 'fear' of language is coupled with a longing for or a privileging of silence. But silence, argues Steiner, is lost in the modern world. The challenge faced by the mod-ern poet is therefore to relocate silence and give it the space to para-doxically reassert itself. It is the poet who 'speaks with the utmost strength' and who therefore relies on words not to become impover-ished. It follows that 'even to the writer, perhaps to him more than to others, silence is a temptation' (ibid.: 58). Steiner presents the art of the poet as a striving towards silence, a constant negotiation with silence against the word.

Sontag's essay traces what she calls 'the pursuit of silence' in mod-ern art: 'The art of our time is noisy with appeals for silence.' (Sontag 1983: 187). Her definition of silence is linked to contempor-ary art's recent discovery of its own 'artness', its own status as art. With this discovery, art lost its innocence as the romantic expression of human consciousness. From the moment the artist becomes con-scious of his or her own expression as 'art', art becomes something other, something potentially *art*ificial that in turn has to be overcome. And to overcome its own 'artness', art must somehow overcome its own material character. This material aspect of art, argues Sontag, is incongruous with the claim of art: 'Practised in a world furnished with second-hand perceptions, and specifically confounded by the treachery of words, the artist's activity is cursed with mediacy. Art becomes the enemy of the artist, for it denies him the realization—the transcendence—he desires.' (ibid.: 182). Silence arises as an alter-native for the artist, a means of silencing the material aspect of his art and of himself as 'artist'. Silence ultimately becomes a 'project of total liberation' in which much is at stake: 'What's envisaged is noth-ing less that the liberation of the artist from himself, of art from the particular artwork, of art from history, of spirit from matter, of the mind from its perpetual and intellectual limitations' (ibid.: 192). Already it is clear how Sontag perceives the high value placed on silence. And although she focuses on numerous art forms, it is the lit-erary artist who is the most disenchanted because he deals with lan-guage, 'the most impure, the most contaminated, the most exhausted of all the materials out of which art is made' (ibid.: 189) Silence again becomes the projected answer to the disenchantment with the materiality of language.

It is clear from these brief summaries that both Steiner and Sontag are dealing with instances of the Dream of Silence. Silence is posited as a beyond, a realm that can, so to speak, save language from itself. But it remains to be seen how they envisage this silence, and whether they point towards alternative understandings of silence.

Steiner relates to silence as a positive choice on the part of the poet. He cites both Hölderlin and Rimbaud as examples.[21] Their abandonment of the word shows that 'Silence *is* an alternative' (Steiner 1985: 74). The only ideal language of the individual poet is silence. Does this imply that the poet should ideally abdicate the word? Steiner concludes his essay by observing that 'When the words in the city are full of savagery and lies, nothing speaks louder than the unwritten poem' (ibid.). The indirect suggestion indeed indicates that it would be nobler of poets to choose silence, to choose the 'unwritten poem'. However, Steiner insists some paragraphs earlier: 'I am not saying that writers should stop writing. This would be fatuous' (ibid.: 73). But is this not what he is saying? Steiner seems to have entered an insoluble dilemma where there seems to be no solution. Writing destroys the necessary silence, but not to write is, after all, no option. As we shall see later, this aporetic stance, this impossible necessity of both writing and being silent, is in fact a potential trigger of literary silence. Steiner, however, does not develop this further as his basic understanding remains dualistic. Silence remains the other of language and the longing for silence remains incommensurable with the necessity of continued writing. Furthermore, Steiner operates with a spatial understanding of silence referring to it as a 'gap', a 'void', a 'shell of quiet', 'far places', etc. The spatial understanding of silence is in accordance with the Dream of Silence which operates with silence as the beyond, a realm or a space that transcends language.

Sontag's essay considers numerous versions of silence, whereby the positive silencing of the poet in the manner of Rimbaud and Hölderlin are only mentioned as one example. 'More typically', says Sontag, the modern artist

continues speaking, but in a manner that his audience can't hear. Most valuable art in our time has been experienced by audiences as a move into silence (or unintelligibility or invisibility or inaudibility); a dismantling of the artist's competence, his responsible sense of vocation—and therefore as aggression

[21] For more on Hölderlin in relation to silence see Thomas Ryan (1988), *Hölderlin's Silence*.

against them. Modern art's chronic habit of displeasing, provoking, or frus-
trating its audience can be regarded as a limited, vicarious participation in
the ideal of silence. (Sontag 1983: 184)

Silence arises as a result of a non-communicative art. When the art
form recognizes itself as an obstacle, a barrier of mediacy, art demonstrates its longing for silence. By making language difficult one indicates a language that seeks to counteract its basic purpose as
instrument of communication and meaning. It is language that seeks
to be something else. This something else can be silence.

   Sontag's observations indicate that she is challenging the Dream of
Silence. She observes that 'the contemporary appeal for silence has
never indicated merely a hostile dismissal of language' (Sontag 1983:
199). Beckett's writing is mentioned as an example of a literary art that
seeks to 'out-talk language, or to talk oneself into silence' (ibid.). The
implication that strikes me as important is that language can somehow become a dynamic of silence itself. However, Sontag does not
develop the thought further. She operates with a dialectical understanding of silence in relation to language that seems to limit her
understanding. She says that ' "Silence" never ceases to imply its
opposite and to depend upon its presence: just as one can't be "up"
without "down" or "left" without "right", so one must acknowledge a
surrounding environment of sound or language in order to recognise
silence' (ibid.: 187). To suggest a dialectic approach to silence is to suggest an intimate relation of dependence between silence and its other.
Ultimately the view implies that silence 'contains' its other and vice
versa. However, as Sontag's essay demonstrates, the dialectic risks
remaining in the dualistic grid that characterized the Dream of
Silence (see Dauenhauer 1980; Van Den Heuvel 1985). To sum up,
Sontag's essay does point towards an understanding of silence that is
not limited to the other of language. However, she does not follow up
this line of enquiry. Rather, silence becomes 'an ever receding horizon' and art can 'verge closer and closer to silence'. Silence remains
the other of language and Sontag's essay is thereby ultimately caught
in the dualistic view of silence.

   We can conclude that these two more literary responses to silence
also ultimately fail to suggest a different framework for thinking silence
in relation to the literary text. The question remains whether it is at all
possible to think a non-dualistic silence in relation to the literary text.
Can silence at all be conceptualized other than the 'unwritten poem',

other than the unsaid that lingers in the interstices of literary discourse, other than the 'before' and 'after' of all utterance? Or can the question be turned around: how, if one operates with a traditional notion of silence, can the text ever be talked of in terms of silence? Simply put, all text is finally and ultimately a linguistic and symbolic construct. Consequently any traditional notion of silence is at odds with the notion of text in itself. This has not, however, reduced the interest in silence in relation to literary texts. Obviously, the relationship is relevant. To further explore this relationship, the challenge is to think an alternative silence that is not reducible to the other of discourse or text. Only then, it seems, can we avoid the risk of speculating about the meaning of the unsaid and make what I believe to be more interesting observations regarding the relationship between silence and the text.

The notion of a literary silence compromises precisely such an attempt to think ourselves 'out' of the dualistic grid that dominates the discourse on silence considered so far. *Literary silence is literary exactly because it arises through the literary, not as the unsaid, but as a dynamic of the literary said. Literary silence is therefore better thought of as inside language, rather than outside it; as coming through literary language, rather than existing beside it.* It is this paradox, this collapsing of dualism that will be explored. And in order to initiate the first positive move towards this literary silence, I suggest that we turn to Maurice Blanchot. I shall argue that Maurice Blanchot's writing represents one of the boldest attempts to move towards a radically different manner of thinking a *literary* silence and that he openly challenges the traditional approach to silence that I have delineated so far.

SILENCE IN BLANCHOT'S 'MORT DU DERNIER ÉCRIVAIN'

The shift away from a dualistic silence that we can trace in Blanchot is especially relevant to the exploration of literary silence in that Blanchot himself is a literary writer. In other words, his theoretical observations are interrelated with his experience as a writer, not primarily as a critic. And since the silence I am concerned to approach is intimately linked with the literary practice of textuality, Blanchot's observations seem particularly relevant.

Blanchot's move towards an alternative silence is not limited to bestowing a positive value on silence (see Picard 1952; Dauenhauer 1980; Van Den Heuvel 1985), but rather to return to the dynamic *relationship* between the literary text and silence. His move is essential to my understanding of literary silence because it radically undermines the notion of silence as an object to be studied or observed. The moment silence is posited primarily in terms of a relationship, it can no longer be thought of in terms of an object or a static, dualistic other.

My intention is to consider some of Blanchot's observations regarding this relationship. This consideration will in turn be developed to indicate the framework that will guide my approach to literary silence. Specifically, I have chosen to focus on his short essay 'Mort du dernier écrivain' that appears in *Le Livre à venir* (1959). It is here, in a condensed but suggestive manner, that Blanchot develops the relationship between the text and silence in a way that is most useful to my exploration. The essay is not theoretical; in fact, it hardly qualifies as an essay. Rather it presents a thought scenario, almost a fable: What happens when the last author dies, and with him the 'mystery of writing'? What is a world without literature? 'Qu'en résulterait-il? Apparemment un grand silence' (Blanchot 1959: 296). When an author ceases to write one tends to talk of the silencing of his pen. It is such a silence both Sontag and Steiner evoke in relation to Rimbaud and Hölderlin. Such a view adheres to the traditional view of silence; language must stop in order to give way to its other, namely silence. But Blanchot moves beyond this view, beyond this *apparemment*, as he dramatically reverses the categories. A world without literature, he says, will be recognized, not by its silence, but by the *absence of silence*: 'Si . . . toute littérature venait à cesser de parler, ce qui ferait défaut, c'est le silence, et c'est ce défaut de silence qui révélerait peut-être la disparition de la parole littéraire' (ibid.: 298). In other words, literature somehow maintains silence; it is the paradoxical dwelling place of silence, the producer of silence, or the guardian of silence. This rather difficult and rich suggestion shows how Blanchot indicates a move that challenges the notion of silence as the opposite of language, as gaps, omissions, or the unsaid in a text. In other words, Blanchot indicates a potential framework that permits a move towards a different manner of thinking silence in relation to the text.

First, it is important to grasp how Blanchot can imagine that the absence of literature should cause the disappearance of silence. What is this disappearance and how does one sense it? When literature ends, says Blanchot, there is 'l'approche d'un bruit nouveau'. It is 'Rien de grave, rien de bruyant; à peine un murmure, et qui n'ajoutera rien au grand tumulte des villes dont nous croyons souffrir. Son seul caractère: il est incessant' (ibid.: 296). The death of the last writer gives rise to a new noise, a murmur. And it is this murmur that deafens silence. Blanchot further describes it as a singular, unique noise that is irreducible to other sounds:

Cela n'est pas un bruit . . . C'est plutôt une parole: cela parle, cela ne cesse de parler, c'est comme le vide qui parle, un murmure léger, insistant, indifférent, qui sans doute est le même pour tous, qui est sans secret et qui pourtant isole chacun, le sépare des autres, du monde et de lui-même . . . L'étrangeté de cette parole, c'est qu'il semble qu'elle dise quelque chose, alors qu'elle ne dit peut-être rien. (ibid.: 297)

As literature ends, this new, impersonal, incessant voice starts murmuring, empty of content, indifferent, but always there. It is a voice that haunts and that cannot be talked about: 'Personne n'ose en discuter, ni même y faire allusion' (ibid.: 298). The voice can never be pointed to or positively identified and therefore *it is impossible to relate to it*. It is everywhere and nowhere. Everyone recognizes it, but not as a phenomenon that can be talked about. It therefore isolates each and every one of us. But whereas the individual is incapable of relating to this murmur, literature can. And Blanchot's point is that literature, through this relationship, can somehow protect us from this noise and give us silence.

In order to understand this relationship, we must consider one final and quite surprising observation that Blanchot makes regarding this voice, namely that it is 'silencieuse, car c'est le silence qui parle' (ibid.: 297). The suggestion seems to be that this incessant murmur is silence itself, alone and raw, unmediated, speaking in its direct form. It is, one might imagine, the unbearable noise of silence itself. We cannot stand in any direct relationship to this silence and therefore constantly risk losing it as we must drown it in noise or simply ignore it. In order to relate to silence a noiseless mediator is needed. And this is the function of literature: 'Il [le livre] s'élève et s'organise comme une puissance silencieuse qui donne forme et fermeté au silence et par le silence' (ibid.: 298). Literature enters into a relationship to this raw, immediate silence and mediates it into a silence that we can relate to. Therefore literature safeguards our relationship to silence. Such, says Blanchot, is the task and responsibility of the author: 'd'entrer, plus que personne, en un rapport d'intimité avec la rumeur initiale. C'est à ce prix seulement qu'il peut lui imposer silence, l'entendre dans ce silence, puis l'exprimer, après l'avoir métamorphosée' (ibid.: 300). Blanchot suggests that literature, because it dares to relate to this murmur, this original silence, transforms it and hence ensures our relationship to it. Without literature, we therefore lose silence. Blanchot underlines that the raw version of silence is potentially dangerous. Only literature can transform 'la parole non parlante en un silence à partir duquel elle peut vraiment parler et laisser parler en elle l'origine, sans *détruire* les hommes' (ibid., my italics). The original unmediated silence cannot speak, nor make itself heard, but it has the power to destroy man. Literature makes silence speak because it mediates it. Furthermore, it protects man from the destructive impact of the unmediated silence.

Blanchot distinguishes literature as that which can silence silence. Inherent in this thought is an understanding of the literary as a specific mode of language. Other modes of language leave us exposed to the incessant murmur as they are unable to silence it. Blanchot refrains from providing a strong definition of the literary as opposed to other modes of language. Nor does he list criteria for the literary. But he does seem to suggest that the literary can be recognized exactly by its being the guardian of silence, the mode of language that seeks the raw silence, that dares approach it more than any other mode of language. It is my suggestion that literary silence must be understood based on a similar understanding of the literary. In other words, literary silence is the silence that we can trace in texts that bears the echo of this raw and unmediated silence, texts that are somehow haunted by it. The silence becomes *literary* as it becomes the silencing of this original silence. Bearing with this vagueness for the time being, I shall return to the notion of the literary and my understanding of it in Chapter 2.

Clearly Blanchot's reflections provide a framework for thinking silence that greatly differs from the critical commentaries considered so far. Essentially, he presents literature, a production of words and language, as a dynamic of silence. Literature mediates silence, makes it a possibility for us, safeguards it. Blanchot hereby draws up a notion of silence that is irreducible to dualistic thought. Silence is not the other of language, not in the gaps, not at the end of the text; it is the result of the text itself. More precisely, silence is a result of a relationship that literature alone can maintain, namely the text's relationship towards the unmediated, raw, dangerous silence. To approach silence as the result of this relationship is also to abandon a spatial understanding of silence. We have seen how such a spatial conceptualization has largely characterized the above-defined dream of a Silence of the beyond (Steiner 1985; Van Den Heuvel 1985). Silence seems to intuitively designate the delineated space that surrounds the text and language. However, the relationship that Blanchot delineates is never static and hence not primarily spatial. Literature's relationship to the raw silence is a constant back and forth, maintained by the movement of literature itself. Silence is the result of this back and forth, this constant relating.

It is important that Blanchot observes different degrees to which texts enter into relationship with the raw silence. Some texts, rather than actually confront the raw silence, seek to distance it. Rhetoric is such a means of protection from raw silence: 'la rhétorique est une protection si parfaite qu'elle oublie en vue de quoi elle s'est organisée: non seulement pour repousser, mais attirer, en le détournant, l'immensité parlante' (Blanchot 1959: 301). Rhetoric is one form that does not actually *relate* to the *immensité parlante*, to the raw silence, but merely excludes it. The point is that not all literature is equally 'courageous' in its relationship to the murmuring, and hence not all literature is equally likely to produce silence. More precisely, Blanchot distinguishes modern literature as the mode that entertains the closest proximity to this raw silence and that is hence the most interesting as a producer of silence. However, he also states that 'il y a, dans chaque grand livre, un autre enfer, un centre d'illisibilité où veille et attend la force retranchée de cette parole qui n'en est pas une, douce haleine de ressassement éternel' (ibid.: 299).[22] Every great literary work relates to the incessant murmur, the immediate silence, and is hence a producer of silence. I have chosen my corpus of texts based on a

---

[22] This observation introduces a more political aspect to Blanchot's essay. The end of literature is linked to the rule of the dictator. The dictator, argues Blanchot, is threatened by literature and will move to ban it. This can be explained with reference to the incessant, impersonal voice or raw silence. The dictator is by definition threatened by this voice and seeks to fight it with order and loud commandments. But, indicates Blanchot, the voice of the dictator is in fact nothing less than a parody of this original voice, 'plus vide encore qu'elle' (Blanchot 1959: 300). In other words, the dictator's voice also relates to this unmediated silence, but it does not silence it; it merely becomes its distorted face and hence offers no protection. Literature is therefore always an alternative to the dictator. It becomes a refuge where one can find real protection from the empty murmur in the form of silence. The dictator is hence threatened by the writer and his book. The power of the writer is exactly to reveal the impotent power of the dictator's voice against the unmediated silence by offering mediated silence.

similar conviction. It is my intention to explore how Pascal's *Pensées*, Rousseau's *Rêveries* and Beckett's trilogy are all literary producers of silence, to discover their various *centres d'illisibilité*.

Blanchot provides a framework for thinking a silence that is not dualistic, not primarily spatial, but rather the result of a movement, a dynamic that literature enacts. This in turn formulates the main presupposition for my move towards literary silence as a silence that defies objectification. Literary silence designates a silence that emerges through the literary and that is hence contingent upon the literary text. It is a silence that arises through a relationship that the literary has with something else, something threatening, unsayable—a raw silence. It is a silence that emanates from the dynamic of words and sentences and that provides and guarantees the experience of silence as an experience of reading. In other words, literary silence is a concept that explores the literary text's paradoxical, almost uncanny, ability to give voices to silence, to say the unsayable.

In the next and last section I shall discuss in more detail why I have chosen the three authors in question. I shall also define more closely some of my basic terminology, focusing on the notions of first- and second-degree silence and the non-symbolic.

FIRST- AND SECOND-DEGREE SILENCE, THE NON-SYMBOLIC, AND THE AUTHORS

A primary and important distinction is between what I shall call *first-* and *second-degree silence*. First-degree silence designates a silence that is described in the narrative. It can be the mention of the word silence, a description of a silent experience, or a silent character. It is, one might say, a silence that 'happens' within the narrative. Second-degree silence, however, describes the silence that is not mentioned or described on the level of the narrative, but rather occurs as a dynamic that arises from the text, that is produced by the text and that takes place in the actual reading of the text. Literary silence ranks under second-degree silence.[23] Needless to say, my interest is first and foremost in second-degree silence.

---

[23] Van Den Heuvel, in his reading of Camus, distinguishes between two comparable silences. One is situated 'au niveau de l'énoncé narratif' and distinguishes in this case the silence of the killed Arab. This is first-degree silence, whereas the second is situated 'au

The second important notion is that of the *non-symbolic*. The authors and texts I have chosen to consider in this study are chosen based on how they all, in different manners, entertain a relationship to a sense that can be described as the *unsayable*. Pascal's *Pensées* are, as most critics agree, a collection of fragments that was intended as an apology for the Christian faith. The apology was addressed to the seventeenth-century *libertin*, the non-believer, as an attempt to convince him of the truth of the Christian religion. However, as Pascal writes, 'Les choses de Dieu [sont] inexprimables'.[24] The result is a text that is constantly relating to a sense of the unsayable, constantly exploring the limits of language and the text. In the case of Rousseau the endeavour has shifted slightly, though it is still concerned with the limits of the sayable and the text. It is now the sense of an inner immediate self that is at stake. As we know, Rousseau initially wrote his *Confessions* in an attempt to make himself understood, in the attempt to make his self available and transparent to the reader. However, his experience was that the project failed. The moment the self was written it was redefined, transformed, and caught in the symbolic, alienating grip of language. In other words, he experienced the self as fundamentally unsayable. The *Rêveries* constitute his final attempt to write his self, this time addressed not to the other reader, but primarily to himself. His aim, however, remains to transform his immediate inner subjectivity into exterior writing. By the time we get to Beckett and his trilogy, there is no longer such a defined sense of the unsayable. However, there is a constant preoccupation with the word silence (first-degree) coupled with a frustration with the dynamics of language. The trilogy develops into an intense exploration of the potential of the text as opposed to everyday language. Without going into further detail here, it is this observation that I shall pursue in my reading of the trilogy and the non-symbolic aspect of the texts.

To sum up, I have chosen texts that are defined in relation to and that constantly 'deal with' a sense of an unsayable, or, as I shall call it, the *non-symbolic*. The non-symbolic designates that which we struggle to translate into words or symbols. It can also be called the untranslatable. Steiner exemplifies a sense of the untranslatable by referring

niveau de l'énonciation' and distinguishes what he calls the 'silence du texte' (Van Den Heuvel 1985: 167 n.). This can be called second-degree silence as it designates a silence that is not actually described. However, as we have seen, Van Den Heuvel's notion of the silence of the text differs significantly from literary silence.

[24] Pascal 1991: fragment 303. I am quoting the Sellier edition of the *Pensées*.

to the development of new mathematics in the seventeenth century. With the discoveries of Newton and Leibniz, mathematics develops as a separate language, 'a fantastically rich, complex and dynamic language' (Steiner 1985: 32). And, continues Steiner, 'the history of that language is one of progressive untranslatability' (ibid.). As mathematics develops its own mode of conception, its own epistemology, it cannot be restated in 'normal' language. With the development of new mathematics, a new reality is born, a reality that resists language, as it can be accessed only through mathematical formulae.

Steiner's example of the untranslatable might help conceptualize the non-symbolic. The non-symbolic defies the symbols of language. Or more precisely, one senses that language distorts and transforms it. Brice Parain, in *Petite Métaphysique de la parole*, indicates the non-symbolic as he reflects upon language in relation to contemplation by the sea: 'Je suis là, sur la rive, à ne rien entreprendre pour affronter l'Océan. Les mots que je pourrais prononcer me paraîtraient une mauvaise revanche' (Parain 1969: 20). Although somewhat commonplace, the observation can help us understand the non-symbolic. Even if the non-symbolic can be described or delineated by language (we can of course talk about God and about the Self), language seems to miss it, to misconstrue it, to leave a surplus.

As an experience, the non-symbolic defies measurement and cannot be pointed to or defined; it is immediate in nature. However, the concept 'non-symbolic' itself is of course a linguistic construct. We can only explain the sense of the non-symbolic through language, or through the failings of language. Language recognizes the non-symbolic and delineates it through its own shortcomings. We create names for God and for Self that serve to point towards the non-symbolic and that create a sense of general acceptance that these are concepts that cannot be explained further. The non-symbolic stands in a dialectic relationship to language. By this I mean that language presupposes the non-symbolic and vice versa. I can *talk* about the non-symbolic by giving it the name 'non-symbolic'. In other words, our experience of the non-symbolic is arguably mediated by language even though its immediacy remains inexpressible.

The non-symbolic can ultimately be viewed as a result of a relationship. Without the symbolic there would be no non-symbolic. In other words, the *Pensées* form and colour the sense of the non-symbolic God, just as the *Rêveries* serve to shape our definition of the non-symbolic self. In a similar manner, Beckett's trilogy determines a more modern, less defined notion of the non-symbolic. To conclude, the non-symbolic designates a sense of the unsayable as it is delineated by the texts in question.

My understanding of the non-symbolic can be linked to some of the descriptions of silence above (see Sontag's dialectic understanding). And it is not incorrect to think of the non-symbolic as the negative other of language. However, as indicated by Blanchot's observations, my intention is to analyse the actual nature of the relationship between the texts and the sense of the non-symbolic. To foreshadow, my readings indicate that this relationship is open to change and that through this change the non-symbolic changes too. At this stage it only matters to underline that the non-symbolic, although initially understood as the negative other of language, can become *something else*.

To give the understanding of the non-symbolic yet another shade, it is possible to return to Blanchot's whispering murmur—the raw silence that we have no means of addressing, but that is always there. Perhaps the non-symbolic is just another name for this unspeakably silent murmur, another attempt to delineate it in order to relate to it? In this case all the names that we construe for the non-symbolic, such as God or Self, are also attempts to relate to and fix the incessant murmur of silence itself. This again would imply that for the investigation of literary silence the different versions of the non-symbolic are of less importance. What I am looking for is rather those instances when these texts stop addressing names such as God and Self, and rather enter into dialogue with the nameless whisper.

The texts that I am going to read all actively relate to a sense of the unsayable. It is the dynamic of this relationship that provides the basis for my readings and for the exploration of literary silence. As they relate to the non-symbolic, the texts are testing and experimenting with their own symbolic potential in face of the non-symbolic; how 'close' can they go? We can imagine that the 'closer' they come to the non-symbolic the more their symbolic ability is challenged: to approach the unsayable is actively to experience the shortcomings of language. We can imagine how we, as speaking subjects, struggle to express a sentiment or an experience, and how our language slowly becomes more and more staccato, less and less coherent, and ultimately rests in a telling, resounding silence. The texts, however, cannot choose this kind of silence; they must go on. Their dynamic is one of repeatedly launching themselves towards the non-symbolic, repeatedly testing how far they can go on. And it is in this 'going on', this continued relating to the non-symbolic, that the texts in question move towards alternative dynamics, creating alternative silences, literary silences.

As indicated above, the authors in question represent three different instances of the non-symbolic. Pascal represents the tradition that has called the non-symbolic God and that has hence placed the non-symbolic outside the self. The self, according to Pascal, is incomprehensible without the external non-symbolic gift of grace. However, with Rousseau's autobiographical project, there is a shift in the non-symbolic. With the new sense of inwardness that characterizes preromantic sensibility, the non-symbolic is called Self and is located inside rather than in an external God. In their *Histoire de la littérature française*, Brunel and his colleagues claim that 'Toute une génération s'est formé dans la lecture des *Confessions*, des *Rêveries* ou de *La Nouvelle Héloïse*: pour la première fois le *moi* prenait la première place dans l'œuvre littéraire et devenait le sujet d'un livre' (Brunel *et al.* 1972: 358).

Arguably Pascal and Rousseau represent the shift between the two major topoi of the non-symbolic: from God to Self. Beckett, however, introduces a new, less definable sense of the non-symbolic. This can be called the transition into modernism. It is characterized largely by a new interest in the dynamics of language and text itself. It is exactly this we shall see happen in Beckett's trilogy. Rather than relate to a sense of non-symbolic that is fixed and that is defined in opposition to the text, the trilogy shifts the non-symbolic and moves to make it an inherent dynamic in language itself. The project emerges as the attempt to liberate language from itself, but to do so within language.

To sum up we can say that the *Pensées* are about God, the *Rêveries* about the Self, whereas the trilogy is about language itself. These shifts in the nature of the non-symbolic of course offer themselves to historical analysis.[25] But, as mentioned earlier, the exploration of literary silence is not primarily historical. I suggested above that for the exploration of literary silence the different names of the non-symbolic are less relevant than those instances when the names are 'forgotten', or at least suspended, and the silence of the nameless whisper is made literary.

---

[25] It is largely this history that we find presented by Charles Taylor in his study *Sources of the Self* (1989).

CONCLUSION

The move towards literary silence has developed against a more traditional notion of silence that I have called the Dream of Silence. Importantly, the Dream of Silence tends to approach silence as an object to be studied. It is the other of language and is talked of in terms of the 'end', the 'unsaid', the 'beyond'—in short, terms that affirm the dualistic opposition between silence and text. However, in Blanchot a new potential framework has appeared. By claiming that literature safeguards our relationship to silence, that indeed without literature there is no silence, Blanchot's view radically challenges the dualism. Before I move on to the theoretical discussion of literary silence, I want to underline that literary silence is the relationship between the text and the non-symbolic to which it relates. Defined primarily as a relationship, literary silence cannot be approached as an object to be observed, measured, or studied. In other words, it escapes an empirical method. Literary silence is not a thing. I underline this to indicate what is required of my theoretical framework. It is necessary to develop a theoretical approach to literary silence that openly questions the value of an objective approach to text and that develops alternative models of thinking silence and text together.

Furthermore, literary silence arises in the relationship between reader and text. It *involves* the reader and its meaning is therefore intrinsically bound up in the movement of back and forth that characterizes reading. As Blanchot says, literature constitutes our primary *relationship* to silence. Literary silence can be thought of as a silence that arises through reading. As such literary silence is an experience of reading. This only underlines how the behaviour of literary silence cannot be accounted for from a positivist or empirical point of view. Rather the dynamics of literary silence require a framework that does not distance or objectify the reader, but rather favours a taking part and a participation in the text that is to be studied. To be able to account for and respond to literary silence, I shall delineate a responsive and flexible theoretical framework that openly seeks to avoid objectifying the text and to privilege the experience of reading as a relationship between reader and text. I will develop this framework in reference to H. G. Gadamer's hermeneutics and the work of various French twentieth-century, so-called post-structuralist thinkers.

THINKING LITERARY SILENCE:
A THEORETICAL EXPLORATION

INTRODUCTION

The overall aim of this chapter is to develop a theoretical framework that can inform a further understanding of the dynamic of literary silence. I consider this aim to be twofold. On the one hand I shall define a general theoretical framework and on the other hand I shall develop and define a set of theoretical concepts. Primarily this will lead to a vocabulary that can stake out the theoretical direction for *thinking* literary silence as a phenomenon. My aim is to create associations and nuances that can describe literary silence as a theoretical concept, and that can distinguish and refine our relationship to the phenomenon. I shall draw on numerous theoretical concepts that can shed light on literary silence.

I should underscore that the theoretical concepts will not be directly applicable when it comes to the textual analysis in Chapters 4–6. Before it is possible to explore literary silence in the texts, a theoretical basis for the concept itself is necessary. (I have therefore reserved for Chapter 3 the aim of developing more specific and practical concepts that highlight the *behaviour* of literary silence in the texts.) The aim with the theoretical framework is therefore not primarily to explain how literary silence behaves in the text, but to trigger the process of understanding, thinking, and actively relating to literary silence as a theoretical concept.

THEORETICAL FRAMEWORK

As I said in Chapter 1, literary silence demands a theoretical framework that does not distance the observer from that which is being studied, but rather views theory in terms of interaction and exchange. It is exactly such a view of theory that is outlined by H. G. Gadamer in his general understanding of theory in *Reason in the Age of Science*

(1993). He discusses the notion of theory with reference to the word's etymology. The word is Greek, *theoria*, and its original meaning relates it to the participation in the procession honouring the gods. In Gadamer's work, theory therefore designates a 'genuine sharing in an event, a real being present' (Gadamer 1993: 18). Vattimo, in *The End of Modernity*, summarizes Gadamer's point by observing that theory originally implies a 'looking at' which is also a 'participating in' and, in a certain way, a 'belonging to', rather than a 'possessing of the object' (Vattimo 1988: 133). Theory is therefore misunderstood if we still treat it as 'the distance from beings that allows what is to be known in an unbiased fashion and thereby subjects it to anonymous domination' (Gadamer 1993: 17). The original meaning of *theoria* reveals the limitations of applying theory as some protective looking glass by which the objectivity of the observer is shielded and through which the text reveals itself without ever reaching the reader. The challenge that Gadamer takes on is to develop a theory/*theoria* that creates affinity and proximity between the reader and the text and that cannot be used as a tool of distant, critical observation. It is exactly such an underlying view of theory that is required as we move towards a theoretical understanding of literary silence.

More specifically it is Gadamer's hermeneutics that I turn to. Gadamer's hermeneutics can accommodate the two basic traits of literary silence mentioned above, namely that it cannot be approached as a defined thing or object and that it does not designate some transcendental, dualistic beyond to language, but rather works through language and has to be understood through language.

Gadamer's work defines itself against Cartesian and positivistic thinking. Gadamer considers the Cartesian ideal of the Enlightenment to be inappropriate to the study of the work of art, be it painting, sculpture or text. Within the subject–object constellation that has dominated the classical methodology of natural science, the work of art loses its voice, its force, as it is reduced to an object. In his main work, *Truth and Method*, Gadamer observes:

the human sciences are connected to modes of experience that lie outside science: with the experiences of philosophy, of art, and of history itself. These are all modes of experience in which a truth is communicated that cannot be verified by the methodological means proper to science. (Gadamer 1994: p. xxii)

Reacting against the Cartesian approach and its procedures of analysing, comparing, and measuring the object at hand, Gadamer is concerned to develop theoretical concepts that might bring us closer to an understanding of experiences or dynamics that cannot be approached as objects. Vattimo, in *Beyond Interpretation*, characterizes Gadamer's main project as one that 'explicitly takes its point of departure in the problem of the truth of those forms of knowledge, like the human sciences, that are not reducible to positive-scientific method' (Vattimo 1997: 4). The experience of reading can be considered as such a form of (non-)knowledge, and literary silence is an intrinsic factor of this non-scientific or non-verifiable aspect of the experience of reading. In its 'no-thingness' literary silence is never here nor there, it is in movement, always already elsewhere, and as such cannot be pinned down as an object to be defined, measured, or analysed. Gadamer's general approach is therefore congruent with literary silence and highlights a basic characteristic of the concept.

The first, in this context, relative aspect of Gadamer's critique of the Cartesian model of knowledge is his so-called 'productive hermeneutics'. Productive hermeneutics sees meaning and understanding as events of production, rather than reproduction: 'understanding is not merely a reproductive, but always a productive activity' (Gadamer 1994: 296). This conception of meaning differs from what is often defined as 'reproductive hermeneutics' (also represented by E. D. Hirsch 1967; 1976). This is a hermeneutic tradition that views interpretation and understanding as the re-creation of an original meaning, and hence operates with the notion of such an original, centred meaning. Gadamer objects that 'hermeneutics that regarded understanding as reconstructing the original would be no more than handling a dead meaning' (Gadamer 1994: 167). Meaning is not stable; it is created through the act of reading: 'Reading with understanding is always a kind of reproduction, performance, and interpretation' (ibid.: 160). Again this informs literary silence. As I have mentioned in Chapter 1, literary silence emerges in the relationship between text and reader. Theoretically it therefore requires a framework that is congruent with productive hermeneutics.

A second aspect of Gadamer's hermeneutics that can fill in the concept of literary silence is his linguistic ontology. In the words of Vattimo, Gadamer posits the fundamental 'connection or identification between Being and language in a direction that stresses ever more emphatically the pole of language rather than of Being' (Vattimo 1988: 130). Borrowing Habermas's term, Vattimo calls this the 'urbanization' of language. It is, he observes, 'a dissolution of Being into language—or, at the very least, a resolution into language' (ibid.: 131). Placing the emphasis on language, Gadamer proposes that all Being that can be understood is language, because *language is the universal medium in which understanding occurs*' (Gadamer 1994: 389). The implication is obviously that there is no outside to language, no valid sense of a beyond: 'Language is not a delimited realm of the sayable, over against which other realms that are unspeakable might stand. Rather, language is all-encompassing' (Gadamer 1976: 67). Rejecting the possibility of an 'other' of language, Gadamer's theory echoes my rejection of the Dream of Silence. Any understanding of silence based on Gadamerian thought will stem from language itself: 'we are always already encompassed by the language that is our own' (ibid.: 62) and can therefore further amplify and nuance my preliminary move towards literary silence.

Gadamer's strong anti-Cartesian approach, his productive hermeneutics, and his linguistic ontology provide a basic and important framework for the theoretical definition of literary silence. However, before I proceed, I would like to draw attention to certain potential limitations that must be accounted for. I choose to bring out these limitations not as a means of dismissing Gadamer, but rather to show how the limitations in question shed further light on literary silence. One could say that Gadamer's hermeneutics can inform the exploration of literary silence to a certain point, it can shed light on major aspects of the dynamic in question. But the more shady regions of this relevance become equally significant and informative as they reveal exactly that which slips away from hermeneutics. It is in the interplay between its applicability and its limitations that Gadamer's hermeneutics can reveal most about literary silence.

Gadamer's productive hermeneutics are based on the identification of understanding with agreement: 'Understanding is primarily agreement' (Gadamer 1994: 180). This is based on Gadamer's so-called 'fore-conception of completeness', which states that all readers expect a text to be coherent and to make sense based on some principle of rationality. The process of interpretation is the attempt to understand what the text as other is saying within the expectation of completeness. In this process the truth of the subject matter will disclose itself as true and some agreement will be reached. Agreement, and hence understanding, is based on the interpreter's ability and willingness to recognize the other as other and 'meet' the other as such. However, Gadamer's linguistic ontology and its link to tradition imply that I can never step outside my own ontological symbolic order, or my historic horizon. I am always already placed within my view, and cannot exchange it for some other view. How then is it possible to completely foreground the other as other, all the while foregrounding my own ontological premiss? How can I approach the other as potentially different, and accept this difference, when understanding ultimately requires agreement? The problem obviously only becomes pertinent when the symbolic horizon of the other radically resists or is at variance with mine.

In his comparative study of Gadamer and Foucault, *The Power of Dialogue* (1996), H. H. Kögler moves towards a new hermeneutics mapped out in between these two thinkers. Kögler also discusses this potential problem evoked above:

> if the ontological premises that the interpreter implicitly introduces in every truth-oriented interpretive act are radically different from those of the symbolic context to be understood, then the interpreter will not be in a position to accept the truth of what is said. . . . because of the truth- and content-oriented perspective, the underlying differences may not be adequately considered and worked out. . . . the other is enclosed within one's own vision of the world in a supposedly open, yet in truth implicitly conservative, manner. (Kögler 1996: 138–9)

Because agreement is the aim of understanding, the risk is that the other can only be affirmed as far as he coincides with my ontological premises, as far as there is '*commonality between other and self*' (ibid.: 144). Clearly, and Kögler sees this too, Gadamer's aim is to react against a hermeneutic that only sought to define meaning in terms of an object. The attempt to recognize and agree with the other is a radical rewriting of the previous mode of understanding. However, the emphasis on agreement potentially limits Gadamer's dialogical model. It advocates unity and identity, and risks reducing the alterity of the other to the horizon of the interpreter's own rationality. Its risk is to diminish the plurality of meaning and perspective; multiplicity is reduced. As Kögler remarks, 'recognition of plurality cannot be achieved through Gadamer's strong model of the truth-oriented fusion of horizons' (ibid.: 148). Rather than advocating understanding as the interpreter's willingness and ability to endure a *radical* in-between movement of difference and conflict, he presents understanding as an amicable meeting. This view risks limiting our understanding of literary silence. It is essential that literary silence can take the form of disagreement, even of discomfort. This in itself distinguishes literary silence from the more appealing Dream of Silence. Literary silence resists understanding to the degree that it resists dualistic thought. If agreement is to be achieved at all costs, this less agreeable potential of literary silence might be overlooked. This signals one limitation that affects the relevance of Gadamer's hermeneutics in relation to literary silence.

The 'fore-conception of completeness' also bears within it a second limitation as far as literary silence is concerned. 'Completeness' implies the attempt to establish a system that can explain the varied aspects of a given text as unified and resolved in completeness. Interpretation and understanding become the imposition of an all-embracing *structure* that is rationally sound. We can draw a parallel with the structuralist approach. And the temptation of the structuralist approach is, of course, that it always 'works': a reader can quite easily locate some structure that can account for various textual features and hence present a virtuoso reading where all differences 'come together' and are erased. However, such neat systems tend to have a surplus; they function so well because they exclude something, something which defies the system, which the structure cannot pin down. The fore-conception of completeness raises a similar risk. As a methodological approach it risks being blinded to those dynamics that resist completeness. And literary silence takes the form of such a dynamic. Because it cannot be pinned down as an object and because it is primarily a relationship, literary silence is always shifting, always 'changing places'. It is therefore incongruent with a sense of the text as a completeness. Again, because it can emerge as conflict, as discomfort, it resists completeness as it tends rather to disrupt any closed structure.

The limitations of Gadamer's hermeneutics have indicated those characteristics of literary silence that are hard to explain positively. The limits that arise due to the centrality of agreement and completeness are therefore not restricitve. Rather they indicate alternative playing fields that unfold in their twilight. A final aspect of literary silence can therefore arise against what Kögler sees as the fundamental 'truth-orientation' of Gadamer's hermeneutics. Kögler observes how Gadamerian understanding 'is the complete presence of *truth* in the identity of one meaning' (ibid.: 148, my italics). Agreement is understanding and understanding is the subject matter revealing its truth. Though this is clearly a notion of truth closer to Heidegger's *aletheia* (i.e. truth as disclosure and unconcealment, see Heidegger 1993: 176–82) than to an empirical, scientific notion, it remains that truth is given priority, and that Gadamer identifies truth with identity, commonality, sameness, and agreement, while it is threatened by multiplicity, difference, and plurality. The suggestion is that literary silence resists a conceptualization that privileges a notion of truth.

One of the first central thinkers to display mistrust in this idea of truth was, of course, Nietzsche. In *The Will to Power*, book 3, part 4, 'The Will to Power as Art', Nietzsche accords crucial importance to art at the cost of the concept of truth: 'art is *worth more* than truth' and 'truth does not count as the supreme value, even less as the supreme power. The will to appearance, to illusion, to deception, to becoming and change (to objectified deception) here counts as more profound, primeval, "metaphysical" than the will to truth' (Nietzsche 1967: 453). Nietzsche's urgency to devalue truth reflects a certain desperation with the stagnation that he considers caused by the notion of truth: 'Truth is ugly. We possess *art* lest we *perish of the truth*' (ibid.: 435). Truth and art are posited as opposites, and truth is seen as that which opposes the 'will to art'. Nietzsche introduces difference where Gadamer relies upon identity (art is truth). Privileging art over truth, Nietzsche is a central figure for what I would now like to introduce as the post-Nietzschean or post-structuralist thinkers.

Turning to post-structuralism, I am obviously less interested in the social and political issues at stake than with the approach to philosophical matters (hence the possible label post-Nietzschean), and more specifically with the hermeneutic issues dealing with understanding and interpretation. As delineated above, structuralism can be summarized as the attempt to analyse texts in terms of systems, categories, and order. Structuralism relies upon an underlying, axiomatic, linear, knowable structure that can account for and embrace all varied and contradicting aspects of the surface of the text. Understanding is the uncovering of this structure and hence the discovery of an underlying all-embracing meaning. Post-structuralist thinking opposes the idea of such a structure by pointing to what it necessarily must expel in order to sustain itself. In their essay 'Introduction: The Class of 1968—Post-Structuralism *par lui-même*', Rivkin and Ryan sum it up as the exploration of 'the unexplainably different counter-example or outside that could never be inside because its negativity allowed the positivity of the inside to define itself' (Rivkin and Ryan 1998: 338). Post-structuralism is the attempt to unravel the structure, to undo the system, and reveal how its seeming stability is always based on excluding elements that cannot be explained by the structure. Structuralism creates 'debris' that it cannot account for, and hence excludes. As indicated above, literary silence is more in the nature of such debris than structure, and my exploration can hence profit from the post-structuralist account.

Of primary interest for the theoretical exploration of literary silence is what we might call the 'vocabulary' of the post-structuralist authors, who question the value of concepts like 'identity', 'structure', 'order', 'sameness', 'original meaning', 'presence', etc.; they allocate value to new terms such as 'multiplicity', 'surface', 'difference', 'force', 'in-between', 'acceleration', 'repetition', 'artifice', 'non-identity', 'transgression', etc. This change of focus reveals how the post-structuralist authors seek to pursue that which slips away from the smooth system of the structure. They irrupt into this system and reveal it as multiple; they undo structures of homogeneity and discover heterogeneity; they see forces of differences, of multiplicity, of *plateaux* (see Deleuze and Guattari 1980), change and movement. These are dynamics that are neither here nor there, neither before nor after; they cannot be grasped within a Cartesian or empirical mode of thinking and hence challenge our concept of analyses and understanding (and hence more traditional scholarly research). The dynamics and forces listed above complement my preliminary understanding of literary silence as the result of a relationship, a constant 'in-between'. This relationship can be further conceptualized in terms of force, difference, repetition. And as the result of such a relationship literary silence creates a dynamic that is always already elsewhere. How can one talk about these dynamics? How can one locate them? How can one observe them? Derrida delineates, and indeed celebrates, a similar problem in his essay 'La Différance':

Comment vais-je m'y prendre pour parler du *a* de la différance? Il va de soi que celle-ci ne saurait être *exposée*. On ne peut jamais exposer que ce qui à un certain moment peut devenir *présent*, manifeste, ce qui peut se montrer, se présenter comme un présent, un étant-présent dans sa vérité, vérité d'un présent ou présence du présent. (Derrida 1972: 6)

The challenge remains to create an academic argument, a 'linéarité discursive d'un ordre des raisons' (ibid.: 7), when the subject matter resists such an ordering and can hence never be grasped by it.

Literary silence provides a similar challenge to thought, a similar mode of (non-)thinking. To talk about it one must *describe* it, and not analyse it. This is why Gadamer's concepts and some of the post-structuralist concepts are so useful. They describe, indicate, and point towards dynamics that are characterized exactly by their slippery nature, by their resistance to analysis, measurement, and observation. Using these concepts I can paradoxically get 'closer' to literary silence as they recognize and underscore the no-thingness of literary silence. Both some of Gadamer's and the post-structuralist concepts can further sharpen our theoretical grasp of literary silence as they supply more resonances and more specific content to the concept. I shall now consider some specific concepts and see how they can further fill in the theoretical understanding of literary silence.

THEORETICAL CONCEPTS: PLAY AND *JEU*

Play is a metaphor used by Gadamer for describing the encounter between the work of art and the person experiencing it. The resonance of the word seems to be twofold. First, it underlines a mode of 'make-believe', of 'let's pretend', a mode in which the player leaves his world behind and enters into another reality that obeys different rules. Secondly, the word designates free movement back and forth, as in the expression 'play of light'. Light is reflected back and forth restlessly on a surface. It has no direction, no purpose, except its own movement. These are the two basic characteristics that Gadamer develops in his definition of play.

Gadamer seeks to free play 'of the subjective meaning that it has in Kant and Schiller and that dominated the whole of modern aesthetics and philosophy of man' (Gadamer 1994: 101). Whereas play has traditionally placed the consciousness of the players over that of the play itself, Gadamer reverses the terms, and brings primacy to the free movement of back and forth that is play. Play is self-sufficient: 'Clearly what characterizes this movement back and forth is that neither pole of the movement represents the goal in which it would come to rest. . . . This freedom of movement is such that it must have the form of self-movement' (Gadamer 1986: 23). The subject of play is play itself. This is essential, as it accords only a secondary importance to the players. The player must lose himself to the play, must 'play along', must 'make believe'. Play, then, 'determines the consciousness of the player' (Gadamer 1976: 53). Questioning the intentional subject, Gadamer insists that the consciousness and autonomy of the player is undermined, defined, by play itself: 'The game is not so much the subjective attitude of the two men confronting each other as it is the formation of the movements as such, which, as in an unconscious teleology, subordinates the attitude of the individuals to itself' (ibid.: 54).

By positing the primacy of play over the players, Gadamer is able to describe art as an event that draws its participants into it. Art as play desires to 'transform the distance of the onlooker into the involvement of the participant' (Gadamer 1986: 24). This provides an essential description of literary silence. Literary silence, again because it cannot be understood as an object, requires that the reader is drawn into the text, that the event of reading is not one of observation and distance, but of participation. Play describes this dynamic of literary silence. To describe the encounter between text and reader in terms of play is to undermine a Cartesian methodology: 'My thesis then is that the being of art cannot be defined as an object of an aesthetic consciousness because, on the contrary, the aesthetic attitude is more than it knows of itself. It is part of the *event of being that occurs in presentation*, and belongs essentially to play as play' (Gadamer 1994: 116). With the concept of play Gadamer bridges the traditional disconnection between the work of art and the viewer by attempting to describe rather how they are connected. He consequently advocates the work's right to address the viewer, to change and touch him: 'the work of art is not an object that stands over against a subject for itself. Instead the work of art has its true being in the fact that it becomes an experience that changes the person who experiences it' (ibid.: 102). Again this is highly relevant for literary silence. Describing literary silence as play is to suggest that the saying of the unsayable can change the reader, can provide an experience that has required the reader to enter into the play, to abandon his own subjectivity in favour of the movement of play.

It is important to underline that Gadamer insists that the game has rules:

The particular nature of a game lies in the rules and regulations that prescribe the way the field of the game is filled. . . . the child gives itself a task in playing with a ball, and as such tasks are playful ones because the purpose of the game is not really solving the task, but ordering and shaping the movement of the game itself. (Gadamer 1994: 107)

This shows that the purpose of the play is not just any movement, but a specific and ordered movement. The play is always playing something, 'something is *intended as something*, even if it is not something conceptual, useful or purposive, but only the pure autonomous regulation of movement' (Gadamer 1986: 24).

Gadamer's play finds a perhaps surprising parallel in Derrida's essay on 'différance', where the movement of difference is described in terms of *jeu*. Derrida's *jeu* is the movement of difference 'qui ne suit pas plus la ligne du discours philosophico-logique que celle de son envers symétrique et solidaire, le discours empirico-logique' (Derrida 1972: 7). The concept of play, he says, 'se tient au-delà de cette opposition, il annonce, à la veille et au-delà de la philosophie, l'unité du hasard et de la nécessité dans un calcul sans fin' (ibid.). Derrida's *jeu* and Gadamer's play have certain parallels, and as such both are important to literary silence. Both play and *jeu* are defined by self-perpetuating movement, and both undermine the Cartesian understanding of the world. Derrida says:

Et nous verrons pourquoi ce qui se laisse désigner par 'différance' n'est ni simplement passif, annonçant ou rappelant plutôt quelque chose comme la voix moyenne, disant une opération qui n'est pas une opération, qui ne se laisse penser ni comme passion ni comme action d'un sujet sur un objet, ni à partir d'un agent ni à partir d'un patient, ni à partir ni en vue d'aucun de ces *termes*. (ibid.: 9)

Jeu is not an act performed by an intending subject on a passive object; rather it undermines these binary oppositions by its differing nature. Gadamer and Derrida both accord primacy to the actual movement, the actual relation being more important than those relating, or that which is related to. However, there are also differences between play and *jeu*, and it is this difference, perhaps more than the similarities, that can add yet another nuance to our understanding of literary silence.

Play and *jeu* are both described in terms of production. However, it seems that Gadamer and Derrida differ regarding what play produces. Gadamer's productive hermeneutics relies on the idea that the movement of play produces *meanings* as the text and reader enter into dialogue. Derrida, on the other hand, defines *différance* as 'le mouvement de jeu qui "produit" . . . ces différences, ces effets de différence' (Derrida 1972: 12). Gadamer's play is productive of 'something' and this something enjoys an independent existence. *Jeu*, on the other hand, merely produces more *jeu*, more differences that have no separate reality outside of play. *Jeu* is immanent in the sense that it operates within its own domain.[1] Literary silence profits from both understandings. As *jeu* literary silence emerges as a repeated production of more movement. It underscores how the relationship between the text and the non-symbolic is *ongoing*, how it finds no final resolution, no end. The idea echoes Blanchot's observation that it is the continuation of text, not the ending of text, that protects our relationship to silence. However, this silence always arises in-between text and reader; it is the reader's access to silence. Similarly, literary silence happens in the relationship that arises between text and reader. Literary silence therefore depends equally upon Gadamer's understanding of play to highlight the movement between text and reader.

As forewarned in the Introduction, play and *jeu* challenge the traditional notion of theory in that they cannot be 'applied' to literary texts. In other words we cannot look for tropes or patterns that designate play in the texts; we cannot use these notions as 'looking glasses' for textual analysis. Rather, play and *jeu* offer potential images, potential 'organic thought models', that enable us to move towards a more complete theoretical understanding of literary silence. In order to 'think' literary silence, we are forced to stretch our thought, and even to use our imagination. There is a need to expand the frame of reference, to stretch our potential field of understanding—a need I suggest is echoed by the project of post-Nietzschean thought (see above) as it has developed in France. One common trait of these thinkers seems to be a pushing towards an alternative understanding of reality through the subversion of ingrained thinking patterns and traditional academic use of language. This explains their occasional difficulty of access. By using new words (see the mention of a new 'vocabulary' above), and by grasping for the middle rather than a beginning or an end, by opting for the fragmentary rather than the seemingly centred argument, by sacrificing linearity and rational order, the post-structuralist thinkers force language towards different, what one might call 'weaker' aspects of reality. The observation echoes the title

---

[1] The difference between the concepts can be linked to Gadamer's definition of the metaphor 'play'. The metaphor is developed by referring to 'two men' who meet in play, and who decide to play something. It seems that Gadamer fails to probe sufficiently the use of this metaphor for the process of reading. Gadamer does not account for the difference between the literal meaning of play as play between two subjects and the metaphoric meaning of play as reading. In fact Gadamer seems to run into a similar problem when he refers to dialogue, and I will discuss this in more detail later.

of Vattimo's *Il pensiero debole*, 'Weak thought' (Vattimo and Rovatti 1983). Without going into detail, it is possible to say that weak thought is a challenge to the powerful and strong dynamic of rational thought. It is, says Stefano Rosso in his article 'Postmodern Italy', 'a way of thinking which has attempted to give up any "strong" concept of reason and being as presence' (Rosso 1990: 82). Literary silence can also be approached as such a 'weak' aspect within the reality of analysis. It is always a slip, never dominant, always more invisible than obvious.

This 'weak' aspect of literary silence emerges in its paradoxical relationship to language. I have already insisted that literary silence operates and works within language. At the same time language struggles to explain it. *Literary silence happens through language, but cannot be paraphrased in language.* Literary silence cannot be explained or summarized because it remains somehow ungraspable within a rational discourse. Derrida observes regarding *différance*: 'En toute exposition elle serait exposée à disparaître comme disparition. Elle risquerait d'apparaître: de disparaître' (Derrida 1972: 6). This, I would argue, applies to all those dynamics that slip away from a Cartesian method of observation. Literary silence, like play and *jeu*, can be ranged under this (non-)category. The challenge is to advance with the awareness of this and hence not aim to expose it or make it appear, as this would risk losing it. Rather one must aim to circle around it, to describe it, and to use other theoretical concepts to highlight and discern its behaviour.

One possible angle of approach is to think literary silence in terms of 'force'. Derrida remarks: 'Or la force elle-même n'est jamais présente: elle n'est qu'un jeu de différences et de quantités' (Derrida 1972: 18). Force cannot be defined or pointed to. It further parallels literary silence in that it defies spatial understanding. Force is a relatively contemporary theoretical concept that is developed in the work of, among others, Derrida, Deleuze and Guattari and Lyotard.[2] In 'Force et signification' (1967*a*) Derrida develops the idea of force by turning to Jean Rousset's structuralist study *Forme et signification*. Jean Rousset seeks to understand and exhaust literary texts based on geometrical metaphors: 'Rousset accorde dans ses analyses un privilège absolu aux modèles spatiaux, aux fonctions mathématiques, aux lignes et aux formes' (Derrida 1967*a*: 29). Although a powerful critical metaphor,

---

[2] For a more thorough discussion of these thinkers' notions of force, see Andrew Gibson (1996), *Towards a Postmodern Theory of Narrative*.

geometry fails to grasp that which defies spatial understanding. Force is one such dynamic: 'La force de l'œuvre, la force du génie, la force aussi de ce qui engendre en général, c'est ce qui résiste à la métaphore géométrique et c'est l'objet propre de la critique littéraire' (ibid.: 35). As I underlined in Chapter 1, literary silence defies spatial and geometrical understanding. Again, to evoke literary silence as force helps clarify this non-spatial behaviour and highlights the importance of literary silence as an in-between movement. As force literary silence is revealed in its constant movement, its speed, its acceleration, and its shifting nature, always already somewhere else. This 'in-between' movement that is emphasized by force has already been evoked several times. Primarily it provides a topological understanding of literary silence that is important. It underscores literary silence as a movement that cannot be pinned down, that resists objectification and teleological thinking. Literary silence is going nowhere yet is always moving.

To conclude, force describes literary silence as movement, as production, and as 'in-between'. The parallel to Gadamer's play can hardly pass unnoticed. However, there seems to me to be one essential difference between Gadamer's concept and those deriving from the French thinkers. *Jeu, différance*, and force do not directly refer to a reader's experience of a text. This is not to say that these concepts cannot enrich our understanding of the process of reading. It remains, however, that they are not aimed primarily at describing what goes on in the reader–text relationship. However, Gadamer's notion of play is developed primarily to describe the reader's 'interaction' with the text. This characteristic of play is, as I said above, central to our understanding of literary silence as play, and not *jeu*. In his article 'Beyond Seriousness and Frivolity: A Gadamerian Response to Deconstruction' (1991), G. B. Madison compares Gadamer and Derrida. He specifically addresses Derrida's hesitancy to turn to the reader, and rather insistently he claims that 'Derrida simply omits to take into account in his theorising (if it can be called that) the fact that texts have *readers*' (Madison 1991: 130). Though this claim deserves some more nuances, it serves to remind us how a further theoretical description of literary silence requires a framework that addresses the actual process of reading and relationship between reader and text. This observation takes us to Gadamer's concept of dialogue.

READING AS DIALOGUE

Dialogue is Gadamer's best known metaphor for explaining the movement of back and forth between text and reader. In the following I will explain Gadamer's concept of dialogue and see how it can further attune the theoretical understanding of literary silence. I shall also point to some potential limits of the notion of dialogue and see how these limits in turn can help indicate the specific literary dynamic of literary silence.

Dialogue presupposes that the reader meets the text within a framework of openness; dialogue is a 'logical structure of openness' (Gadamer 1994: 362). This openness is directly linked to the ability to ask questions: 'to question means to lay open, to place in the open' and 'questioning makes the object and all its possibilities fluid' (ibid.: 367). The art of reading, says Gadamer, is discovering the question to which the text is an answer, and then to state this question:

As the art of asking questions, dialectics proves its value because only the person who knows how to ask questions is able to persist in his questioning, which involves being able to preserve his orientation towards openness. The art of questioning is the art of questioning even further—i.e., the art of thinking. It is called dialectic because it is the art of conducting a real dialogue. (ibid.: 367)

Real dialogue is the ability to listen for questions indirectly formulated by the text and to formulate new questions.[3] Gadamer underlines that the question cannot be premeditated, but rather must come from the text itself: 'We can understand a text only when we understand the question to which it is an answer. . . . this question can be derived solely from the text' (ibid.: 370). In other words, dialectics is a path of risk in the sense that it invents itself during the course of reading; its outcome cannot be predicted. This quality of dialogue as openness and unpredictability can inform literary silence. Literary silence, like dialogue, cannot be predicted to the extent that it cannot be observed, analysed, or measured. Literary silence emerges in the back and forth movement that is dialogic reading; it does not exist 'outside' this relationship. Entering dialogue means shedding the control that seeks to define the course of the process because 'conversation has a spirit of

---

[3] A similar focus on the question can be found in Heidegger (see 'The Origin of the Work of Art', Heidegger 1993).

its own' (ibid.: 383). As such it echoes play: partners in dialogue must be willing to sacrifice their autonomy: 'To conduct a conversation means to allow oneself to be conducted by the subject matter to which the partners in the dialogue are oriented' (ibid.: 367). This view of reading is implicit in the notion of literary silence.

The possibility of real dialogue relies on what Gadamer calls 'good will'. Basically this concept designates an attitude which consists 'not in trying to discover the weakness of what is said, but in bringing out its real strength'. Rather than seek to affirm one's own view, goodwill implies that one is interested in learning from the other, even in hearing something that can modify one's own view. Goodwill therefore indicates that there is potential for learning, for gaining new insight, even for changing, as a result of reading; it can be summed up as an active *listening* to the text.[4] Rather than seek to disprove the views of the other with the aim of proving one's own, listening in goodwill is the willingness to remain open to the voice of the other, to really hear what the other is trying to say. Listening is also an activity intrinsically linked to literary silence. Again, because literary silence slips away from the more dominant textual dynamics, it requires careful attention and thorough listening in order to emerge. As I have said, literary silence, although it emerges through language and relies upon the text, loses its dynamic once it is explained or analysed. Consequently, literary silence requires that the reader listen for it and to it. Literary silence does not announce itself loudly, but is rather soft-spoken and can therefore easily be ignored amid the assuredness and sometimes self-important tone of analytic discourse that forgets to listen.

Dialogue describes reading as an active event of goodwill and of listening. Literary silence happens in such a dialogue and is congruent with this theoretical understanding. Furthermore, Gadamer's definition of dialogic reading implies that the reader sheds his or her analytical inclination to structure and control the outcome of the text and the process of reading and rather is led by the dynamic of the text itself. Dialogue treats the text in terms of another subject with its own voice, its own right to *address* the reader: 'The understanding of a text has not begun at all as long as the text remains mute. But a text can begin to speak' (Gadamer 1976: 57). But this advantage of dialogue also points to its potential limitation as a

---

[4] For a thorough and innovative study that actively pays heed to the activity of listening, see Gemma Fiumara, *The Other Side of Language: A Philosophy of Listening* (1990).

metaphor. The concept of dialogue by definition designates an interpersonal exchange and as such posits two subjects addressing each
other. However, Gadamer's reproductive hermeneutics exchanges
the one subject (traditionally often thought of in terms of the subjectivity of the author) with the text itself: the text has the ability to
address the reader outside of the author–reader dialogue. However,
Gadamer does not directly discuss this exchange of a thinking,
speaking subject with a text, and hence fails to probe the limits of his
metaphor. We recognize the same potential problem that characterizes play. The metaphor literally designates the meeting between two
men and is then transposed to the meeting between text and reader.
It is this seemingly unproblematic replacement of reading with conversation that can indicate the limits of the notion of dialogue. Again
my aim is to delineate these limitations in order to arrive at a more
nuanced understanding of literary silence.

Although Gadamer develops dialogue as a description of reading,
the risk is that the *specificity* of the process of reading is lost as it is
described as an ideal interpersonal dialogue. It is worth noting that a
similar objection to dialogue was raised by Proust in his short pastiche
'Journées de lecture' (1947), where he responds to some of the claims
made by Ruskin in *Sesame and Lilies*.[5] Ruskin views reading as a dialogue with great past thinkers. Proust responds to the claim:

J'ai essayé de montrer dans les notes dont j'ai accompagné ce volume que la
lecture ne saurait être ainsi assimilée à une conversation, fût-ce avec le plus
sage des hommes; que ce qui diffère essentiellement entre un livre et un ami,
ce n'est pas leur plus ou moins grande sagesse, mais la manière dont on com-
munique avec eux, la lecture, au rebours de la conversation, consistant pour
chacun de nous à recevoir communication d'une autre pensée, mais tout en
restant seul, c'est-à-dire en continuant à jouir de la puissance intellectuelle
qu'on a dans la solitude et que la conversation dissipe immédiatement.
(Proust 1947: 256–7)

The interest of the passage lies exactly in Proust's claim that dialogue
is a reductive understanding of reading because it risks overseeing or
missing that which is singular to reading. Reading, continues Proust,
is 'l'impulsion d'un autre esprit, mais reçue au sein de la solitude'
(ibid.: 265). Reading takes the form of a specific friendship of which
'L'atmosphère . . . est le silence' (ibid.: 275). These descriptions of

---

[5] 'Journées de lecture' first appeared as the preface to Proust's translation of Ruskin's
Sesame and Lilies, *Sésame et les Lys*, which he completed in 1906.

reading circle closer towards the dynamic of literary silence. Because literary silence is a dynamic that is exclusive to the text and to the activity of reading, the notion of dialogue risks overlooking it. Literary silence arises in the solitude and silence evoked by Proust that are exclusive to the relationship formed between reader and text.

It is also worth adding that dialogue is a concept that stems from Gadamer's view of understanding as agreement. Although dialogue often occurs between two people of different opinions it is ordered back-and-forth with the goal of creating understanding as agreement. Dialogue is teleological in the sense that it moves towards this goal of understanding. Literary silence, however, can best be approached as a topological movement. It is a roaming movement, going nowhere in particular, but incessantly moving, around and about itself. Dialogue reduces the freedom of this topological movement into topics for discussion. It is a mode that presupposes a rational, meaning-oriented exchange of arguments. As a saying of the unsayable, literary silence is not the articulation of arguments, observations or clear ideas, but rather the dissolution of such agreement-orientated, symbolic discourse. Where dialogue is largely a productive and rational exchange conducted in a shared language, literary silence emerges when this functional language shuts down, when dialogue dissolves and gives way to a non-ordered movement.

Dialogue, we have seen, is an inter-subjective exchange between two distinct, reflective subjects. Literary silence, however, and this foreshadows the next chapter, introduces a dissolution of such reflective subjectivity that stands in distanced relationship to its surroundings. Literary silence invites, or permits, the reader to abandon the position of reflective critic and interpreter and rather become part of the text's dynamic and movement. Literary silence is the force that moves the text in relation to the reader and the reader in relation to the text. This predicates a collapse or breakdown of dialogue as a dualistic exchange between two distinct subjects. More is at stake as the reader gives in to the disquiet, the constant tension, the playful force of the text and lets these dynamics take over in a roaming visitation of textual topoi.

Again the understanding of literary silence has profited from a discussion of the limits of more traditional hermeneutics. Proust's observations have drawn attention to reading as a solitary, silent exchange that is irreducible to dialogue. I have indicated that literary silence belongs precisely to this silent and solitary aspect of reading.

Literary silence, because it slips away from explanation, happens when reading becomes a movement that cancels ordered discourse as it becomes *literary*. With this observation we inevitably come to the question: what is the literary? And clearly the question cannot be avoided, as my understanding of what defines the literary is bound up with my approach to this silence that is specifically literary.

THE STATUS OF THE LITERARY

The status of the literary, or of literariness, is not given or predetermined. On the contrary, the question of deriving criteria that can discern poetry and literature and provide a stable descriptive notion dates back to Aristotle and continues to inspire theoretical debate. My intention is not to provide an overview of the critical issues and directions that arise from this.[6] Rather I aim to outline an understanding of literariness as it pertains to literary silence.

Literariness, as a descriptive term, aims to distinguish that which is literature from that which it is not. Roman Jakobson launches the term: 'Ainsi, l'objet de la science de la littérature n'est pas la littérature, mais la littérarité, c'est à dire ce qui fait d'une œuvre donnée une œuvre littéraire' (Jakobson 1977: 16). It is a question of drawing lines and deriving criteria. Historically the problem arose with renewed sense of urgency in the late eighteenth century, the century in which literature became an academic discipline. Thinkers and writers such as W. Wordsworth and S. T. Coleridge,[7] and of course the Jena romantics Friedrich Schlegel and Novalis, start exploring the status of what they then call poetry, or *Dichtung* (a notion arguably close to our notion of literature). The romantic period can be recognized by a dissolution of the distinct classical genres that until this time had organized most writing and the understanding of it. In the wake of this dissolution various literary practices emerged, and with

---

[6] Some useful references are Jacques Rancière, *La Parole muette: essai sur les contradictions de la littérature* (1998) and the chapter entitled 'La littérature' in Antoine Compagnon's work *Le Démon de la théorie* (1998) and Jonathan Culler's essay 'The Literary in Theory' (2000).

[7] Coleridge, in *Biographia Literaria* (1817), poses the question: 'What is poetry?', and thereby instigates a new critical reflection regarding the status of the literary. Novalis, to a similar end, questions the status of his own critical text *Monologue* (1798): 'Could this in the end, without my knowing or believing, be poetry?'

them a staking out of a new, larger genre called romantic, gothic, poetic, or just literature.[8]

In their central study *L'Absolu littéraire*, Lacoue-Labarthe and Nancy suggest that the Jena romantics were not so much concerned with defining existing literary texts, but in investigating new premises for the *production* itself of literature: 'La pensée du "genre littéraire" concerne donc moins la production *de* la chose littérarire que *la* production, absolument parlant' (Lacoue-Labarthe and Nancy 1978: 21). Rather than discern and describe the literary object, Lacoue-Labarthe and Nancy seem concerned to explore the conditions of literariness. According to them, the Jena romantics did not primarily perceive literature as a thing, but as a coming into being, a movement. Friedrich Schlegel writes in fragment 116 of his *Athenäums Fragmente*, here translated by Lacoue-Labarthe and Nancy, that romantic poetry:

Veut et doit aussi tantôt mêler et tantôt fondre ensemble poésie et prose, génialité et critique, poésie d'art et poésie naturelle, rendre la poésie vivante et sociale, la société et la vie poétiques, poétiser le Witz, remplir et saturer les formes de l'art de toute espèce de substances natives de culture, et les animer des pulsations de l'humour. . . . Le genre poétique [*Dichtart*] romantique est encore à devenir; et c'est son essence propre de ne pouvoir qu'éternellement devenir, et jamais s'accomplir. (Lacoue-Labarthe and Nancy 1978: 112)

Poetry, or literature, arises as a new ideal of mixture, plurality, and surplus where the old genres, as well as the separation of philosophy and poetry, dissolve. It is not something to ever be completed but something that must always repeatedly become.

Since this unsettling but inspiring 'discovery' of literature's more or less undefined status, literary theory has been orientated towards defining and delineating its object of study and hence justify its own status as academic discipline. I propose that we can distinguish two general approaches to literariness, one that I shall describe as strong and another that is weak. The former, which is reflected in Jakobson's comment quoted above, seeks to arrive at a list of criteria that in turn can define the quality of literariness. Primarily this strong approach has been developed within the critical movements of Russian formalism,

---

[8] Many critics see the Jena or early German romanticism as inaugurating a certain way of questioning or approaching literature which has been retraced in (post)modern literary theory and its reflective and critical agenda. In addition to Philippe Lacoue-Labarthe's and Jean-Luc Nancy's *L'Absolu littéraire* (1978), see also Andrew Bowie's *From Romanticism to Critical Theory* (1997) and Critchley's chapter 'Unworking Romanticism' (1997: 85–138).

structuralism, and new criticism.[9] The weak approach, however, can be traced through voices that shy away from categorical thinking, that rather wish to retain the lack of any stable definitions and criteria. These are weak voices in Vattimo's sense of the word; they do not wish for their object of study to be defined, in fact they do not wish for an object of study at all. They do not believe that literature is something that can be pointed to and identified, and hence repeatedly seek the instability of the literary, the literature that questions itself as literature. According to Lacoue-Labarthe and Nancy, the question 'qu'est-ce que la littérature?' is a question that must persist and be maintained and to which the answer is 'interminablement différée, toujours décevante, rappelant sans arrêt la question' (Lacoue-Labarthe and Nancy 1978: 266). This weak approach to literariness can be recognized amid the so-called post-structuralist or deconstructive thinkers, such as Derrida, de Man, Deleuze and Guattari, and Lacoue-Labarthe and Nancy, and their historical points of reference such as the Jena romantics and Mallarmé.[10] It is such a weak understanding of literature that underlies this exploration of literary silence and that I shall attempt to describe further.

Derrida, in the interview 'This Strange Institution Called Literature', remarks: 'even if a phenomenon called "literature" appeared historically in Europe, at such and such a date, this does not mean that one can identify the literary object in a rigorous way. It doesn't mean that there is an essence of literature, it even means the opposite' (Derrida 1992: 41) Literature's lack of essence does not mean that it does not exist, but it does call into question the nature of this existence. Literature is not a presence. Is it then an absence? Blanchot writes: 'La littérature va vers elle-même, vers son essence qui est la disparition' (Blanchot 1959: 266). Blanchot describes literature as a continual vanishing, a disappearance towards itself. Literature now emerges as a constant retreat from its proper definition, from the world and towards itself. Is this the paradoxical existence of literature—a movement that disappears, that comes, that is before us and ahead of us, but never present? We might describe literature as a

---

[9] For a good selection of critical essays by representatives of these critical movements such as Boris Eichenbaum, V. Shklovsky, V. Propp, Mikhail Bakhtin, Cleanth Brooks, Roman Jakobson, and Lévi-Strauss, see Rivkin and Ryan 1998: 8–115.

[10] Mallarmé's thoughts about literature and what we might call literariness will be explored in the Interlude where I shall describe the idea of poetic language as it emerges through Blanchot's readings of Mallarmé.

stirring, a movement just beyond our field of vision, that which attracts our gaze towards it, but that is never there to be looked upon. Or again, in the words of Lacoue-Labarthe and Nancy, 'une *chose* indistincte et indéterminable, reculant indéfiniment à mesure qu'on l'approche, susceptible de (presque) tous les noms et n'en tolérant qu'un: une chose innommable, sans contours, sans figure—à la limite "rien"' (Lacoue-Labarthe and Nancy 1978: 266). Such a description of literature repels all strong definitions, all talk of criteria. The literary, a no thing, slips inbetween the demarcations and definitions.

This description of literature gives associations to the literary aspect of the silence I am tracing. Literary silence can be described as a silence that follows the literary movement, the constant disappearing that eludes the objective analysis, and that hence suggests the need for a different critical approach. Its possibility is linked to the conditions of the literary and to its production. If we return to the notion of dialogue, we can conclude that whereas 'dialogue' presupposes agreement as understanding, text as completeness and dialogue as meaning-orientated, literature is irreducible to such a conversational mode. Literature disappears, slips away, resists paraphrase; and it initiates, or liberates, a mode of language that can also be silence.

CONCLUSION

Above I suggested that literary silence was a 'weaker' aspect of reality. I referred to Vattimo's notion of weak thought, and found that this notion was descriptive also of an understanding of the literary. By describing literary silence as such a weak dynamic, I hope to highlight two things. First of all, literary silence is never a dominant textual dynamic. It is always a slip away from any overt, productive structure. Secondly, literary silence cannot be explored within the underlying framework of 'strong' thought. Strong thought relies upon a rational system to make sense, to produce lasting meaning. Again it is telos-orientated. It presupposes a rational subject that remains in control of and superior towards the produced system of thought. Strong thought therefore guarantees the reader's subject status as thinker and inter-preter, and the stable relationship to the text as an object. By now we sense that literary silence is irreducible to this mode of thinking.

The paradoxical power of weak thought is that it can destabilize the relationship maintained by strong thought. Weak thought, because it challenges the control of the rational, superior subject, introduces different constellations and movements. As a slip, it has the potential to collapse the powerful, linear narrative of strong thought. Literary silence *moves* the subject and undermines his or her control in relation to the object of thought. Finally, literary silence does not have the power to create systems of thought. Rather it always undermines any system, always destabilizes it, troubles its rational foundation, and disrupts its teleological, productive impetus. In light of this it should be noted that Vattimo's notion potentially reduces literary silence. The movement of literary silence cannot be grasped in terms of *thought*, be it strong or weak. The limitations of the dialogue metaphor and the weak understanding of the literary have indicated literary silence as a movement that is irreducible to any rational exchange. To think of literary silence as thought ignores this important aspect of the movement. It is therefore preferable to talk of literary silence as a weak *dynamic* or weak movement.

A last fitting description of reading is again provided by Proust in 'Journées de lecture'. He describes the childhood experience of reading, of being completely immersed in a book, only to be interrupted by the maid who asks if he wants a table moved closer:

Et rien que pour répondre: 'Non, merci bien', il fallait arrêter net et ramener de loin sa voix qui, en dedans des lèvres, répétait sans bruit, en courant, tous les mots que les yeux avaient lus; il fallait l'arrêter, la faire sortir, et, pout dire convenablement: 'Non, merci bien', lui donner une apparence de vie ordinaire, une intonation de réponse, qu'elle avait perdues. (Proust 1947: 238)

In order to respond, the voice with which one reads must, with great effort, be called back to normality, away from its own silence. It is this silent experience of the literary, of reading, this ability to relate with a different voice to text, in solitude, apart from the world of others, that can create a clearing for our understanding of literary silence.

To conclude, we can say that this theoretical exploration of literary silence has provided theoretical associations and nuances to the concept. Different theoretical notions have provided different shades and tones that indicate the dynamic of literary silence. But, as the quotation from Proust indirectly suggests, literary silence is not primarily a theoretical concept. It can first and foremost be explored as a concrete phenomenon that occurs in reading. The concept can therefore only be explored so far theoretically, only be circled in so far, and never positively be pinned down. The most informative and all-embracing description or image of literary silence is as a 'weak', topological movement that invites the reader into a playful, disruptive movement that is irreducible to everyday language. It is exactly these observations that point us in the direction of the next chapter. The aim now is to turn to the more concrete manifestation of literary silence in texts.

THE BEHAVIOUR OF LITERARY SILENCE:
REPETITION, APORIA, IMPLOSION

INTRODUCTION

The theoretical understanding of literary silence indicates a path along which we might trace literary silence. One might say that the previous chapter established a set of associations, perhaps a certain 'mind set', that in turn will enable us to understand, or at least approach, literary silence. Concepts like force, difference, and *jeu* now describe and point towards literary silence. However, these theoretical concepts do not directly reveal or address how literary silence positively can be explored in the text. The next step is therefore to explore the more concrete *behaviour* of literary silence in texts and to indicate how literary silence emerges in the text, what dynamics it produces and is produced through. By behaviour, I mean the textual dynamics or 'patterns' of literary silence as a textual phenomenon. I will develop three such dynamics, namely *repetition, aporia*, and *implosion*.

In a sense these markers or indicators of literary silence function as methodological guidelines. They delineate my method, in the etymological sense of *methodos*, the way to walk, or, in this case, the way to read. However, the concepts cannot map the entire way or lead to the end of the road because they cannot be exhaustively explained, or exhaustively explain literary silence. These are not systematical concepts, but rather function as different perspectives on the dynamic of literary silence. The primary aim of the following is therefore not to provide a set of defined and clearly delineated methodological concepts. Rather they are pointers that can lead me only so far into the exploration of literary silence. Each concept is in itself an angle, a level of literary silence. Consequently there is only so much that can be said about each concept as they all, in the final instance, become literary silence. As such they open onto that which can only be further explored by turning towards the text and by *reading* literary silence. This, in turn, will lead us to the next main section, namely the reading of the three texts in question.

Repetition will be developed mainly with reference to Kierkegaard's work *Repetition*, or *Gentagelsen* (literally *the taking again* or the *taking back*) in Danish. I choose initially to define repetition based on Kierkegaard rather than maybe more obvious thinkers like Derrida and Deleuze. I do this because I believe Kierkegaard's *Repetition* is more directly relevant to the *behaviour* of literary silence. This is due to Kierkegaard's interest in the moment, *øieblikket*, the blink of an eye, and its relation to repetition. This Kierkegaardian moment will take on increasing importance as we explore the actual experience of literary silence that is congruent with the temporal category of the instant. Furthermore, *Repetition* was published alongside *Fear and Trembling*, which appeared under the, in this context, suggestive pseudonym Johannes de Silentio. I will refer to this work in order to develop further the parallel between silence and repetition. I will distinguish two types of repetition, namely simple and complex repetition. The second dynamic is the aporia, literally meaning the impasse. Aporia is a concept that has had specific importance for those thinkers concerned with deconstructing Western metaphysical philosophy's claim to a final truth. However, my aim is limited to defining the aporetic experience in its relation to literary silence. Finally I will turn to the actual experience of literary silence that I have chosen to designate as the *implosion*. The implosion describes the moment in which literary silence actually *happens* as it creates, opens up, or produces the experience of the non-symbolic between text and reader. The implosion will be defined in relation to both Kierkegaard's repetition and the aporia. In addition it will introduce a fourth category, namely the idea of a *sacrifice*. I believe that the implosion demands a sacrifice on the part of the reader, a sacrifice that is specifically related to the reader's relationship to language, to the actual book and the reading of it. I will here refer mainly to Bataille's concept of sacrifice as it is developed in *Théorie de la religion*.

KIERKEGAARD'S *REPETITION* AND THE IMPORTANCE OF THE INSTANT 'NOW'

Published in 1843, under the pseudonym Constantin Constantinus, *Repetition* is a surprising and challenging text. This is partly due to an increasing complexity in the actual concept of repetition as it develops throughout the text. Although we all arguably have a common sense of what is meant by repetition, the word seems to slowly dissolve from such an anchored, stable, recognizable meaning. It is my aim in the following to grasp some of these nuances of the Kierkegaardian repetition and show how they inform literary silence. It is important to be aware that *Repetition*, like many of Kierkegaard's works, operates on a highly biographical level. Again it is the story of Kierkegaard and his relationship to the young Regine.[1] However, there is a certain ironic twist that leaves us unable to account for the text as mere biography. Furthermore the text defies genre. It is, again like most of Kierkegaard's corpus, too intriguingly literary for it to be dismissed as an essay on theology or philosophy, but also too philosophical to be read as fiction. As the text might be unfamiliar to some, I will give a general summary of its content and structure.

Repetition is divided into two sections. In the first Constantin tells us the story of a young man, his friend, who is deeply in love. But, as Constantin discovers, this young love is tainted by melancholy; it is the love of the poet: 'The young girl was not his beloved: she was the occasion that awakened the poetic in him and made him a poet' (Kierkegaard 1983*a*: 138). The young man is in love with the idea of love and not the girl herself. The consequences of this 'love of the poet' are lethal for the girl: 'thereby [she] had signed her own death sentence' (ibid.).[2] Constantin deems it necessary for the young man to be released from this situation and proposes the following procedure: pretend to be in love with someone else in order to make the girl leave you. In other words, say the opposite of what you feel and mean: be ironic. The young girl will be upset, surely, but not *abandoned*—she, not the man, ends the affair. Subsequently she, and the young man, reasons Constantin, will have the reward of freedom—she from the love of the poet, he from his unhappy obligation to the girl. But the young man cannot handle this ironic operation, because, in the words of Constantin: 'My young friend did not understand the power of

---

[1] Regine Olsen was the young girl with whom Kierkegaard fell in love and got engaged. It did not take long, however, for Kierkegaard to realize that the happiness he had imagined in married life remained an impossible ideal for him. He could not be released from his melancholy, could not live the reality of others, and therefore his destiny was that he could make no girl happy. But the thought of breaking the engagement and the pain it would cause Regine seemed impossible. Instead he behaved in such a way as to cause Regine to break up with him. The story haunts Kierkegaard and reappears to different degrees in almost all his work.

[2] The scenario is clearly similar to that of Johannes and Cordelia in the 'Diary of the Seducer' in *Either-Or*. However, where Johannes possesses a chilling self-awareness regarding the nature of his love, the young man in *Repetition* preserves a certain naïvety. Still the consequences for the beloved of such a love remain symbolically, if not literally, lethal.

repetition; he did not believe in it and did not powerfully will it' (ibid: 145). This leads Constantin into a reflection concerning the actual nature of repetition. It is this reflection that is of most value to my understanding of repetition. It is also here that Constantin tells of his own attempt to experience repetition by returning to Berlin to relive memories of a happy time spent in the city. However, the city and the experiences it stages fail to duplicate the memories. Sameness and identity give way to difference. Constantin must hence dispel this type of repetition: 'I had discovered that there simply was no repetition and had verified it by having it repeated in every possible way' (ibid: 171).

This leads to the second section, also, ironically, or suggestively, called 'Repetition'. This is the collection of letters received by Constantin, addressed to My Silent Confidant, from the young man. He is in despair. He has left the young girl and is now haunted by the thought of her miserable fate. His only solace is in the Book of Job, which he rereads and rereads. He here finds described the ideal of repetition. This is the *gentagelse*, the taking back, whereby Job receives *everything* double and thereby comes back to himself and finds God: 'Job is blessed and has received everything *double.*—This is called a *repetition*' (ibid.: 212). The example of Job reveals how Kierkegaard's repetition slips away from a conventional understanding of the word. This 'slippage' is only taken further in the young man's last letter, where he describes his own repetition. Reading through the news-paper, he accidentally learns of the young girl's marriage to someone else: 'I am myself again. Here I have repetition' (ibid.). The question as to how this can be *repetition* will be addressed later. For now it is suf-ficient to remark that the young man's jubilant celebration of repeti-tion contrasts Constantin's failed attempt to repeat the trip to Berlin.

The text ends with a letter from Constantin addressed to 'Mr X, Esq., the real reader of this book'. This seems to be a certain 'manual' on how to read the book. The most important comment is the encour-agement that the book's order is *inverse*: 'He [the ordinary reviewer] will also find it difficult to understand the movement in the book, for it is *inverse*' (ibid.: 226, my italics). It seems that the reader is strangely encouraged to read the book again, to start at the end maybe? To read it inversely: I will return to the importance of this notion.

Repetition is a rich text, and a challenging one. It leaves few answers, numerous insinuations, and even more questions. It is hard to know whose words (if any) we are to identify with Kierkegaard himself—the ironic Constantin or the romantic young man. And most likely

Kierkegaard would answer neither, wishing to leave us hovering in-between the two. My interest in the text is mainly concerned with Constantin's observations regarding repetition as it is these that can inform the behaviour of literary silence.

Constantin starts his observation on repetition by referring to the example of Diogenes, who, when the Eleatics denied motion, opposed this viewpoint. He said nothing, but 'paced back and forth a few times' (Kierkegaard 1983a: 132). The importance of movement is repeated later as Constantin questions the actual meaning of media-tion (referring to Hegel's system of dialectics) and observes: 'In this connection the Greek view of the concept of *kinesis* corresponds to the modern category "transition" and should be given close attention' (ibid: 149). Kierkegaard's critical (but therefore also fascinated) atti-tude towards Hegel's dialectical system is well known, and we recog-nize here an attempt to bring more sense of movement into the dialectic synthesis. What the reference to Hegel reveals is the empha-sis placed on movement. It seems that repetition is to be understood primarily in terms of movement.

As movement, repetition is defined in contrast to recollection: 'Repetition and recollection are the same movement, except in oppo-site directions, for what is recollected has been, is repeated backwards, whereas genuine repetition is recollected forward' (ibid.: 131). The opposition between recollection and repetition is essential. Repetition implies a re-peat, a re-make of what has been *into the present*. In this sense it projects into a future, and therefore moves forwards. Recollection, however, remains in the past as it constantly returns without actively repeating, or *taking back* and making new. Three kinds of movement have been defined so far: movement backwards (recol-lection), movement forwards (repetition), and, as shown by the exam-ple of Diogenes, movement back-and-forth.

The contrast between recollection and repetition might also explain why Constantin's trip to Berlin failed as repetition: his trip took the form of recollection. It became a movement backwards, fail-ing therefore to realize or repeat the past as *present*. Furthermore, this trip was the attempt to repeat something, a memory, an experience, a content; it was, as Constantin himself observes, 'a repetition of the wrong kind' (ibid.: 169). In other words, the disavowal of repetition does not concern all repetition, but specifically the repetition that is not defined as *movement forward*. Constantin's name of course suggests this permanence that accompanies recollection, this lack of forward movement that characterizes the absence of repetition. Melberg, in the study *Theories of Mimesis*, presents a perceptive reading of *Repetition* and asks whether the trip to Berlin is not 'a demonstration that "repetition" of *something* whatever it is, is doomed to failure, although "repetition" as such—as movement, as strategy—is necessary?' (Melberg 1995: 133). This is one of the main conclusions to be drawn from Kierkegaard's *Repetition*. Repetition is usually thought of as dealing with a certain 'content' that is repeated. Kierkegaard's text challenges this more substantial understanding of repetition by insisting rather on movement. In other words, the more traditional notion of repetition is discarded in favour of a different, less intuitive understanding.

That a different understanding of repetition is at stake becomes obvious as we turn to the final, successful representation of repetition as occasioned by the announcement of the girl's marriage to someone else. The young man reads of this marriage in the newspaper and celebrates it as his repetition. How are we to understand the girl's getting married as being repetition? Kierkegaard's repetition must be thought in terms of the original Danish *gentagelse*, meaning, as stated above, to take something back, to take it again. So how does the marriage occasion such a *taking* back, and what is taken back? After reading the announcement, the young man exclaims: 'I am myself again. This "self" that someone else would not pick up off the street, I have once again' (Kierkegaard 1983a: 220). It seems that it is in relation to his own self that the young man experiences repetition. By marrying another man the girl has absolved the young, unhappy man, she has released him from the bond to her. As long as the girl remained unmarried, the young man's self was still defined in relation to her, still caught, and therefore unfree. By marrying she creates the redemptive occasion where he can take back his self from this guilty bond. It is an indirect forgiveness that permits him to repeat his relationship to his own self, and reclaim his self. In other words, repetition, or taking back, is a movement through which the individual can reclaim his/her self as, what Kierkegaard would call, an 'authentic' self. In this case the movement is initiated when the young man *repeats* his relation to the girl in the sense that the relation undergoes change. But, as concluded above, it is not the repetition of the relation, not the repetition of *anything*, that matters: the marriage is merely the *occasion* whereby the young man experiences repetition. Whereas he formerly was caught in the relationship of betrayal (he was the 'betrayer', she the 'betrayed'), the marriage has the effect of freeing his self from this relation. And through this double movement he *takes* himself *back*, receives, as Job 'everything double'. His self is returned to him anew; repetition makes him free.

Let me be clear: the marriage and its link to repetition remains, in a typical Kierkegaardian way, enigmatic. It can be helpful to note that repetition also figures in *Fear and Trembling* as it describes the case of Abraham. Abraham's repetition is clearly deeply religious and existential. In the case of the young man, the movement of repetition is not so clearly achieved as a *religious* movement. Despite his jubilant last letter, the question of how he fulfils the movement of repetition, whether it brings him to the religious stage, is left vague. And although it can be assumed that the movement of repetition is essentially a religious movement,[3] we are left with a notion of repetition that can best be described in terms of movement. The marriage is not a repetition of *something*, but it does cause a movement whereby the young man experiences repetition and movement. Repetition is *movement void of content whereby something is taken back*.

We can now explore in more detail what Constantin observes regarding this movement. So far, it has been defined as movement forwards. Constantin further defines it as dialectic, which, we should not forget, he has just defined in terms of *kinesis* and transition:

> The dialectic of repetition is easy, for that which is repeated has been—otherwise it could not be repeated—but the very fact that it has been makes the repetition into something new. When the Greeks said that all knowing is recollecting, they said that all existence which is, has been; when one says that life is repetition, one says: actuality, which has been, now comes into existence. (Kierkegaard 1983a: 149)

In order for something to be repeated it must have been. But in the actual repetition it becomes new. This is the temporal understanding of repetition. Repetition is the transition from old to new, it is the *movement* by which the past transforms into present existence. It is the coming 'into existence', the producer of existence: 'If God had not willed repetition, the world would not have come into existence' (ibid.: 133).

---

[3] It is worth noting that in the only work where he comments on his activity as an author, namely *Point of View for my Work as Author*, Kierkegaard claims: 'The content of this little book affirms what I truly am as an author, that I was and am a religious author, that the totality of my authorship is related to Christianity, to that specific problem of becoming a Christian.' Although the link to Christianity is less obvious in *Repetition* than in *Fear and Trembling*, one is right to assume that the religious aspect still weighs heavily.

So repetition is the category of *becoming* and as such it refers both backwards and forwards. It relates backwards to what is repeated, and forwards to the new becoming of this past. Repetition, one might say, *trembles* between past and future. It is the suspension of temporal sequence, the mark of the paradoxical re-versal of the past into the future. In linear sequence the present becomes the past, but through repetition the past becomes present. Repetition corresponds to the instant of becoming and hence relates to the temporal category of the instant, or the 'now', the actual moment when time advances, transforms the past into the future. Repetition is the topos of the 'now'.

We are now dealing with Kierkegaard's concept of the 'øieblikk', literally meaning the blink of the eye, which designates the overwhelming and yet completely elusive sense of 'now'. Repetition is linked to this 'øieblikk' in Constantin's following words: 'Repetition's love is in truth the only happy love. Like recollection's love, it does not have the restlessness of hope, the uneasy adventurousness of discovery, but neither does it have the sadness of recollection—it has the blissful security of the moment' (Kierkegaard 1983a:132). Repetition's love is the constant reclaiming of the present. It is the process through which the past is constantly reappropriated and made new. Constantly hovering between the past or the 'has been' and the new, repetition's love is in the instant of becoming. Melberg gives a clear summary of this 'now's' relationship to repetition: 'The temporal dialectics of "repetition" suspends temporal sequence: the *now* that is always an *after* actually comes *before*—it is the *now* of the instant, the sudden intervention in sequential time, the cesura that defines what has been, makes it possible to tells its story and makes way for the "new" ' (Melberg 1995: 137). Repetition relates to the 'has been' and the 'becoming' as the actual movement by which this shift from past into present takes place. We might say that repetition is the producer of this paradoxical *now*: 'with "repetition" existence *now becomes*' (ibid.). With its pointing both forwards and backwards and yet being essentially in the 'now', repetition is not reducible to linear, or teleological, time. One might say that its telos is the constant 'now', and that therefore this telos is one of constant evaporation and constant becoming. There is no stable telos *beyond* repetition, no unchanging aim towards which it advances. One might hence claim that repetition, if not teleological, is *topological*. But its topos is 'unstable'. Its topos is the instant: a forever shifting place to which it must constantly return only to constantly flee.

The instant is a caesura that 'opens' time up and gives it the promise of the moment. And the moment's paradox is that in its 'now' it is also the promise of eternity. As Kierkegaard's pseudonym Vigilius Haufensius says in *The Concept of Agony*: 'Nothing is as quick as the glance of the eye and still the glance is compatible with the substance of the eternity.' The 'now', which we tend to deem too short to be grasped or measured, is strangely linked to eternity, which we tend to deem too long to be comprehended. They are linked because eternity, like the instant 'now', is not a linear construct. It belongs to a different sense of time that radically escapes man's measurement of time. Therefore the instant can accommodate an experience that is inversely comparable to the experience of eternity. From this it is possible to conclude that the 'now', like eternity, is an experience that is seemingly 'outside' of time.

There is a clear sense that the 'now' escapes explanation and therefore language. In many ways it is a silent experience that always slips away from articulation. I would, however, like to make it clear that the 'now' is not to be equated with a metaphysical ideal of presence. In the words of Melberg: 'The temporal dialectics of "repetition" is . . . not a metaphysics of presence of the sort that Jacques Derrida has recently criticized and deconstructed as the stigma of "Western thinking" since Plato' (Melberg 1995: 140). Although the 'now' is silent and although it is not reducible to linear time, it is actually *not* outside or beyond time. Rather it is an intense 'being in' time. The experience of the *øieblikk* is the result of the rather dizzying back-and-forth of repetition, the highly accelerated movement between a 'has been' and a 'will be'. It is therefore quite the opposite of the plenitude and wholeness postulated by the dream of presence. Repetition rather negates the presence it suggests because it radically precludes rest or standstill. It is always movement—*kinesis*. So although the 'now', and its inverse relation to eternity, is seemingly *outside* time, it is always a result of repetition. It is haunted by repetition's buzz of minuscule back-and-forth. A potential image is that of an electric current accelerating between two poles. It is by remaining in this (rather unbearable) movement of back-and-forth that we might experience the 'now'. In other words the 'now' is a result, one might say, of daring to remain *inside* the temporal sequence of repetition, whereas the metaphysical presence was postulated as a beyond time.

The description of the instant as always evaporating and disappearing from the present echoes the description of the literary in

Chapter 2. The literary, I suggested, emerges in a manner congruent with every now—never present or available for objective analysis. Their essence is the movement of disappearing, of slipping away, but of still existing. As repetition is the dynamic of the instant, it is also possible to approach repetition as the dynamic of the literary and of literary silence.

KIERKEGAARD'S *REPETITION* AND LITERARY SILENCE

As I said above, the actual experience of the 'now' escapes articulation and explanation. The moment it is stated in words, or measured, it is lost. As such it might be defined as an experience of the non-symbolic. And importantly, this non-symbolic, non-temporal experience of the 'now' happens *through* repetition. This observation delineates a further 'meeting point' between the discussion of repetition and the 'now' and literary silence and the non-symbolic. The general hypothesis is that although the 'now' is the opposite category of time (hence its intimate link with eternity), it *requires* time, takes place *through* and *within* time. Similarly, the non-symbolic, arguably the opposite of language, requires language. But it requires language to behave in specific ways, just as time must behave as repetition in order to become the 'now'. Based on what I mentioned above, language must behave in what we might call a 'literary manner' for it to become the expression of the non-symbolic, and time must behave like repetition for the non-symbolic instant to come into relief. It is with this congruence in mind that I will further explore the relationship between literary silence and repetition.

One of Constantin's most important and also most enigmatic observations is relevant to literary silence: 'If one does not have the category of recollection or repetition, all life dissolves into an empty, meaningless noise' (Kierkegaard 1983*a*: 149). First of all, repetition and recollection are again comparable as *movements*, although, as we remember, they are movements in opposite directions. Secondly, this movement is a protection against 'empty, meaningless noise'. We are reminded here of Blanchot's observations in 'Mort du dernier écrivain' (see Chapter 1) regarding literature and its acting as a *silencing* shield against pure noise. We recall his suggestion that without literature, and we might borrow the words from Constantin, 'all life dissolves into empty, meaningless noise' as we *lose* our relationship to silence. Blanchot opposes pure noise and literature, suggesting that literature secures our relationship to silence. Constantin expands the opposition by suggesting a contrast between pure noise and movement: stillness and immobility produce *empty meaningless noise*. Repetition protects against this noise.[4] Does this imply that repetition, like Blanchot's concept of literature, can safeguard our relationship to silence? That it can be a dynamic of silence? I believe the answer requires a digression via Kierkegaard's *Fear and Trembling*.

The pseudonym Johannes di Silentio suggests the importance of silence that runs throughout *Fear and Trembling*. Johannes posits two types of silences, one that is related to the aesthetic and one that is related to the religious.[5] To simplify one might say that the aesthetic silence, or hiddenness, is a free act that rewards its hero with a 'happy end': 'Aesthetics then demanded the hiddenness and rewarded it' (Kierkegaard 1983*b*: 86). Aesthetic silence 'makes everything possible for the lovers' (ibid.: 85). This 'optional silence' stands in contrast to the religious silence exemplified by Abraham, the true 'knight of faith'. Abraham's act of faith is, of course, his trip to Mount Moriah where he will sacrifice his son, Isaac. In order to understand the nature of Abraham's silence we must digress once again in order first to explain the essence of the religious act.

Johannes defines Abraham's religious act as double. First, Abraham will sacrifice his son. He will do it not for any specific reason, not for any highly proclaimed decree, but for the sole reason that God has *silently* demanded it of him, and of him only. Secondly, and this is the true paradox of the act of faith, he, against all reason, knows that he will get his son back: 'He [Abraham] climbed the mountain, and even in the moment when the knife gleamed he had faith—that God would not require Isaac' (ibid.: 36). Abraham's faith is not so much the renunciation of his son, as the *knowledge* that, beyond all logic, God will return his son. This is the true act of faith by which Abraham abandons the

[4] Isak Winkel Holm's Danish study *Tanken i billedet, Søren Kierkegaard's poetik (The Thought in the Picture, The Poetics of Søren Kierkegaard)* (1998) explores this problem further. (As it is not translated, the study is available only to readers of Danish.) Especially interesting is his reading of the musical Don Giovanni topos in *Either/Or* (157–205). The problem revolves around how the immediate, musical force is made apparent in the figure of Don Giovanni, and, furthermore, how this musical apparition can emerge and take form in text. Holm explores the relationship between a so-called 'unarticulated noise', a chattering murmur, and the aesthetic-poetic writing.

[5] As is probably known to many, Kierkegaard operates with three stages, the aesthetic, the ethical, and the religious. Whereas the first and last can be described in terms of silence, the ethical stage is defined in terms of disclosure.

universal, ethical, and rational parameters and enters the absurd: 'He had faith by *virtue of the absurd*, for all human calculation had ceased long ago' (ibid., my italics). 'Human calculation' cannot guarantee that Abraham will get his son back, that Abraham, by sacrificing his son, will not become a murderer. Abraham has thereby 'transgressed the ethical altogether' (ibid.: 59) and entered the religious. Ethically, sacrificing one's son based on a silent summons from God is not valid; ethically Abraham is a potential murderer. Religiously he is 'a knight of faith' because: 'faith begins precisely where thought stops' (ibid.: 53). So, based on his faith that God will return his son, Abraham steps out of thought, out of the universal and its codes of ethics in order to 'exist as the single individual in contrast to the universal' (ibid.: 61). This is the extreme loneliness of the 'knight of faith', who has 'simply and solely himself, and therein lies the dreadfulness'. The religious act requires that the individual sacrifice belonging and relinquish community in order to become 'the single individual'. Johannes describes the fate of the religious individual:

he knows that up higher there winds a lonesome trail, steep and narrow; he knows it is dreadful to be born solitary outside of the universal, to walk without meeting one single traveller. He knows very well where he is and how he relates to men. Humanly speaking he is mad and cannot make himself understandable to anyone. (ibid.: 76)

From the perspective of 'rational discourse', 'humanly speaking', the religious individual is labelled mad. He cannot explain his absurd act without receiving the diagnosis of madness, so he finds himself consigned to loneliness, his life 'like a book under divine confiscation [that] never becomes *publice juris* [public property]' (ibid.: 77).

This is the backdrop for religious silence. By choosing to become the 'single individual', silence becomes an imperative: 'the single individual simply cannot make himself understandable to anyone' (ibid.: 71). If Abraham spoke, if he warned his family, he would have to *explain* the absurd. However, human language is based on the universal, on shared codes that cannot express this transgression into the absurd. As Johannes di Silentio says: 'As soon as I speak, I express the universal' (ibid.: 60). And because the religious is exactly the act by which the individual must abandon the universal and enter the absurd, Abraham must remain silent:

Abraham remains silent—but he *cannot* speak. Therein lies the distress and anxiety. Even though I go on talking night and day without interruption, if I cannot make myself understood when I speak, then I am not speaking. This is the case with Abraham. He can say everything, but one thing he cannot say, and if he cannot say that—that is, say it in such way that the other understands it—then he is not speaking. (ibid.: 113)

The movement of faith is therefore by necessity silent. Because it requires the entry into the absurd, and the relinquishment of the universal, there is no language available in which to express it. The 'knight of faith' has 'no higher expression of the universal that ranks above the universal he violates' (ibid.: 60)—he must remain silent. We can conclude that whereas aesthetic silence is a reversible choice, religious silence is not. Religious silence emerges as a necessity in face of the limits of ethical language. Although he speaks, the religious individual is always silent because he cannot share the one thing that matters.

It is this that Constantin is close to expressing as he claims that without the movement of repetition we drown in *meaningless noise*. Does not this meaningless noise reflect the universal, ethical language as reified and inauthentic? It is the same despair repeatedly voiced by the young man: 'I could despair over these written symbols, standing there alongside each other cold and like idle street-loafers' (Kierkegaard 1983a: 193), 'What kind of miserable invention is this human language, which says one thing and means another?' (ibid.: 200), 'What kind of wretched jargon is this human speech called language, which is intelligible only to a clique?' (ibid.: 201). The young man is caught in the ethical and still trying to express himself in ethical language. And as we now know, Kierkegaard sees only one way of relating to this dilemma, namely the religious act whereby one reclaims oneself in face of the ethical and universal. This is the *taking back* of the self, the reclaiming of the individual over the universal—repetition.

Johannes di Silentio describes the act of Abraham in terms that recall repetition: 'By virtue of the absurd, you will get every penny back again—believe it!' (Kierkegaard 1983b: 49), or: 'through a *double-movement* he had attained his first condition, and therefore he received Isaac more joyfully the second time' (ibid.: 36, my italics). This echoes the young man's description of Job: 'Job is blessed and has received everything *double*—This is called a *repetition*' (Kierkegaard 1983a: 212). In other words, the absurd, religious act of Abraham is also an event of repetition. At stake is the relationship to Isaac and to God.

Through the silence that characterizes the act of faith, through the willingness to sacrifice and the belief that Isaac would be returned, Abraham receives his self *again through God*. Through his relationship to Isaac and to God, he returns from the ethical to his authentic, religious self.

To sum up: repetition emerges as the movement of the act of faith, which, because it is absurd, requires silence and hence gives release from the 'meaningless noise' of universal language. As the young man exclaims: 'So there is repetition, after all. When does it occur? Well that is hard to say in any *human language* [my italics]. When did it occur for Job? When every *thinkable* human certainty and probability were impossible' (ibid.: 212). Repetition is a movement that is intimately related to the absurd, to the end of universal, ethical language: to silence.

But so far, the religious silence emerges in dualistic opposition to language. If Kierkegaard's repetition is to be finally relevant for literary silence, it must reveal a movement that challenges this opposition. This aspect of repetition can be traced in Johannes di Silentio's description of Abraham's breach of silence.[6] Abraham once speaks as he replies to Isaac's question regarding where the lamb for the offering is: 'And Abraham said: "God himself will provide the lamb for the burnt offering, my son"' (Kierkegaard 1983*b*: 116). These are Abraham's only words during the three and half day journey towards the designated place of sacrifice. So how are we to understand these words? Johannes shows that these words make up the only possible, religiously speaking, reply Abraham can give. If he remains silent at this point it would risk becoming an aesthetic silence aimed to protect himself and Isaac. He must answer Isaac's question, but, as we know he cannot do so in the language of universal ethics because his answer is the absurd, the inexpressible. He cannot say 'I don't know' because he does know, but it is exactly this knowledge that human language cannot impart. Neither silence nor speech is possible. But in this impasse, Abraham speaks. He speaks, says Johannes di Silentio, 'in a divine language, he speaks in tongues' (ibid.: 114). He speaks without speaking: 'So he does not speak an untruth, but neither does he say

---

[6] Dauenhauer's study *Silence: The Phenomenon and its Ontological Significance* (1980) offers a reading of this silence. Briefly put, he argues that it is an example of silence being 'determinate' and discourse 'nondeterminate', i.e. that silence is strong enough to overshadow the spoken words. Although interesting, the analysis again reveals the limitations of the dualistic view point: it is *either* silence or discourse that must be determinate and stronger.

anything, for he is speaking in a strange tongue' (ibid.: 119). This is essential as it implies that there is a language, or a *mode* of language, that is not reducible to the ethical. In other words, there is a language that can challenge the ethical, that can express the 'single individual'—a language that speaks without speaking, *a language that becomes silence*. The text indirectly implies that this language, due to its intimate link to the religious act, is a language intimately tied to the movement of repetition.

Abraham's silence is described in a manner that further indicates the parallel between this silence and literary silence. He is, as quoted above, confined to silence 'like a book under divine confiscation [that] never becomes *publice juris* [public property]' (ibid.: 77). The book, which is of course a topos of the literary, here becomes a perhaps surprising metaphor for silence. The book which never becomes 'public property', that never becomes available for the universal or ethical language, is a book that promises a different language, a, for Kierkegaard, divine language and a, for us, *literary* language, through which silence can be sustained.

The example of Abraham suggests that the religious silence of repetition is not reducible to the *end* or opposite of language; Abraham still speaks and his silence is that of a book. This suggestion is indirectly exemplified or echoed by the actual construction of the text *Repetition*. As mentioned above, the text ends with a final letter addressed to the 'Mr X Esq., the real reader of this book'. Again we are confronted with Constantin's voice telling us that the movement in the book is 'inverse'.[7] In other words, the text proclaims itself as one that must be oddly repeated, suggesting that it has no linear progression: *it dismantles its own ending by questioning the concept of an ending*. To come to the ending is not to end. So we are thrown back to Constantin's observations, and to the young man's tale—back-and-forth, in-between in an endless repetition. The text enacts the repetition of which it talks by refusing, one might say, to end. There is no end to repetition and no end to the text. The repeated denial of an ending further affirms that the silence of repetition, like literary silence, is not outside of language, not an end. Repetition, one might say, has no outside, merely more movement. In the words of the young man, repetition heralds 'three cheers for the dance in the vortex of the

[7] For a more thorough and in-depth analysis of the significance of this inverse order, see Melberg 1995: 147–53.

infinite, three cheers for the cresting waves that hide me in the abyss, three cheers for the cresting waves that fling me above the stars!' (Kierkegaard 1983a: 222). Repetition is dance and waves, non-dualistic movements, and the potential of a silence that is literary.

Both repetition and literary silence have been described as dynamics whereby the non-symbolic and non-temporal are mediated *through* language and *through* time. We might imagine that literary silence and repetition are dynamics of *transformation*. To think literary silence is also to think a transformed notion of language as the expression of the non-symbolic, and to think repetition is to think a transformed notion of linear time as the topos of eternity. Literary silence is the transformation of the traditional Dream of Silence into a silence that emerges through language. It follows that through literary silence the universal language is transformed into a different language, a, in Kierkegaard's vocabulary, 'divine language', that is also silence. Repetition, in a similar manner, is the transformation of the notion of eternity (the beyond-time) into the 'now'. Like eternity the now is an atemporal category (it cannot be measured), but whereas eternity is beyond duration, the moment is the basic component of all duration. It follows that repetition, as a movement of the 'now' transforms linear time into a dynamic of eternity .

To sum up, literary silence and repetition are linked as both are modes of transformation that set afloat the dualistic understandings of the temporal–atemporal and language–silence. In other words, the description of Kierkegaard's repetition has revealed repetition as a movement closely related to literary silence. Repetition, in the Kierkegaardian sense, therefore introduces the *temporality* of literary silence. As we shall see, literary silence is intimately linked to repetition as movement and hence to the topos of the moment. It is the moment, the 'now', that decides both repetition and literary silence as modes of transformation. In order to approach this temporality, I shall develop two different types of repetition, simple and complex repetition, and describe how they relate to literary silence.

SIMPLE AND COMPLEX REPETITION: DYNAMICS OF LITERARY SILENCE

Overall the exploration of literary silence can be summed up as the exploration of how certain literary texts relate to the non-symbolic. As stated in Chapter 1, the authors in question are chosen based on the way their texts interact, approach, dream of, or problematize the non-symbolic that they strive to express. Simple and complex repetition describe specific patterns of this relationship between the literary text and the non-symbolic it strives to express. They designate the manner in which the text *repeats* the non-symbolic as well as the actual repetition of this relationship. Again we must suspend a more traditional concept of repetition, at least as far as complex repetition is concerned. Basically I use repetition to designate a certain 'textual behaviour', a dynamic that arises in the interstices of the relationship non-symbolic–literary text. I am concerned to identify and describe a movement that has the potential to shift, and this shift will be from simple to complex repetition. In his *Samuel Beckett: Repetition, Theory and Text*, Steven Connor remarks: 'While to a large extent repetition determines and fixes our sense of our experience and representations, it is also the place where certain *radical instabilities* in these operations can reveal themselves' (Connor 1988: 1, my italics). It is exactly such places of instabilities that I am interested in and that will be explored in terms of simple and complex repetition.

Simple repetition might be generalized as the standard or dominating movement by which the literary text deals with the non-symbolic, with that which it cannot express. This is therefore often a relationship of frustration, delineating the 'limit' of the literary text. It is the text's relationship, one might say, to its own end, its defeat in face of the unsayable that it strives none the less to say. Caught in this frustration, the text must create a dynamic or a gesture by which it indirectly says: 'out there, beyond me, is the truth of what I am trying to say.' The intention is to indicate the silence of the non-symbolic as the negative other of the text. The text attempts to gesture towards this silence, hint at it, point its readers in a special direction, lead them outside itself. Furthermore simple repetition is an overt system that can often hypothetically be linked to the intentions of the author.

Simple repetition is this dynamic in the text by which the non-symbolic is placed and defined as outside the text. It is the text's way of 'gesturing' towards the unsayable, of creating a certain 'logic' or 'system' that refers the reader to the beyond. The reader is asked to seek an 'outside' of the text where truth might be found. As the text affirms its own limit, it bestows existence to that which lies beyond the limit. Simple repetition is the text's means of affirming the non-symbolic *negatively* as that which cannot be stated: the non-symbolic is what lies beyond me, it is the black against which I become white, it is the boundary against which I become literary. An obvious example, then, of simple repetition would be negative theology. By insisting on God's Otherness, his inaccessibility from human discourse, negative theology does not deny, but rather affirms God's existence. Similarly, simple repetition, by insisting on the non-symbolic in its complete distance from language, is a negative affirmation of the non-symbolic. The example of negative theology risks being misleading in that it is more obvious than simple repetition tends to be. The complexity of simple repetition is related to the fact that its movement of negative affirmation is often subtle and indirect and rarely takes the form of an obvious or direct 'gesturing' towards the beyond.

Simple repetition emerges as a dualistic dynamic. It operates according to dualistic opposites such as inside–outside, within–beyond, present–absent, silent–speaking, me–other, etc. According to these dualisms, the text defines the text according to its inside (the actual text) and its outside (the non-symbolic), and consequently defines language in terms of an inside and an outside: the expressible versus the non-expressible. Simple repetition relies upon and keeps reproducing, *repeating*, this dualistic machinery that maintains the non-symbolic as the opposite of language. The dualistic system ensures the most important function of simple repetition, namely that it is *stabilatory*. We might for a moment imagine that the text and its relationship to the non-symbolic behave in regards to each other like water and oil. In other words, their boundary is absolute, but fluid. Simple repetition ensures the stability of these two elements by continually reaffirming them as opposites, by making sure that no 'reaction' takes place that would destabilize the relation.

The question remains: how are we to think simple repetition as *repetition*? It is as a dualistic dynamic that simple repetition actually *repeats*. The repetition in question is the *repetition* of the dynamic that *repeatedly* ensures the negative existence of the non-symbolic. It is the text's repeated effort to sustain itself in opposition to the non-symbolic, to gesture towards it as its other. It describes how the text 'works' to maintain the boundary that stabilizes the text as text and the non-symbolic as the unsayable. Are we, then, to understand simple repetition as a repetition of *something*? In a sense simple repetition is the repetition of a dualistic dynamic, hence of something. However, this dynamic changes and varies from repeated instance to repeated instance. It is therefore more appropriate to say that by repeating a dynamic simple repetition *produces something*, a concrete end-product, namely the delineated, negatively defined non-symbolic as that which lies beyond the text. Simple repetition can be thought of as a well-functioning 'machinery' that repeatedly produces a stable, negatively defined notion of the non-symbolic.

We can conclude that simple repetition is a dynamic that repeatedly ensures and stabilizes the Dream of Silence as the other of language. It follows that it is a dynamic that precludes literary silence. If the non-symbolic is posited as the dualistic opposite of the text, silence becomes the beyond. Within such a schema literary silence cannot take place. Literary silence requires a certain shifting of the border between the text and the non-symbolic. A certain reaction must take place whereby the 'water mixes with the oil'. Only in the destabilization of this border can literary silence happen as the expression of the non-symbolic through literature. In other words, the dualistic system must somehow break down or dissolve in order for literary silence to occur. This destabilization describes the work of complex repetition, namely to transform or destabilize simple repetition and the stable conditions it has procured and thereby create the potential for literary silence.

Complex repetition is, as the name indicates, harder to grasp than simple repetition. First of all let me underline that the following descriptions are a theoretical attempt to describe a dynamic that takes place in the texts in question. The terminology and imagery are motivated by a need to develop a means of talking about and recognizing these abstract dynamics that constitute the movement of literary silence. As I shall try to show, the opposition between simple and complex repetition is less absolute than it might seem based on these more theoretical descriptions.

Abstractly, complex repetition might be described as the movement through which the border between the text and the non-symbolic is momentarily suspended. In other words, it is a movement that disrupts, disorganizes, and destabilizes the simple, dualistic repetition whereby the non-symbolic is affirmed as a beyond. We might imagine that due to some chemical reaction oil and water suddenly infiltrate each other. No longer affirmed negatively in relation to each other, the beyond and the text can potentially transform into one another. Imagine that the border 'desolidifies', that it is revealed as porous, thereby causing a certain 'flooding' between the text and its beyond: this is the movement of complex repetition, the dynamic of literary silence.

Complex repetition is first and foremost a movement. In other words, it is not a repetition of something. It has nothing to repeat, no pattern to reinstall. Furthermore, complex repetition, unlike simple repetition, is not productive. If we return to the image of simple repetition as a well-functioning machine that keeps producing stable versions of the beyond, complex repetition designates a certain flaw in this machinery, or rather a *derailment*. Rather than producing anything the machine derails and is hence unable to complete the successful 'production line'. It is this actual moment of derailment that I designate as complex repetition. It is the moment of a destabilization of the system, a moment when simple repetition turns into complex.

As I indicated above, it is important that simple repetition actually *becomes* complex. The two dynamics are not two distinct movements that replace each other. Rather they are intrinsically linked. Simple repetition is the stronger, dominant dynamic that produces something (see above). It is a grand movement of repetition that ensures a system. It corresponds to 'strong' rather than 'weak' thought (see Chapter 2). However, as repetition, it is also movement, the movement of repetition. And, as described above, the movement of repetition, as movement void of content, is always in the 'now', the instant before that which has been is repeated into that which will come. It is the transition between a past and future. Simple repetition, although a stable repetition of something, is therefore also a series of instants, of 'nows'. And in this now, the productive system of dualism is at its most fragile. In every now something can always happen that disrupts the repetition; strong dynamics become weak. Within the stable system, this 'now' emerges as a category of openness and fluidity, it is the moment just after and just before the border is (re-)affirmed. The 'now' of simple repetition is complex repetition. Complex repetition is the instability that introduces itself in every now of the productive system.

Complex repetition is therefore the potential derailment of the production line. In every 'now' simple repetition is unstable, fluid, and hence also complex repetition. However, it is important to underline that any derailment or destabilization is never final—this is not a derailment that causes the production line to stop. Rather we have to imagine a production line that keeps producing while it derails, and a derailment that keeps derailing despite the production line. This double movement can only take place in the opening and destabilization introduced in the instant 'now'. We might picture this as a hologram that presents changing images according to the angle of the light. One angle reflects the well-functioning production line—the product being the silent beyond. The other angle shows how this production line is, in every 'now', a series of potential interruptions, derailments, tensions, discontinuities that disrupt the production line and preclude the end product. The advantage of the hologram is that it shows how both movements exist at the same time, and that whichever one you see is dependent upon the perspective from which the system is observed. It shows how complex repetition always happens within or alongside simple repetition. It is the constant potential of simple repetition, the opposite reflection, the hidden dynamic. Simple repetition is also always complex, and vice versa.

The observation suggests that it might be more correct to think of complex repetition not first and foremost as derailment, but as the movement that is *in between* (see Chapter 2) production and derailment. Complex repetition cannot completely derail the dynamics of simple repetition as this would mean ending the text's movement. As the text ends, one gets either a traditional silence or Blanchot's and Constantin's unbearable 'meaningless noise'. Therefore, as a marker of literary silence, complex repetition can never completely derail. However, at the same time, it constantly disrupts the smooth, uninterrupted production of simple repetition. To see complex repetition as an in-between movement of production and derailment also provides a better image of how it is a potential of every 'now' of simple repetition. To repeat: in the instant before and after the border to the non-symbolic is (rea)-ffirmed, simple repetition bears within it an unstable 'now'. In this 'now' simple repetition is potentially open, potentially *in between*. It can either derail or continue. This is complex repetition.

As said above, complex repetition must be thought of as repetition as movement, rather than production. Complex repetition can be thought of in terms of play and force as these were defined in Chapter 2. It is an in-between movement where the movement in itself is primary. But in order to understand how complex repetition behaves as a textual, repetitive movement, let us return to the young man's experience of repetition. The young man's experience of repetition was the movement by which he received again his self. Suddenly reading in the newspaper of the girl's marriage to another, he was freed from the bond to her. No longer defined by his tie to the other, he was free in himself and could *change*, could become different.

Though somewhat far-fetched, the story can function as an image that can conceptualize further the movement of complex repetition. Complex repetition is the repetition whereby the text is momentarily freed from the dynamic of simple repetition. To be more precise, it is the movement whereby the text is no longer bound in its dualistic relationship to the *negative* non-symbolic. It designates the possibility the text has to liberate itself from the negative dynamic of simple repetition. In simple repetition the text is defined in relation to the negative non-symbolic. However, in complex repetition the text is freed from this defining relationship and can therefore *change*. We recall that repetition in Danish—*gentagelse*—means a taking back. Through complex repetition the text takes back the wordless silence, reclaims it, and makes it literary. Complex repetition designates the possibility the text has to reclaim the silence that has been defined as the dualistic other. Consequently, complex repetition is the potential for literary silence, for the text to become silence. Silence, like water, infiltrates porous stone and leaves its trace in caverns and canals that it traces through the text.

We recall Blanchot's image of the author as one who enters into dialogue with the raw, unmediated silence in order to silence it. Although the perspective is slightly different, this can also be understood as an image of complex repetition. The literary text can bestow silence on silence, and hence ensure that the reader can relate to silence. Blanchot recognized this moment of silencing and described it as 'un autre enfer, un centre d'illisibilité' (Blanchot 1959: 299). Evoked are those interstices where the text talks to and grapples with the silence that surrounds it. Instead of repeatedly placing this raw silence as a negative beyond, the text has the potential, the *literary* potential, to give voice to this silence and thereby to create silence. Blanchot's description offers a slightly different description of the dynamic that I have named complex repetition and which is the dynamic which makes silence literary.

To sum up, let us exemplify the dynamics of simple and complex repetition by turning again to the example of Abraham. Simple repetition designates the silence Abraham is forced to maintain as he cannot explain his absurd act of faith in universal language. Repeatedly he must keep the silence, thereby maintaining the dualistic opposition between silence and language. But this dualistic repetition is also a series of nows, a series of instants. And in each instant, the system has the potential to destabilize. When he finally speaks, it is by virtue of this potential destabilization that I call complex repetition. As Abraham cannot speak the universal language of the others, he speaks in a manner that maintains the silence. One could say that he has used the potential instability, the 'now', of the dualistic system in favour of a 'third option'—neither speech nor silence, speaking 'a strange tongue' (Kierkegaard 1983*b*: 119), a 'divine language' (ibid.: 114). The example also shows how simple and complex repetition do not rule each other out, but rather are closely interrelated. By speaking, Abraham has not broken with the dualistic system in the sense that he has not chosen either speech or silence. The dualism is therefore still valid on one level; he must still be silent as he cannot speak the ethical language of others. But exactly within this dualism he sees a parallel option: to speak while maintaining silence. On this level the dualism is destabilized by an in-between option: to speak in a language that is not universal. In this act of speaking, the relationship between language and silence changes from the strict either–or opposition to a new fluidity: he can speak silence. Indirectly Abraham's silent words describe the dynamic of complex repetition as the potential for a silence that is literary.

The conclusion is that complex repetition designates the potential of a text to *transform,* to be neither language nor silence, but somehow in-between. No longer defined against the non-symbolic, the text can behave differently. Using its potential as play or *jeu*, the text changes, its boundaries become fluid. This implies that my further exploration of literary silence will be concentrating on passages where the text behaves *differently*, where it somehow slips away from, or transforms, the system of simple repetition. These can be instances in which the simple gesturings towards the beyond suddenly 'slip' or become seemingly meaningless. Such weird or disturbing moments are the keys to literary silence. They mark the manifestation of the 'now' of complex repetition and its interference with the smooth production line.

Simple and complex repetition have been defined as simultaneous movements of repetition. Simple repetition is the repetition of a dualistic system according to which the non-symbolic is negatively affirmed in relation to the text. Through simple repetition both the text and the non-symbolic are ensured their 'identities' as stable. However, as a *movement* of repetition, simple repetition always has its essence in the 'now', that is, in the constant becoming of the system. And it is in this instance of becoming, this 'before' and 'after' that the system reveals itself as potentially fragile. This 'now' indicates the potential that is complex repetition. It is in this 'now' that the text can take back, repeat itself, and liberate itself from its negative relation to the non-symbolic. The text will then change, lose its stable identity as the other of silence, and emerge as a potential 'divine language'—a language of silence—literary silence.

THE APORIA

Complex repetition has been described as a moment within a text that is a potential destabilization of the smooth-running machine of simple repetition. Taking the form of the actual 'now', complex repetition is always a moment of openness in the sense that in this 'now' the system might either derail or continue its production. It is a movement of in-between, a suspended 'now' that is characterized not by being either productive or unproductive, but strangely both. As said above, it cannot derail or continue the stable simple repetition. It is as such that complex repetition is essentially aporetic and that the importance of the aporia enters into the behaviour of literary silence.

The aporia originally means impasse and hence designates the place from which no further advance is possible. It has been used as a rhetorical term to signify the doubt arising from two incompatible but equally valid views on a subject matter. The aporia arises when there are two potential outcomes, both of which rule the other one out, but both of which are true. In other words, both outcomes, both 'paths', are true, but they are incompatible; choosing one, I am immediately thrown back on to the other, and so on. The only possible locus within the aporia is therefore the *in-between*. Again I can draw a parallel between play and aporia. Like play, aporia has the advantage of focusing on, even of privileging, the movement rather than the two poles between which the movement occurs.

As mentioned in the Introduction, the aporia is well chosen to describe the venture of post-structuralist thought and its attempt to dismantle the notion of a single truth. Aporia reveals that any truth always exists in relation to another truth, hence undermining any universal claims. In her study on Pascal, *Discourses of the Fall*, Sara Melzer perceptively describes the aporia in a footnote: 'Aporia, in the modern deconstructive sense, is born of the knowledge that there can be no certain knowledge. It brings to light the failure of our attempts to

seize that truth of the world' (Melzer 1986: 4). Central to my understanding of the aporia is also de Man's observation in *Allegories of
Reading* (1979*b*). Reading, suggests de Man,

will always lead to the confrontation of incompatible meanings between
which it is necessary but impossible to decide in terms of truth and error. If
one of the readings is declared true, it will always be possible to undo it by
means of the other; if it is declared false, it will always be possible to demonstrate that it states the truth of its aberration. (de Man 1979*b*: 76)

In other words, reading emerges as the oscillation between incompatible meanings or paths—the experience of the impasse. If you choose
one way, then you are thrown back onto the other, etc. There is no resolution. This defines the aporia.

I would like to extend the definition of repetition with reference to
the aporia. Complex repetition was defined in terms of the
Kierkegaardian 'now', the moment of mediation between a past and
a future. It is a certain suspension that is the essence of the 'now'. And
this suspension, I would like to argue, is also aporetic. It is the impasse
between a past and a future. Repetition cannot be identified merely
with the past as this past is always also a becoming into a future.
Furthermore it cannot be identified merely with the future, as it is also
always a past. In other words, repetition, as described by Kierkegaard,
is an aporetic experience. It is the constant experience of an impasse
between a past and a future that leaves one suspended in the present,
in the *in-between*. The actual 'now' therefore becomes the only 'true',
or possible experience of repetition. It is the only position that can
account for repetition's relation to the past and the future. So the
'now' is the aporetic position of a constant in-between, a constant
mediation between a past and a future. To experience the 'now' is to
bear the full pressure of the aporia, to remain standing in the impasse,
to not think the past or the future, but be absorbed in the in-between
movement of the aporia.

If the 'now' is aporetic, this implies also that complex repetition can
be further understood in terms of an impasse, an aporetic movement.
We recall that complex repetition designates the moment of instability
where the system can either derail or continue, but does neither. In
order to take place, complex repetition requires the system of simple
repetition to continue. But the essence of complex repetition is still
the moment of disruption or instability of this system. In other words,

complex repetition is defined as the moment when the system can
neither break down nor merely continue. This is its essence, and as such
it is aporetic. Complex repetition is the ongoing *repetition* of this impasse.
It is, one might say, the constant hesitation, the constant in-between, of
these two mutually exclusive options that describes complex repetition.

As far as the actual reading of the texts is concerned, the aporia can
be the presence of two mutually exclusive relationships to the non-
symbolic beyond. It emerges as a figure of the unthinkable. It is the
instance in a text, the instance of complex repetition, when the text's
attempt to gesture towards the silent beyond continues, yet also
derails. In other words, it describes the instance when the positioning
of silence as the other of the text destabilizes and potentially shifts. As
the dualism breaks down, we can no longer think silence in terms of a
beyond. But neither can we think of it as in the text, because the text
is still text. The situation is again comparable to Abraham: silence is
no longer an option, nor is speech. This is the true aporetic instance.
However, and this is important, the aporia is not a 'barren' situation.
Rather than a dynamic of frustration, the aporia behaves as a fruitful
moment. Abraham, when caught in the impasse, discovers what we
called above the 'third' option, the language that remained silent.
Although an impasse, I therefore believe the aporia is always an opening, a fruitful moment. However, this opening takes the form of the
impossible, or the *unthinkable*. It is the non-dualistic, the infiltration of oil
into water, water into rock, the discovery that the membrane that
divides is porous. I propose that the third way requires a 'leap of logic',
a suspension of rational understanding. In the case of Abraham the
'third' option is a language that does not speak. In the case of complex
repetition it is literary silence. This 'third' option arises when one
remains in the aporia, when one stands in the 'now' of the impasse
and thereby experiences how both potential paths, hitherto incompatible, 'merge' and transform, providing a 'new' opening. In Chapter
2 I defined literary silence in terms of force. The back-and-forth of the
aporia, already described as play, can also be thought of as the topos
of this force and hence the producer of the dynamic of literary silence.

I have chosen to introduce the term aporia specifically because it
designates a *logical impasse*. That is to say, it describes moments which
radically challenge our rational capacity to understand. My intention
is to explore how the literary text is a dynamic that can bear the
aporia, that can indicate the third option that defies dualism, namely
literary silence. Where everyday language and everyday logic require

a choice—either one is silent or one speaks, either one continues or one ends—the literary text appears as a dynamic that can stand in the aporia and rather take advantage of it. Literary silence assumes this continued, persistent aporetic dynamic that is the privilege of the text over everyday language. The texts in question move towards a language that can both be and not be silence, towards a silence that can both be and not be language.

The aporetic dynamic of literary silence suggests that literary silence is not a phenomenon we can exhaust rationally. Arising in the 'now' of complex repetition, literary silence is aporetic in the sense that it is the constant *in-between* of the silent non-symbolic and the literary text. Literary silence is the third way that arises in the aporetic moment. It requires us to remain in the 'now' of the aporia, and it therefore also requires that we abandon a mere rational understanding. It is these moments of rational 'collapse' that I now propose to discuss further in terms of what I will call 'implosions'.

THE IMPLOSION

The implosion can best be defined as the dynamic that arises through literary silence. It is not therefore a textual marker for literary silence like repetition or aporia. Rather implosion describes how literary silence addresses the reader and how the reader is invited to respond to literary silence. It delineates those dynamics instigated and created by literary silence in relation to the reader. Implosion therefore describes the relationship between text and reader that arises through literary silence. It is inherent in the Gadamerian view of dialogue as a moment of *interaction* between text and reader. In Chapter 2 I said that literary silence is not an identifiable object within the text, but rather a result of play, force, and dialogue. We have seen how complex repetition and the aporia are fields of such force and play and therefore markers of literary silence.

Complex repetition and aporia transform the text from the positive other of the non-symbolic and thereby indicate how the text can become silence while continuing. The implosion, on the other hand, describes how literary silence also changes the relationship between reader and text, or at least how it implies a specific view of this relationship. Literary silence can therefore only be approached on the basis of this understanding of the reader–text relationship. Simply put, the implosion releases the reader from the often superior position of interpreter and it follows that the text is no longer an object of interpretation. The 'critical distance' between text and reader implodes, collapses. In order to explain this I will describe the implosion in terms of *sacrifice* as it is defined by Bataille, namely as an act through which both the sacrificed and the sacrificer undergo transformation. But first I will attempt a general description of the actual implosion.

The Oxford English Dictionary defines implosion as 'The bursting inward of a vessel from external pressure', and to implode is 'To burst inwards'. Although brief, these definitions suggest the essence of implosion as a bursting *inward*. *Webster's Collegiate Dictionary* defines implosion as '1: The inrush of air in forming a suction stop 2: the action of imploding 3: the act or action of bringing to or as if to a centre.' To implode is '1 a: to burst inward b: to undergo violent compression 2: to collapse inward as if from external pressure.' These definitions point to a movement that signifies a *collapse* in space caused by a force that moves inwards, towards, or as if towards, a centre. An implosion 'sucks' space together and causes it to 'cave in'. It is this sense of *collapsing* and *bursting inwards* that provides such adequate and powerful descriptions of the experience of reading literary silence.

As a 'bursting inwards', the implosion describes the relationship between text and reader. It is the movement that causes the reader somehow to 'collapse' towards the text, to be pulled towards the aporetic dynamic of complex repetition. We might imagine the implosion as the result of the mounting 'pressure' of the aporia. Again, the implosion evokes notions of force. As said above, the text can sustain the aporia because it can transform it into a third option which is literary silence. But when the reader is asked to relate to this aporia, he or she must accept to stand in the unthinkable, must accept a text that continues while it derails, that continues while it is silence. The aporia invites the reader to stand in and to accept the constant in-between that is a repeated challenge to rational thought and understanding. In other words, the aporia, as a marker for literary silence, creates a movement that slips away from rational analysis. Literary silence therefore summons the reader to abandon the situation of critical observer. It is this movement that takes the form of the implosion. Usually the relationship between text and reader is characterized by a certain 'distance', a 'space' that separates the two. This distance ensures the respective roles of 'reader' as reader, as interpreter, and of 'text' as that which is read, that which is interpreted. Relating to literary silence, this distance collapses and the text is no longer a separate object facing the reader, but rather the two 'merge' together. We can recognize literary silence because it invites this implosion, this transformation in the traditional analytical relationship between text and reader.

In order to grasp the implosion as such a radical collapse, we must again recall the observations in Chapter 2. I there claimed that literary silence cannot be understood within a subject–object constellation. Literary silence always belongs to that surplus of a text that cannot be analysed and interpreted according to the empirical view of the text as an object. I suggested that the experience of literary silence required a different way of conceiving the relationship between text and reader. I referred to Proust and the sense of reading as a silent, solitary experience in which the reader's voice is far removed from the sphere of everyday communication. Reader and text merge together, mixing, so to speak, their voices. The implosion is intrinsic to this view of reading. It is the moment through which the subject–object constellation actually collapses. It is a moment of a certain 'trembling' between text and reader, a dissolution of roles as the reader is no longer the interpreting subject and the text no longer the object to be interpreted. Implosion marks the end of rational and meaningful dialogue. It shows literary silence as *play* in the sense that the player abandons his or her subjectivity as the movement of play itself becomes primary. It is a moment then of a certain 'floating' and destabilization which is congruent with complex repetition. The implosion is therefore playful because it is always surprising, never foreseen, never as expected, always new.

So far we can conclude that because the aporetic dynamic of literary silence defies rational and logical mastery, literary silence requires a different approach on the part of the reader. This approach encompasses a willingness to accept the implosion and to enter into an uncertain relationship with the text. This uncertain relationship can be further explored in relation to the category of the Kierkegaardian instant. As we mentioned above, Kierkegaard defines the instant as the inverse experience of eternity. In other words, the instant, because it cannot be objectively measured, is, like eternity, the experience of a 'non-time'. The instant escapes linear time because it is an experience that is not governed by thought. On the contrary, it requires a certain abandonment of rational thought. *The moment one thinks about the instant one has lost it*. The experience of the instant therefore presumes a suspension of reflection. And the implosion can be approached as an experience of the instant in that it also requires that the reader abandon his or her position as rational 'interpreter'. The implosion is therefore also a movement that is not primarily *thought*, but rather experienced. To think the implosion is to lose it and re-enter the realm of reflection and control. Literary silence is the dynamic that invites the reader to perform a certain unmediated 'jump' away from the firm ground of reason, and into the free fall, scary or relieving, of non-rational control.

This is the essence of the implosion. It is not only a collapsing inwards of text and reader, but also of the reader's rational ability to reflect. It is a fall into a certain immediacy, a 'simpleness', or even 'imbecility', that knows no reflection. The implosion creates this lack of reflection and thereby becomes the experience of literary silence.

Already it is clear that the implosion relies upon the willingness of the reader to change not only the relationship to the text as an object, but also to him- or herself as an interpreting, reflecting, rational reader. The dynamic of literary silence can be recognized by how it invites and solicits these changes or transformations in the relationship between text and reader. I shall now describe these dynamics further in reference to Bataille's notion of sacrifice.

I have chosen to refer to Bataille's notion of sacrifice because it delineates a release from 'thingliness' that in turn can nuance our understanding of the implosion.[8] Central to Bataille's understanding of the sacrifice is the power of the act of sacrifice to release the sacrificer and the sacrificed from their status as *things*. The sacrifice is an act that transcends the realm of the reified, or *le monde profane*, as Bataille calls it, and brings liberation from reification. I turn to Bataille's notion to borrow this resonance and highlight how the implosion is a similar movement.

The immediate question to be raised is: what is actually sacrificed in the implosion? It is after all not a physical act of transgression in the sense of a sacrifice of an animal. However, as we have seen, the implosion requires a radical abandonment of rational thought and rational

---

[8] Bataille's *L'Expérience intérieure* (1943/1954) is of course also relevant. His description of the experience clearly parallels the implosion: 'Le sujet dans l'expérience s'égare, il se perd dans l'objet, qui lui-même dissout' (Bataille 1943/1954: 76). However, I shall focus on the sacrifice as it is developed in *Théorie de la religion* (1973). The image of the sacrifice is richer in that the act itself provides associations that can throw new light on the understanding of the implosion. The notion of sacrifice also brings us back to the story of Abraham and Isaac.

approach to the text. In other words, it requires a *sacrifice of rational control*. It is the momentary loss of subjective mastery. The power of observation and analysis that greatly characterizes our subject–object approach to the world must be sacrificed. We must dare, one might say, to enter a world that is floating and unfixed and that undermines rational control. Based on the previous section, we might define the implosion as a double collapse or 'bursting inwards'. First it designates the collapse between the subject-reader and text-object, causing them momentarily to merge. Secondly it is the collapse of the reflective relationship the subject has to himself as rational observer and interpreter. Both these reflective relationships must be sacrificed in the implosion.

Both these relationships are basically predicated by our relationship to what I will designate as *reifying* language. By this I mean the mode of language that corresponds to a Cartesian way of thinking, that is, the language that defines the world as objects, as *things*. Reified language is in many ways our 'everyday language'. It is the language that we rely upon to give meaning and signification. It is a teleological language in the sense that it is always orientated towards the goal of creating meaning and communication and the sharing of feelings, needs, ideas, etc. It is the language that defines, categorizes, and measures the world. It is the language that ensures our control in regards to this world by keeping it so to speak at a 'distance', an objective reality against which we stand as subjects.

Reified language is intimately linked to the first part of the sacrifice, namely the sacrifice of the text as thing. It is through reified language that the text becomes an object that stands against us as subjects. But it is not only the text that becomes an object in this reified relation. Also the subject is locked in the constellation and is thereby equally reduced to a thing. This is the valuable observation made by Bataille in his *Théorie de la religion* (1973) when he talks of *le monde profane*. The profane world basically consists of subject–object relationships. He develops these in terms of subordination and differentiation. He specifically describes the object as the tool with a purpose of utility. To relate to the tool as an object is to establish a difference between the self and it, and to subordinate it. The ultimate consequence of this approach is that the subject also becomes an object, subordinated and caught within the subject–object constellation:

D'une façon générale, le monde des choses est senti comme une déchéance. Il entraîne l'aliénation de celui qui l'a créé. C'est un principe fondamental:

subordonner n'est pas seulement modifier l'élément subordonné mais être modifié soi-même. L'outil change en même temps la nature et l'homme: il asservit la nature à l'homme qui le fabrique et l'utilise, mais il lie l'homme à la nature asservie. . . . . S'il met le monde en son pouvoir, c'est dans la mesure où il oublie qu'il est lui-même le monde: il nie le monde mais c'est lui-même qui est nié. (Bataille 1973: 55)

Reification, therefore, not only affects the objects in question, but also the subject that uses and relies upon this language. Referring to agricultural production, Bataille summarizes: 'Le produit agricole, le bétail sont des choses, et le cultivateur ou l'éleveur, au moment où ils travaillent, sont aussi des choses' (ibid.: 56). As far as the relationship between text and reader is concerned, this observation implies that the reader, when relating to the text as a thing, also becomes a thing. In the thought of Bataille, the sacrifice is the potential 'escape' or release from this locked chain of reification. In other words, the sacrifice constitutes a release from 'thingliness' for both object and subject, for both text and reader. It is in light of this that it is useful to think of the implosion in terms of sacrifice.

But what is actually destroyed in the act of sacrifice? According to Bataille: 'C'est la chose—seulement la chose—que le sacrifice veut détruire dans la victime' (ibid.: 58). It is only *as a thing* that the sacrificed object must be destroyed. It is noteworthy that Bataille postulates the subject–object separation as the necessary state *against* which the sacrifice operates: 'Le séparation préalable du sacrificateur et du monde des choses est nécessaire au retour de l'*intimité*, de l'immanence entre l'homme et le monde, entre le sujet et l'objet' (ibid.: 59). Because the subject–object constellation is the presupposition of the sacrifice, it is what is *destroyed* in the sacrifice. The subject-object constellation is in itself reifying. It is a dynamic that locks both subject and object as things. Again, this implies that the implosion invited by literary silence can be viewed as a sacrifice to the extent that it destroys the respective positions of reader-subject and text-object. Literary silence offers the potential for a transgression whereby both reader and text undergo a change. No longer separated as things in relation to each other, they 'melt' together, towards each other, and the border that ensured the various positions implodes. Text is no longer text, reader is no longer reader. This floating, undefined 'state' is the experience of literary silence.

Bataille continues to develop the sacrifice by insisting that what is sacrificed is always that which is useful, which has a purpose: 'C'est si bien le sens du sacrifice, qu'on sacrifie *ce qui sert*' (ibid.: 67). This purpose corresponds to the sense of a 'telos' implied in any useful *production*. What one sacrifices, therefore, is the teleological, the linear sense of purpose. This recalls my definition above of reified language as teleological or goal-orientated. It is this language that must be sacrificed in the implosion. We must destroy our relationship to language as *ce qui sert* and thereby enter into a sense of language as *something else*. My suggestion in this project is that the text, because it does not rely upon the criteria of usefulness that determine everyday language, can move towards this *something else*, can become the site of the sacrifice of reified language. This describes the precondition of literary silence. Only as non-reified language, as non-useful language, can language become literary silence—the writing of the unsayable.

The link between literary silence and sacrifice can of course also be traced in Kierkegaard's story of Abraham. First of all, reified language can be compared to Kierkegaard's version of ethical language: both ensure the universal. The ethical language, like the reified language, guarantees the community, but is incongruous with the religious, which begins, as we recall, 'exactly where thought stops' (Kierkegaard 1983*b*: 53). The story of Abraham is of course first and foremost a story of the sacrifice. And, as I have insisted earlier, the exigency of this sacrifice is silence. The sacrifice of Isaac also demands a sacrifice of the ethical, reified language. Derrida's response to *Fear and Trembling*, 'A qui donner (savoir ne pas savoir)' in *Donner la mort* (1999) focuses on this sacrifice and its implications for ethics. He observes that 'Abraham doit prendre la responsabilité absolue de sacrifer son fils en sacrifiant l'éthique' (Derrida 1999: 95). The scandal caused by the summons to perform the sacrifice of the son indeed entails, even presupposes, the sacrifice of the reified, ethical language.

Two aspects of Abraham's sacrifice are important here. First of all, the unthinkable necessity of the sacrifice of Isaac is linked to the necessary silence of Abraham. Where thought stops, the sacrifice of reified language takes place. As Derrida says: 'Le paradoxe, le scandale ou l'aporie ne sont autres, eux-mêmes, que le sacrifice: l'exposition de la pensée conceptuelle à sa limite, à sa mort et à sa finitude' (ibid.: 98). Derrida here indirectly supports my understanding of the implosion as a necessary result of the aporia and as sacrifice. The second important aspect of Abraham's sacrifice of ethical language is a more direct link to literary silence. We recall that Abraham's one answer to Isaac arises as neither ethical (reified) language nor silence.

In its in-between mode this 'speaking in silence' indicates the possi-bility of literary silence. The suggestion seems to be that the sacrifice of ethical language is intimately linked to literary silence.

To sum up, the implosion is the invitation issued by literary silence to sacrifice first the relationship to the text and to oneself as objects caught in a subject–object relationship, and secondly the relationship to reified, useful, everyday language.

Not surprisingly the sacrifice is described in terms of fear and anxiety. To sacrifice is threatening: 'Sans nul doute, ce qui est sacré attire et possède une valeur incomparable, mais au même instant cela apparaît vertigineusement dangereux pour ce monde clair et profane où l'humanité situe son domaine privilégié' (Bataille 1973: 48). To sacrifice is to leave the (profane) world of measurable, empir-ical facts, of control, of observation, and of verifiable realities. This constitutes at once the attraction of the sacred world, but also its deep sense of horror. To sacrifice one's relationship to reified lan-guage is to abandon the universal and to risk the loss of understand-ing and shared meaning. It is the entry into a different 'realm' of language that, unlike the language of the *cogito*, offers no guarantee. In addition there is a second dimension to the fear of the sacrifice that is linked to the necessary destruction of oneself as a subject in relation to the object. To sacrifice is momentarily to 'dissolve' as an individual as far as this individuality, this selfhood is defined through reified language (i.e. as 'reader', 'critic', 'interpreter', 'scholar', etc.). This is the deep fear of the sacrificer: 'L'homme a peur de l'ordre intime qui n'est pas conciliable avec celui des choses' (ibid.: 70). The sacrificer must lose his identity in the sacrifice. This is obviously related again to the destruction of rational control and mastery. Through the sacrifice the sacrificer becomes immediate, non-reflective and hence loses control of himself as an object in the world. Importantly, this fear acts as the precondition of the sacrifice. The fear indicates that something *is* to be sacrificed. Again, the rei-fied status of the subject (in relation to the object) is always the 'start-ing position' of the sacrifice: it is that which is to be sacrificed. Therefore, without the fear of this destruction 'il n'y aurait pas de sacrifice, et il n'y aurait pas non plus d'humanité' (ibid.). To sum up: the sacrifice is defined as a moment of anxiety and this anxiety is linked to the transformation and dissolution of the sacrificed victim and the sacrificer that is always implied by the sacrifice. The obser-vation indicates the experience of literary silence, of the implosion,

as one that might emerge as threatening in that our identity as interpreting, rational, academic readers is challenged.

To describe the implosion caused by literary silence as a sacrifice
implies three major suggestions. First, I suggest that literature has the
power to trigger a sacrifice. Secondly, I postulate that literary silence,
by triggering the implosion, is a textual dynamic that invites and permits (!) a sacrifice of something, and that this can be experienced as
threatening on the part of the reader. And finally, I suggest that reading can be compared to the experience of the sacred in the sense that
the sacred is a release from thingliness and from reified language. As
stated above, I believe that literature can 'stage' a language that is not
goal-orientated towards a shared meaning. Literary silence is congruent with this 'performance'. It designates moments in the literary text
when the literary language does not behave as reified language, but
rather transforms and shifts. It designates moments therefore of a certain 'meaninglessness' in which the purpose of language no longer is
to signify a universal meaning. *Relating to this language that is literary
silence, the reader is forced to sacrifice the relationship to reified language.* This
involves momentarily 'entering' a language that does not obey the
rules of the universal, that does not signify, but rather that 'floats' and
in fact dissolves meaning. By 'entering' into this language I mean let-
ting it move you around and through its movements. It is a question
of taking it seriously and listening to it (see Chapter 2) and then of participating in its consequences. Listening to literary silence, accepting
the invitation that is the implosion, the reader must also sacrifice his
or her subject status that is guaranteed by the reified language.

Described as a sacrifice, it is clear to what extent the implosion is
demanding of the reader. To sacrifice implies that one gives something away. It is a loss. In the case of the implosion it is the loss of the
'security' and 'control' guaranteed by the reified language and the
subject–object constellation. It follows that the implosion does not
simply 'happen' without the willing interaction of the reader, without
the courage to perform the necessary sacrifice. Finally, I believe that
the implosion is congruent with sacrifice also to the extent that it does
create an opening to the sacred, although not necessarily a religiously
defined sacred. As sacrifice the implosion dissolves the relationship to
the object, it transforms the subject, and it performs a language that
says the unsayable. In other words, the profane world, as defined by
Bataille, dissolves in the implosion and the experience of literary
silence becomes a potential experience of the sacred, of the non-

reified, of the unsayable. Such, argues a reader of literary silence, is the potential of literature.

CONCLUSION

Chapter 3 concludes what can be called the explicatory section. Literary silence has now been explored and circumscribed according both to theoretical concepts and to so-called textual 'markers' or textual behaviour. I shall now turn to the literary texts as I start the more exploratory section of the book.

Based on the above descriptions of the behaviour of literary silence I can delineate the following general approach. Moving on to the literary texts, I will be looking first for patterns of simple repetition. Having recognized and described how the texts relate to the silent non-symbolic in a negative manner, I will see how this system also consists of slips, discontinuities and derailments that indicate the behaviour of literary silence. I shall then explore how these instances behave as playful, aporetic dynamics and movements. I shall see how they produce incompatible meanings as they can be approached as both simple and complex repetition—a constant in-between. In addition the dynamics of complex repetition are aporetic in that they produce instances that challenge our rational ability to synthesize and conclude an acceptable meaning. If we accept the force of this irresolvable aspect of the aporia, it will be possible to delineate a potential implosion. I shall see how the passages in question challenge the ability of the reader to remain an interpreting reader in relation to an object and how the language emerges as non-reified. The passages in question invite the readers to commit the sacrifices described above and hence indicate the potential of the text to become something else that is not symbolic or non-symbolic, not language nor silence, but a silent language, a third option, a non-reified, non-rational movement that is literary silence.

II

Exploring Literary Silence

4

LITERARY SILENCE IN PASCAL'S *PENSÉES*

INTRODUCTION: '*LE SILENCE ÉTERNEL*'

One of the most celebrated and most quoted fragments of Pascal's *Pensées* resounds with silence: 'Le silence éternel de ces espaces infinis m'effraie' (Pascal 1991: 233).[1] At the simplest level, the fragment recognizes the silence of a newly discovered, infinite universe,[2] in which man risks further estrangement from God, and from his prelapsarian 'voice'. But despite this rather straightforward understanding, the fragment has caused various interpretative problems (see Sellier 1991: 256 n. 19). The issue at stake is the unnamed identity of the *me* of the *m'effraie*, that is, of the speaking subject. The question arises as to who is experiencing this fear—surely it cannot be the Christian believer? Is Pascal lending his voice to the libertine? Maybe it is merely a rhetorical move? Paul Valéry, in his 'Variation sur une Pensée', encounters this frustration and concludes that the experience of fear is certainly not that of a true believer, and hence accuses Pascal of artificially forging identities as part of his apologetic project.

Valéry is dealing with a problem that confronts all readers of the *Pensées*—who is talking to me? What, or who, one might ask, hides behind the first person? Who speaks? (See Parish 1986; Marin 1975.) The *Pensées* are always playing out a multiple range of voices, be it in obvious dialectic form like the famous *pari* or the more mysterious cases like fragment 233. The question of who is speaking is further complicated by the unfinished state of the text.[3] Whether considered

---

[1] I am refering throughout to the fragments from the Sellier edition of the *Pensées*, by fragment number.

[2] Michel Serres (1968: 648–712) draws attention to the important role played by the contemporary astrological discoveries of a decentralized, infinite universe in the *Pensées*, and also draws specific attention to this fragment.

[3] When they were found in 1662, the *Pensées* were to a large extent unorganized, barring certain preliminary classified sections (we cannot be sure they were definitive), the *liasses*, twenty-eight of which were named. Since the appearance of the first edition in 1670, numerous editions have appeared all claiming a higher degree of original order. Predictably, the issue of editions and order of the fragments occupies a central position in Pascal studies. For a good introduction and overview, see Sellier's Introduction (Sellier 1991: 5–92), the Pléiade edition (Le Guern 2000), and Mesnard's Introduction (Mesnard 1993: 15–55). Mesnard also

a result of Pascal's death or an inherent principle,[4] the fragmentary style of the *Pensées* contributes to the play of interrupted voices in endless substitution. The complexity increases, as we also have to ask who listens (see Parish 1986; Michon 1996: 10–14). In other words, the identity of the mysterious *me* of *m'effraie* remains suspended as we do not know whether it belongs to the writer or the reader, the believer or the non-believer.

I propose that this unidentifiable *me* can be explored as an indicator of another silence that displays a behaviour closer to literary silence. The fragment presents a *me* that is 'silent', or secretive, about its own origin. This is a silence that is not based on the absence of words, but rather a silence that operates through language, that is inherent in the operation of discourse. This indecisiveness of the *je*, this tussle between writer and reader, creates a suspension at the core of the fragment. It is this suspension that I propose to think of in terms of silence. We might imagine that the *silence éternel* of the infinite universe also appears within the linguistic composition of the fragment, namely the unnamed, or unsaid, identity of the *je*. In fact, there is no *je* in the fragment, as the *silence éternel* is the grammatical subject of the sentence. All that is left is the short *m'* that has no fixed belonging. Silent and absent, the *je* returns in the unfixed *m'* which then becomes a marker for the silence that haunts the fragment and that has confused various readers.

Read as such, the fragment stages a silence that is in fact *double*. The first silence, which corresponds to what I in Chapter 1 designated as first-degree, is named and refers to God's retreat from the world. It is, as mentioned, a strong silence that is accorded subject status in the

summarizes (apps. IV and V: 389–404) the most important discoveries during the last fifty years, namely those of Pol Ernst (1996) in his *Les Pensées de Pascal: géologie et stratigraphie*, and Emmanuel Martineau's work (1992) which resulted in an alternative reconstruction of the *Pensées* named *Discours sur la religion et sur quelques autres sujets*.

[4] This passing comment raises a central debate which has created two opposing tendencies among Pascal readers (Mesnard 1993: 396). The issue is the degree to which the *Pensées* should be read as an intentionally fragmented text, or as an unintentionally fragmented text. The latter tendency, exemplified and strengthened by the recent research of Pol Ernst (1996), aims to recreate an original order of the text. The supposition is that the *Pensées* were written with a larger structure in mind that was not based on the fragment. This tendency is opposed by those who argue for an aesthetics of the fragment. The argument claims that the *Pensées* are intentionally fragmented, and see this fragmentation as intrinsic either to the apologetic project or to Pascal's theology. The fact remains that we still have no complete structuring of the fragments and that we are still dealing with an unfinished text. My conclusion is therefore that, whatever Pascal's intention, the experience of *reading* the *Pensées* remains fragmented.

sentence and that has the power to inject fear into the *m'*. The silence represents a postlapsarian, unspeaking, and unknowable God who is 'infiniment incompréhensible' (Pascal 1991: 680); he is completely other; 'il n'a nul rapport à nous' (ibid.). The silence of God designates his inaccessibility from within human discourse: only 'Dieu parle bien de Dieu' (ibid.: 334) and 'Les choses de Dieu . . . [sont] inexprimables' (ibid.: 303). However, I suggest that this same difference between human discourse and God further elucidates the second silence of the *me*, of the writing subject. As I said in Chapter 1, Christianity operates with a fallen notion of language. By this is meant a fundamental aspect of all discourse, namely the gap or distance between the signifier and the signified that precludes language from ever attaining a transparent relationship to the reality that is signified. In the case of fragment 233, this dynamic of language is first evoked by the terrifying *silence éternel* that leaves man forever separated from God. But fallen language is indirectly referred to also in the second silence as the fragment specifically *enacts* the problem of the first pronoun 'I' and its lack of coincidence with a speaking subject. Louis Marin, in his article 'Voix et énonciation mystique: sur deux textes d'Augustin et de Pascal', describes the locus or the origin of the speaking subject as 'cette insaisissable et constante présence absente de la voix de l'énonciation, voix d'origine et de commencement inaudible dans les signes du texte' (Marin 1990: 171). So the silence of the *m'*, the second-degree silence (see Chapter 1), which is symptomatic of the indeterminacy and multiplicity of voices, of the difference between the sign 'I' and the actual speaker, is also intrinsic to the 'appareil formel de l'énonciation' (ibid.: 176)—the playing out of 'le mystère et le secret où cet appareil s'articule' (ibid.).

Valéry's aggressive response to the fragment overlooks this dimension. The silence is more than an apologetic tool as it reflects language's fallen status, the impossibility of saying 'I' without calling forth a multiple range of personae. Understood as such, the silence in fact describes the gap or difference created by any act of enunciation between the (im)personal pronoun and the proper name of the speaker, between the *je* and the identity of the speaker. The second-degree silence in the *Pensées* emerges as an indirect reflection of the operation of discourse.

For the moment I conclude that the *silence éternel* first designates the silence of a God inaccessible to language. This designates the non-symbolic God, transcending language and articulation and about whom one must remain *silent*. This silence is then transformed into a different silence that appears when the discourse of the *Pensées* actually 'plays out' its own distance from an origin or truth. This is the silence of a language that can never coincide with its origin and hence must remain silent about this origin. Fragment 233 evokes this silence by acting out the inherent gap or *écart* that characterizes the relationship between discourse and its indiscernible locus of origin (see Marin 1975: 135). This double movement compresses a more general movement that takes place throughout the *Pensées*, namely the simultaneous positing of, on the one hand, the non-symbolic in terms of a certain silence and, on the other, a reflection regarding the possibility of a discourse on God and Christianity. Marin, in another study entitled ' "Pascal": Text, Author, Discourse . . .' remarks that 'The *Pensées* speak of God and religion while positing the question as to how and even if it can be possible to speak of God and religion' (Marin 1975: 130). This is the simultaneous double operation of the *Pensées*. On the one hand the text speaks of the non-symbolic and on the other it draws our attention to language's inability to talk about the non-symbolic. This is a first, general indication of how simple repetition becomes complex in the *Pensées*. Simple repetition designates those means by which the text evokes the *silence éternel* as the stable opposite of the text, and complex repetition arises as the text questions its own ability to even maintain this stable relationship to such a silence. My intention can therefore largely be summarized as the following: to consider how the *Pensées* perform this reflexive mood of on the one hand questioning the possibility of their own apologetic purpose (complex repetition) and on the other overtly aiming to fulfil this purpose (simple repetition).

The apologetic aim of the *Pensées* exerts considerable strain on language and logic in order to make them gesture towards a transcendent truth that is beyond the grasp of fallen humanity. It is this strain or stress that language is subjected to that I am primarily interested in throughout the *Pensées*. As a modern reader of theory and critical texts on the *Pensées*, I cannot enter into Pascal's overt apologetic aim. Yet I am a startled, fascinated, and engaged reader of the text: it *means* something to me. My larger aim is therefore to articulate this experience of meaning without referring to a sense of *beyond* outside the text, but rather engage in the strain exerted on language and see how this further elucidates literary silence. I hope by this to show that the traditional experience of the non-symbolic beyond can potentially take place also within and through language. Let me specify that my

aim is not to present a new, truer, or more complete reading of the
Pensées, but to try to understand the power and meaning the text holds
for a modern reader by showing how the silent beyond can be understood as a textual experience. It is important to underline that my
reading is not a dismissal of the apologetic project in the name of the
libertin. Some so-called modern readings of Pascal have been accused
of seeking to demonstrate that Pascal's basic enterprise was a failure
(see Lagarde 1993; Wetsel 1993). This is not the intention of my reading. I believe the richness of the *Pensées* lies in their power to startle
even the reader who is not engaged in the overt apologetic gestures of
the text. To me this indicates that the apology also operates on
another level. By exploring this level I will hope to show that the
Pensées can be read in a celebratory yet modern way.

It is first of all necessary to determine what kind of silence figures in
the *Pensées* and whether or not it is largely a dualistic notion, and see
to what extent the more traditional silence is openly challenged. In a
first section I shall therefore consider examples of first-degree silence
throughout the *Pensées*. I shall also provide a general description of the
operations of simple and complex repetition in the *Pensées*. Already the
introductory consideration of fragment 233 has shown an example of
how the transformation of first-degree silence into a different silence
is related to the notion of a fallen language. This sense of fallen language will be developed further in reference to Sara Melzer's study
Discourses of the Fall: A Study of Pascal's 'Pensées' (1986). I shall consider in
more detail Melzer's development of the aporia in the *Pensées* and her
concept of the 'atextual heart'. It is my conviction that the exploration
of literary silence requires me to move beyond Melzer's study, and I
will do this specifically by challenging the notion of the 'atextual' heart
and further dwell on the aporetic dynamic she delineates. This in turn
will further indicate the behaviour of literary silence in the *Pensées*. I
shall trace this behaviour by focusing specifically on the *contrariétés* and
on the *point fixe* and shifts between simple and complex repetition.

SILENCE IN THE *PENSÉES*

Already in Chapter 1 I showed how the ineffable nature of God and
the sense of a limit to discourse are Christian topoi, and how they are
specifically central to mystical thought. The mystical experience of a
union with God is defined by its transcendental nature, unavailable to

language. This manner of thinking is echoed by Pascal's words 'Les
choses de Dieu . . . [sont] inexprimables' (Pascal 1991: 303). Pascal, like
the mystics, experiences a limited language that is incapable of articulating the ineffable nature of God. This experience calls for a notion
of a beyond, an other to discourse, and silence is raised as an alternative mode of being with God. Implied is the Dream of Silence as presented in Chapter 1, and hence a dualistic understanding of silence as
the opposite of discourse.

The link between Pascal and mysticism has been much discussed
and any in-depth consideration transcends the scope of this chapter.
Mesnard, in his commentary *Les Pensées de Pascal* remarks: 'Il nous
semble . . . impossible de ne pas découvrir dans l'œuvre de Pascal une
pensée mystique' (Mesnard 1993: 333). And although numerous
critics agree with Mesnard's stance,[5] he himself states, 'La critique a
toujours éprouvé une grande répugnance à employer le mot "mystique" à propos de Pascal' (ibid.: 331). Mesnard refers specifically to
Henri Gouhier, who in his *Blaise Pascal, commentaires* argues against a
mystical reading of Pascal's 'Mémorial'.[6] However, the study of André
Bord, *Pascal et Jean de la Croix* (1987), establishes important parallels
between the Spanish mystic and Pascal, hence making implausible
any simple rejection of mystical thought's influence on Pascal.
Similarly, Michon's study *L'Ordre du cœur* convincingly argues the presence of a mystical discourse that runs throughout the *Pensées*, but that
does not necessarily define Pascal as a mystic:

nous ne nous posons pas la question de savoir si Pascal peut être ou non rangé
parmi les auteurs mystiques; nous aimerons découvrir en revanche si, dans
les *Pensées*, existe un type de discours qui ne relève ni d'une critique de la
philosophie, ni de la théologie spéculative, mais bien d'une approche mystique de la connaissance de Dieu. (Michon 1996: 271)

For the purpose of our investigation, the importance of mysticism
lies in its recognition of a non-symbolic or ineffable nature of God
(Mesnard 1993: 333–6; Bord 1987: 281–2). Y. Congar, in 'La Mystique
rhénane', posits such a 'spiritual ontology':

---

[5] For a more comprehensive list of those who agree with Mesnard and define Pascal as
a mystic, see Gouhier 1966: 51.
[6] Gouhier's text 'Le Mémorial est-il un texte mystique?' first appeared in *Blaise Pascal,
l'homme et l'œuvre* (1956) in the Cahiers de Royamunt series. Most other contributors
(Goldman, Koyré, Birault, Cognet, etc.) adopted a comparable viewpoint.

Les spirituels cherchent à exprimer une réalité spirituelle qui consiste dans leur rapport d'union avec un Autre, vraiment un Autre . . . Tout se passe comme s'il y avait une ontologie propre du rapport spirituel, qui a son unité, sa certitude, mais au-delà de l'ontologie naturelle, de telle sorte qu'elle est antinomique et paradoxale pour celui-ci. (Congar 1963)

The spiritual ontology is imagined in terms of another, supernatural order that cannot be grasped by the epistemology of what is here referred to as the natural ontology. Hence 'la seule manière pour l'homme d'atteindre la divinité cachée est de l'aimer' (Michon 1996: 316). The strong experience of our limited epistemology in turn posits a *beyond*, a sense of *au-delà*, a realm of transcendent truth. This in turn elucidates the mystical silence as a silence that discourse must surrender to, that 'surrounds' discourse. It now remains to be seen whether Pascal, in his confrontation with the limits of discourse, reverts to a similar notion of a silence of the beyond, or whether the *Pensées* suggest an alternative understanding of silence that is closer to what I am calling literary silence.

As far as a more mystical silence is concerned, Pascal objects in one fragment that such a silence presupposes faith: 'On n'entend les prophéties que quand on voit les choses arrivées. Ainsi les preuves de la retraite et de la direction, *du silence*, etc. ne se prouvent qu'à ceux qui les savent et les croient' (Pascal 1991: 751, my italics). As a planned apology,[7] the *Pensées* must be wary of any persuasive argument that presupposes faith. Pascal therefore rejects, if not in principle, then at least as far as the apologetic project is concerned, a more traditional monastic and mystical silence.[8] Fragment 751 hence refers to this traditional, dominant understanding of silence, but then questions it. Although efficient for the believer, this silence is discredited as a persuasive apologetic tool. In other words, the mystical, or even more general monastic silence, is not a universal. Pascal will find more

---

[7] For the problems concerning the use of this term in relation to the *Pensées*, I refer to Sellier who claims: 'Ce mot d'*apologie* se révèle indispensable pour désigner, au sein des *Pensées*, le massif des textes orientés vers la *Défense et illustration* de la vision catholique du monde' (1991: 25).

[8] It is worth mentioning that this traditional silence played a large role in the Port-Royal monastery. Courcelles's portrait of the Mère Angélique, *Le Sang de Port-Royal* (1994: 83–93) reveals the importance of silence: 'Le silence était bien la présence d'un présent par impression d'une vie nouvelle . . . Elle [la Mère Angélique] avait soin de faire garder un parfait silence dans la Maison' (ibid.: 87–8). Courcelles also quotes letters from Abbé de Saint-Cyran (Jean Duvergier de Hauranne) on the importance of silence, and we know from the correspondence of his succesor, Martin de Barcos, that he also valued silence as essential for the monastic retreat (Barcos 1956: 370–6).

apologetic 'use value' in the negative and terrifying *silence éternel* as this is a silence the non-believer recognizes and can relate to. We might conclude that the apologist does not privilege a mystical silence.

A second mention states: 'Le silence est la plus grande persécution. Jamais les saints ne se sont tus' (Pascal 1991: 746). Not mystical or despairing, this silence is a means of censorship used against the Christian believer. Silence is a tool of repression, a persecution, which was meant to repress belief through the silencing of discourse.

A third mention of silence gives more complexity to the notion. In fragment 230, 'Disproportion de l'homme', Pascal talks about man's position between the two infinities of the universe, the infinitely small and the infinitely big. He remarks that he who considers himself in comparison to these infinities 'sera plus disposé à les contempler en silence qu'à les rechercher avec présomption' (ibid.: 230). This is the silence that can somehow contain that which language cannot express. In other words this fragment establishes congruence between the non-symbolic, the *infiniment incompréhensible*, and silence. This reproduces the understanding of silence as a privileged other to discourse: 'il faut se tenir en silence autant qu'on peut et ne s'entretenir que de Dieu' (ibid.: 132). Here the more traditional silence is advocated.

Pascal's understanding of silence, though in different guises, is repeatedly defined as the other of discourse: silence is the terrifying end of language or the beginning of the immediate. It is a silence that is born through the 'repression' or cessation of language, that is *outside* language. In other words, a simple, dualistic, or traditional under-standing of silence is dominant. This is a first indication of simple rep-etition in the *Pensées*. It underlies the repeated definition of silence in negative opposition to the text. Complex repetition would take the form of a potential shifting of this silence. A general, but quite clear, example of such a shift from a negative, dualistic silent to a different silence can be recognized in the above discussion of fragment 223. The first-degree *silence éternel* was defined as the terrifying silence that arises against the limits of fallen language. So although not the imme-diate silence of God, it is still a negative, dualistic silence, and as such an example of simple repetition. However, this silence transforms or shifts and arises in the undefined m'. This second silence cannot be defined in opposition to language as it is a result of language itself. Language itself creates this second silence as it reveals itself as fallen. This shift from one silence to another shows how the dualistic *silence éternel* is not only the opposite of fallen language, but can actually become a result of it. The fragment reveals a silence that is both beyond language and a dynamic within language, a constant play or movement between these two mutually incompatible definitions. Without going into further detail, the fragment is a good introductory example of how the *Pensées* move between simple and complex repetition and thereby towards a different, non-dualistic silence.

On a more general level, simple repetition in the *Pensées* can be traced through the overt proceedings of the apologetic project. It is the system by which Pascal defines God and transcendent Christian truth as beyond the text. As the other of discourse, God becomes equated with the permanent, the unfragmented and unchanging whole that language can never attain. In the words of Congar, this beyond has both *unité* and *certitude* (see Michon 1996: 257). The role of simple repetition is to preserve this stability and silence of a non-symbolic God that is unattainable by language, defined as a constructed beyond. The purpose of simple repetition is to point the reader towards the limits of the text and the sayable, thereby inviting the reader to relate to a beyond as the only possible Truth. This is the only means of talking about the non-symbolic Him. Simple repetition, as producer of such a beyond, therefore constitutes the 'confident mode' of the apology as defined in the Introduction.

Complex repetition, on the other hand, designates instances that indirectly question language's ability to talk about God and even to posit a stable sense of a beyond. It can, as it did in the above example, produce a dynamic that reveals the instability of language itself by, for example, showing the undefined status of the first person pronoun. By revealing this fragility of language, complex repetition threatens the stability and credibility of the dualistic hierarchy that relies on language to indicate the negative non-symbolic. Consequently the productive system falters and displacements take place that again are conducive to literary silence. It is in these interstices that we perceive a transformed apologetic function that again might help me articulate the sense of meaning and edifying force that I experience reading the *Pensées* without referring to a sense of the beyond.

'*LE DISCOURS DE LA MACHINE*': A FALLEN DISCOURSE

The questions of language that appear in the *Pensées* are related to a larger, more general linguistic debate within Jansenism. Although the

Jansenist movement sought to present itself to history in terms of unity, it has been argued that internal dissonances existed (Goldmann 1956). Lucien Goldmann relates these dissonances specifically to the two factions of Arnauld/Nicole on the one hand and the lesser-known, but equally central, Martin de Barcos on the other. Melzer, in *Discourses of the Fall* (1986), adopts Goldmann's view. She considers the views of Barcos and Pascal on language and develops them specifically in relation to the original Fall of man into sin.[9] As I have already indicated, the Fall serves to underline an imperfectibility that lies at the centre of all discourse and that figures our estrangement from God: 'l'homme est déchu d'un état de gloire et de communication avec Dieu en un état de tristesse, de pénitence et d'éloignement de Dieu' (Pascal 1991: 313). The essence of the Fall is the loss of direct knowledge of God: 'La distance infinie des corps aux esprits, figure la distance infiniment plus infinie des esprits à la charité, car elle est surnaturelle' (ibid.: 339). *Surnaturelle* and hence unbridgeable, this infinite distance has set its mark on language: 'The evocation of the Fall was necessary to account for what was perceived as the fundamental flaw of language, that signs are separated from the real world to which they refer' (Melzer 1986: 9). This observation is central to the linguistic debate mentioned above. Melzer, although admitting the risk of simplification, identifies 'two opposing attitudes regarding the separation between signs and objects' in seventeenth-century discourse (ibid.: 10). For the purpose of this chapter, I will adapt her somewhat artificial classification of two main, different factions.[10]

The first theory has retrospectively been constructed as the classical, Cartesian doctrine of a transparent, pure language that coincides with the signified.[11] Melzer aligns Arnauld's *Logique de Port-Royal* with Descartes's thoughts on language.[12] Melzer refers to a

---

[9] For the more general importance of the doctrine of the Fall in the *Pensées*, see Wetsel 1981.

[10] For a more detailed and nuanced outline of the different critical views, see the Introduction of Nicholas Hammond's study *Playing with Truth* (1994: 10–22).

[11] Alexandrescu argues that this faith in language stems from Aristotle and his principle of non-contradiction: 'En s'appuyant sur le principe de correspondance de la vérité des énoncés et de la réalité des choses, Aristote va passer des mots aux choses représentées, en supposant un monde d'essences ou quiddités correspondant de manière univoque à celui des sens' (Alexandrescu 1997: 18).

[12] The grouping together of Arnauld/Nicole and Descartes is largely a result of Chomsky's influential work *Cartesian Linguistics: A Chapter in the History of Rationalist Thought* (1966). However, his conclusions are disputed by Miel (1969b), who accords more value to the influence of St Augustine in the *Logique de Port-Royal* than that of Descartes.

letter from Descartes to Mersenne, from which the following passage is worth quoting:[13]

Et si quelqu'un auoit bien expliqué quelles sont les idées simples qui sont en l'imagination des hommes, desquelles se compose tout ce qu'ils pensent, et que cela fust receu par tout le monde, i'oserois esperer ensuite une langue universelle fort aisée à aprendre, à prononcer et à écrire, et ce qui est le principal, qui aideroit au iugement , luy representant si distinctement toutes choses, qu'il luy feroit presque impossible de se tromper . . . ie tiens que cette langue est possible, et qu'on peut trouver la science de qui elle dépend, par le moyen de laquelle les paysans pourroient mieux iuger de la vérité des choses. (Descartes to Mersenne, 20 Nov., 1629, in Descartes 1969)

The aspiration towards a transparent language is also symbolized by the foundation of the Académie Française in 1635. The aim of the Academy was to ensure rules and guidelines that would propagate a precise and clear language. The quest for clarity of language also figures in Arnauld and Nicole, and their work on language theory, *Logique de Port-Royal*. Louis Marin concludes that according to the *Logique* 'le mot renvoie nécessairement à l'idée. Le signifiant est lié nécessairement au signifié' (Marin 1976: 170). The ideal of a transparent language is not coloured by original sin and is hence able to transmit truth directly. Arnauld's faction 'values the mind and correspondingly the mental side of the linguistic sign, the signified, over the body or the material aspect of the linguistic sign, the signifier' (Melzer 1986: 27).

The second faction is associated with an opposing current of thought within Jansenism, headed by Martin de Barcos.[14] This faction places 'obscurity and distance at the centre of their linguistic theory' (Melzer 1986: 27). Language is saturated by sin and corruption, hence 'questioning the possibility of a pure thought that transcends the body of language' (ibid.) Barcos's view is most clearly set forth in his letters to Le Maistre de Saci regarding the translation of the Bible. The question revolves around the actual *possibility* of translation (Marin 1976). Barcos holds that 'correct' translation is impossible because language

---

[13] Spellings of correspondence will not be changed into modern French but rather quoted as they have been rendered by the editors in each case.

[14] It is worth noting that Barcos's position is ignored, or only marginally considered, in some of the major works on Pascal, Port-Royal, and questions of language and rhetoric (see e.g. Topliss 1966; Norman 1988; Koch 1997). This does not indicate that his position is of less importance, but rather supports Goldmann's view that Barcos has been repressed throughout the history of Port-Royal (Goldmann 1956).

cannot reproduce or coincide with its meaning. To attempt to translate would be to ignore this aspect of language and try to recreate a sense of original meaning (Barcos 1956: letters 78,102). Implied is the view that there is no stable, unchanging signified in relation to the signifier. This indicates a rejection of Arnauld's and Nicole's attempt to transcend fallen discourse by transposing it into a transparent language.

Pascal's view of language has been placed within both theoretical perspectives and is often aligned with the more dominant faction of Port-Royal (Norman 1988: p. xvii; Miel 1969*a*: 267). In his study *Pascal and Rhetoric*, Koch, although recognizing the validity of such claims, disputes them: 'The calm certainty of such claims can only be maintained by overlooking the treatise that Pascal has written on rhetoric' (Koch 1997: 15). Force's careful analysis in *Le Problème herméneutique chez Pascal* points out how Arnauld and Nicole consider that 'l'idée qui est exprimée par le mot, si elle est claire et distincte, est le principe d'une adéquation parfaite entre les choses et les mots', whereas Pascal claims that the regular 'usage des mots est un fait de coutume, et en cela il est arbitraire' (Force 1989: 148). Pascal hence sees no *natural* link between signifier and signified, only one formed by habit. With these factors in mind, it is possible to imagine a potential affinity between Pascal and Barcos (Goldmann 1956; Melzer 1986; Marin 1976). However, this also raises problems. Mesnard (1977–9) shows how Barcos was opposed to the *Pensées* and Hammond, in his study *Playing with Truth*, quotes a comment by an anonymous writer saying, 'M. Barcos dit que M. Pascal a été foudroyé de Dieu comme un pygmée, que ce n'était pas à lui de parler de la religion' (1994: 11). However, this does not preclude parallels between the two writers. As Hammond states, in reference to Melzer, to approach Pascal and Barcos has the advantage of challenging 'the preconceptions of those who see clarity of language as central to an understanding of the *Pensées*' (Hammond 1994: 11). Although I hesitate to propagate an overestimated affinity between Barcos and Pascal, I believe that Barcos's thought can be used to further elucidate the view of language that is presented in the *Pensées*, and especially inform my exploration of literary silence.

One fragment is particularly relevant as it shows how Pascal is closer to Barcos than to the authors of the *Logique*, namely fragment 141, which rejects the idea of a transparent discourse:

toutes les fois que deux hommes voient un corps changer de place, ils expriment tous deux la vue de ce même objet par les mêmes mots, en disant l'un

et l'autre qu'il s'est mû. Et de cette conformité d'application, on tire une puis-
sante conjecture d'une conformité d'idée. *Mais cela n'est pas absolument convain-
cant de la dernière conviction.* (Pascal 1991: 141, my italics)

In other words, language, although seemingly stable, is no final
guarantee for a shared universal meaning.[15] The word *mouvement* is
introduced in a new light of doubt: does it convey the same idea to all
participants in discourse? Marin observes in reference to the fragment: 'Même au niveau des mots primitifs, se diffuse, dans la lumière
de la certitude, une "certaine obscurité douteuse" qui compromet la
thèse transcendantale d'Arnauld et Nicole' (Marin 1976: 172). Pascal's
rejection of transparent language hinges on the rejection of any
potential direct knowledge of God through language. Language can
never reach this ideal, as it is doomed to obscure the thought or idea
that it is trying to express. Vlad Alexandrescu, in his study on the role
of scepticism and the paradox in Pascal's thought *Le Paradoxe chez Blaise
Pascal*, recognizes in Pascal 'une méfiance à l'égard de la capacité de
la parole d'exprimer la vérité' (Alexandrescu 1997: 229). Another concrete example from the *Pensées* (discussed more closely by Marin 1975)
is the reflection on the word *campagne*: 'Une ville, une campagne, de
loin c'est une ville et une campagne, mais à mesure qu'on s'approche,
ce sont des maisons, des arbres, des tuiles, des feuilles, des herbes, des
fourmis, à l'infini. Tout cela s'enveloppe sous le nom de campagne'
(Pascal 1991: 99). The word *campagne* hides a multiplicity of referents.
The word refers to an infinite set of other signifieds, and hence is
never present in one signified. Marin imagines Pascal's view on
language as 'un *jeu* (au sens où une charpente a du jeu) . . . entre le signifiant et le signifié, mot et idée' (1976: 173). All that is required is a
change of perspective for the seemingly stable word to slip away from
its original referent and point to a multiple range of new referents,
which again slip away, and so on.

We can conclude that Pascal rejects language as a transparent or
clear bearer of a permanent meaning: 'Les sens. Un même sens
change selon les paroles qui l'expriment. Les sens reçoivent des
paroles leur dignité au lieu de la leur donner' (Pascal 1991: 645); 'Les
mots diversement rangés font un divers sens. Et les sens diversement
rangés font différents effets' (ibid.). To change the order of words

---

[15] It is important to underline that Pascal heads this fragment 'Contre le pyrrhonisme'
to indicate that although we might doubt language or 'la faiblesse de notre raison', this does
not indicate 'l'incertitude de toutes nos connaissances' (Pascal 1991: 142).

potentially creates different, multiple meanings. Such transformation is primarily due to the lack of coincidence between the signifier and the signified. This can be traced in the *Pensées* by considering the concept of *La Machine* (see Melzer 1986: 58–64). 'Le Discours de la Machine' describes the human psyche as partly ruled by habit, like an automaton.[16] It is closely related to the important concept of *custom*, developed throughout the *Pensées*. The mention of machine in the following is important:

Ordre. Une lettre d'exhortation à un ami pour le porter à chercher. Et il répondra: 'Mais à quoi me servira de chercher? Rien ne paraît.' Et lui répondre: 'Ne désespérez pas.' Et il répondrait qu'il serait heureux de trouver quelque lumière, mais que selon cette religion même, quand il croirait ainsi, cela ne lui servirait de rien et qu'ainsi il aime autant ne point chercher. Et à cela lui répondre: 'La machine.' (Pascal 1991: 39)

La Machine is presented as the alternative route to faith when active searching fails. The Machine primarily refers to the body: 'nous sommes automate autant qu'esprit' (ibid.: 661). This body is in turn decided by habit, or *coutume*: 'la coutume fait nos preuves les plus fortes et plus crues: elle incline l'automate, qui entraîne l'esprit sans qu'il y pense. . . . C'est donc la coutume qui nous en persuade, c'est elle qui fait tant de chrétiens' (ibid). Custom informs the body, like a machine, and makes it function in a specific way. By changing our habits, we can therefore 'train' or 'programme' our bodies, our machines, to different beliefs and principles, 'Une différente coutume en donnera d'autres principes naturels' (ibid.: 158). Hence custom is one road to faith: 'Il y a trois moyens de croire: la raison, la coutume, l'inspiration' (ibid.: 655). Because we believe our custom to be the given and 'natural' reality, the power of custom is such that, by changing it, we can change our beliefs.

From this discourse on psychological automatism arises a possible view of language and semiological codes as comparable to habit. Melzer says that 'the machine refers both to human beings who function as automatons and to the conventional structure of their discourse' (Melzer 1986: 60). This implies that language, like a repeated habit, has the power to shape our experience of the world and determine our sense of reality: 'discourse is a major mechanism

---

[16] Sellier names the famous *pari* fragment the 'Discours de la machine', based on fragment 45 which states: 'Après la lettre qu'on doit chercher Dieu, faire la lettre d'ôter les obstacles, qui est le discours de la machine, de préparer la machine'.

of control which shapes human desire and belief' (ibid.: 63). Fragment 69 plays out this power of language: 'Talon de soulier. Ô que cela est bien tourné! Que voilà un habile ouvrier! Que ce soldat est hardi! Voilà la source de nos inclinations et du choix des conditions. Que celui-là boit bien! Que celui-là boit peu! Voilà ce qui fait les gens sobres et ivrognes, soldats, poltrons, etc.' (Pascal 1991: 69). The fragment plays out oral, commonplace exclamations and cites them as sources for our inclinations and impressions of a sober or drunken person, a soldier or a coward. Language—expressions and observations—creates our categories, our experiences and potentially order our world view. We can now appreciate Pascal's claim that the obstacles to faith can be removed by instigating a change in the machine-like habit, and that this also applies to discourse: by changing the semiological codes, we can change our beliefs. The *Discours de la Machine* hence indirectly challenges the view of fallen language as a mere obstacle to revelation. Exactly because it is fallen, because it never coincides with a reality, but rather produces new realities, it can lead to faith.

This reversed view of fallen language calls for a closer consideration of Barcos's observations on translation. Barcos's letters to Saci particularly address the translation of St Paul. Barcos argues against any translation that endeavours to clarify the inherent obscurity of the passage: 'la Traduction des Epistres de S. Paul me semble dangereuse, premierement parce que le dessein que vous avez de les rendre claires et faciles paroist contraire à celuy du St. Esprit qui les a voulu rendre obscures et difficiles' (Barcos 1956: 290). Barcos hence privileges the difficulty, 'des expressions foibles, informes et obscures' (ibid.: 374) as mark of the 'sagesse' of the biblical language. The language relies upon obscurity in order to show man 'combien la vraye sagesse est de soy cachée est disproportionnée aux Esprits des hommes' (ibid.: 371). The obscurity of the original biblical language shocks its readers who are used to the clear language of biblical commentaries or translations: 'Il ne leur est pas si difficile de concevoir les veritez dogmatiques, par ce que le raisonnement et le sens humain les y peut aider: mais la morale de l'ecriture leur est sans comparaison plus obscure et plus impenetrable' (ibid.). This in turn leads Barcos to argue that the edifying aspect of language differs from that which brings contentment. Whereas the latter consists 'en parlant proprement et clairement' (ibid.: 373), the former lies in obscurity, frustration, and confusion—the beginning of humility.

We can conclude that Barcos actually embraces fallen language as a mark of *sagesse*.[17] Divine language uses and relies upon the dynamics of fallen language as a means of imparting divine truths. Specifically Barcos identifies 'des hyperboles, des raisonnemens interrompus, des comparaisons imparfaites, des periodes sans suite et sans ordre, des expressions courtes et difficiles dont elles sont remplies' (Barcos 1956: 290). Marin, in 'La Critique de la representation classique: la traduction de la Bible à Port-Royal', observes how the characteristics mentioned by Barcos all somehow refer to the unsaid, 'ce qui n'est pas dit dans le dire . . . ce qui est hors de l'usage, ce qui ne doit pas être dit . . . ce qui est dit mais n'est pas entendu' (Marin 1976: 186). He concludes: 'Barcos insiste donc sur ce qui n'appartient pas à la surface visible du texte, mais relève d'une dynamique profonde du discours dont la caractéristique est de se signifier en surface par le silence, par une sorte de hachure de texte par son propre silence et c'est cependant ce silence, intérieur au texte même, qui est le sens vrai' (ibid.). Marin's conclusion points towards an understanding of silence that is closer to literary silence. It is *intérieur* to the text and it is the obscure 'signifier' or marker of the *vrai sens*. Furthermore, this Barcosian silence is linked to language practising itself as fallen, playing out its distance from order and clarity. This suggests that Pascal also could view fallen language itself as the *means of edification*. Rather than rejecting language as fallen and removed from truth, this reading of Barcos suggests that there was a current within Jansenism that viewed language as a potential means of edification if only it foregrounded its fallen status rather than attempting to overcome it.

We might conclude that with Barcos's comments and the concept of the *Machine* the view of fallen language propagated by Melzer can be taken further. Melzer's analysis hesitates to perform the reversal whereby the flaws of fallen language become the mark itself of 'divine' or 'sacred' language. Consequently her analysis risks reducing fallen language by defining it in terms of restriction. This is echoed by the quotation from Nietzsche that heads Melzer's study: 'We have to cease to think if we refuse to do it in the prison-house of language.' This suggests language as entrapment and the only possible escape becomes a beyond. However, we can see how Barcos's observations

---

[17] Clearly Barcos's observations on language are first and foremost referring to biblical language. However, his observations still place the advantages of this biblical language in its fallen status, hence indirectly proposing that fallen language, in its fallenness, can be edifying in matters of religion. This is of course important for the apologetic project.

indicate that the 'true meaning', the sense of the revelation, hence of the non-symbolic, also hides *within* biblical language, in a potential silence of this within. This shows how the notion of fallen language is congruent with the double operation of simple and complex repetition. In Melzer's sense, fallen language posits the beyond as its other. However, with the notion of the *Machine* and with Barcos's comments, fallen language in itself becomes a dynamic of the unsayable beyond. This suggests that fallen language can become the topos of a transformation from simple to complex repetition and hence a potential dynamic of literary silence. The notion of fallen language provides a manner of thinking about language that propagates the exploration of literary silence.

Indirectly grasping this potential of fallen language, Marin, on Barcos, talks about a 'sens suspendu' (1976: 185–8). He argues that Barcos's rejection of translation is not based on a sense of Hebrew as untranslatable, or on a sense of polysemy, but rather on the grounds that *meaning is always suspended in the writing itself.* Attempting therefore to translate this meaning is necessarily to state the meaning and hence reduce or change it. He concludes. 'Il n'y a pas plusieurs autres sens possibles, c'est là le problème de la polysémie, mais le sens est le possible même, le pluriel en instance et en latence' (ibid: 187). The meaning lies in the *possibility* of multiple meaning. Barcos himself states the danger of trying to discern 'la liaison et l'enchaînement des pensées' in the Bible without reducing biblical language to that of man, that is with pretension to order, clarity, and transparency. He compares the indiscernible, obscured (non-)order of the Bible to a trace left in water: 'Dieu marche souvent comme sur la mer sans qu'on puisse voir ses traces' (Barcos 1956: 372). It is this invisible trace that is the suspension of meaning. In other words, it is crucial to 'accept' the obscurity, the seeming lack of order as the meaning itself: 'Comme il y a une sagesse qui est folie devant Dieu, il y a aussy un ordre qui est desordre; et par consequent il y a une folie qui est sagesse, et un desordre qui est un reglement veritable' (ibid.: 140). Whereas language is primarily a means of signification, it can change or shift onto a plane where the primary function is not to signify directly but rather to perform the inherent flaw of all signification: the lack of coincidence between language and world. In this moment language transforms as it loses its primary function of signification. This, in turn, becomes the opening for dynamics like the aporia that are basically untranslatable. This moment of transformation is the opening of 'sacred' language or literary silence within fallen language.

Rather than a sense of a 'prison-house' Barcos's observations can lead us to view language as an infinite arena. We might imagine the beyond shifting into the 'within' that no longer relates to any outside. Language, in its fallenness, through its *désordre* and *sens suspendu*, potentially enacts the non-symbolic *sagesse* and *ordre* that is the outside of the prison. And in this instance in which there is no longer an active sense of a beyond, language no longer borders onto a silence but rather has the potential to become this silence. To sum up, the notion of fallen language arises as the most fruitful indication of how literary silence can be approached in the *Pensées*. Barcos's views as expressed in his letters show a potential lifting of the prison walls that Melzer describes as limiting. And if the walls are lifted, then we can imagine a language that 'seeps' into the beyond, 'mixes' with it, and potentially enacts its silence.

Barcos's letters act as important 'witnesses' indicating that a variety of thoughts on language were circulating in Pascal's immediate milieu. They attest that Pascal's views on language would be informed by a more general trend or discourse that developed in opposition to Arnauld and Nicole. Although I am clearly rereading Barcos's letters from a modern point of view, his observations still lay the historical ground for my exploration of literary silence in the *Pensées*. And in the following I will show more closely how Melzer's development of fallen language can be developed further through a more careful consideration of Barcos's comments on translation and their potential influence on Pascal. Specifically I will focus on Melzer's description of the aporia in the *Pensées* and on the ensuing notion of the 'atextual heart', which can be thought of as the escape from fallen language, the topos of the beyond. This designates Melzer's attempt to get out of the 'prison-house', and thereby restore the value of the apology. I will argue that by positing this beyond she risks reinforcing the 'prison-house', and hence precludes the possibility that the apologetic value of the *Pensées* lies within their potentially infinite language.

THE APORIA AND THE 'ATEXTUAL HEART'

In order to explore further Melzer's view of fallen language, I shall now turn to her notion of the aporia. Obviously the idea of an aporia at the centre of the *Pensées* is pivotal to the exploration of literary silence, and Melzer's observations in this regard are central. In the following I shall trace Melzer's definition of the aporia and see how her perceptive reading of the *Pensées* nonetheless fails to realize the potential of the aporia as a marker for literary silence.

The aporia is derived directly from fallen language and is one of the strongest points in Melzer's argument. She here refers to Pascal's fragments 230 and 479:

The realization of our imprisonment in language gives rise to two conflicting situations. On the one hand, it breeds the desire to escape and find a transcendent truth: 'nous brûlons du désir de trouver . . . une dernière base constante pour y édifier une tour qui s'élève à l'infini'. On the other hand, it constantly reveals that we cannot attain a transcendent truth that would decide the meaning of our signs: '. . . à la fin de chaque vérité il faut ajouter qu'on se souvient de la vérité opposée'. The result is an aporia that presents two incompatible logics of our relation to a transcendent truth. The aporia undermines the belief that we can satisfy our desire for truth, as it becomes impossible to decide rationally which of the two logics is true. (Melzer 1986: 75)

The aporia implies that thought can never reach a synthesis. Because we are trapped in language, we desire truth. But this desire cannot be gratified as we are always thrown back into language and imprisonment away from truth. Again the desire arises, and again we are thrown back into language. Language gives us the means of articulating our desire for truth, and it constantly reveals that this truth is unattainable because we cannot transcend language. This endless back-and-forth movement is the nature of the aporia in the *Pensées*.

Melzer develops the aporia more specifically with regard to the story of the Fall. On the one hand, she argues, the desire for truth figures the story of the Fall and Redemption: 'It figures the Fall by virtue of the fact that it cannot be satisfied, and thus it underlines *la misère* of our distance from truth and God' (Melzer 1986: 76). This is the perspective of uncertainty. However, because it breeds the desire, our entrapment in language also suggests that we can be raised above it, if only in that we can perceive the existence of a transcendent truth and desire to be released from our epistemological codes: 'It also figures the possibility of Redemption because we are not satisfied with our fictions of truth; we desire to go beyond them in order to recapture a transcendent truth. Our desire for Redemption suggests that we contain *la grandeur* of a former state wherein we had access to truth and God' (ibid.). This is the perspective of faith. The *Pensées*, according to Melzer, play out this aporetic impossibility by refusing the reader the comfort of choosing one of the perspectives at the cost of the other: 'the text is so constructed that the readers, once they feel they have discovered the certainty of a particular story, are thrust into the opposite. They cannot help but realize that neither story is totally true and thus neither can subsume the other' (ibid.: 80). Herein lies the heuristic value of Melzer's argument for our exploration. She shows how the *Pensées* invite the reader into a never-ending vicious circle and concludes that, 'although we are trapped in a fallen language where truth can only be other than what it says or implies, this fallen language is, paradoxically, the only tool available to help us approach an understanding of God' (ibid.: 143). By arguing here that the non-symbolic nature of God can only be approached through fallen language, Melzer suggests the potential richness of fallen language. However, the further development of her argument reveals how it ultimately precludes the understanding of literary silence.

Despite the astuteness of its insights, Melzer's study ultimately seems unable to bear the weight of its own conclusions. In Chapter 3 I said that the force of the aporia, its potential to become literary silence, only emerges if one has the 'stamina' to remain in the aporia. The challenge is to tolerate and accept the unthinkable state of the aporia without attempting to transcend it by help of reason. The essence of the aporia for literary silence is exactly the fact that it cannot be resolved. However, Melzer's analysis ultimately seeks to resolve and transcend the aporia. She observes that 'Pascal belongs to that group of individuals who, according to Derrida's famous characterization, do not experience "the joyous affirmation of the freeplay of the world . . . without truth, without origin"' (Melzer 1986: 8). This necessary origin for Pascal is of course Christian truth and God. Melzer draws on this need for an origin and, seeing that all language is fallen, places Pascal's origin outside language: 'Pascal . . . seeks a solution outside language; he wagers to go beyond textuality' (ibid.). Rather than challenging this traditional perception of Pascal, she adapts to it as she herself opts for simple repetition by creating a principle that enables her to transcend the aporia and 'save' it from 'meaninglessness'. She does this by developing the notion of the heart as an 'atextual origin of certainty' (ibid.): 'The heart, the seat of the most fundamental knowledge, can apprehend its truths outside language' (ibid.: 139). In other words, the heart becomes the commonplace topos of a certain silence that is the other of language, atextual. We might say that with the 'atextual heart' Melzer's analysis repeats the view that the non-symbolic is congruent with a traditional, dualistic Dream of Silence.

The heart is of course central to the *Pensées* and Melzer's argument draws upon the basic opposition heart–reason that runs throughout the fragments. Pascal's appeal to the non-rational side of the individual has been highly attractive to thinkers of later centuries who recognize a rare challenge to what was often thought of as the supremacy of rational thinking in the seventeenth and eighteenth centuries. Briefly stated, Pascal defines reason as the faculty that ensures reflection and rationality, while the heart represents the idea of an essence of our being, thereby grasping the immediate that precedes and transcends reflection and reason.[18] Philippe Sellier states: 'Le *cœur* représente donc la profondeur et l'intimité, notre être véritable. . . . *Cœur* désigne toute la profondeur de l'âme' (Sellier 1995: 135). The heart defines man, and as such it is also the source of his wretchedness: 'Que le cœur de l'homme est creux et plein d'ordure' (Pascal 1991: 171). This is the fallen state of the heart and designates what Norman calls the *attraction* of the heart to 'pleasures that are neither reasonable nor moral nor religious' (Norman 1988: 39).

However, the heart is also a faculty of knowing, and specifically of knowing through *loving*. The heart ensures the human capacity to love that which we do not rationally grasp and to embrace the immediacy of the inexplicable. The heart can be described as both the lowest and highest in man. There is consequently a tendency to designate the heart as the 'seat of all the faculties of the soul' (Miel 1969*a*: 158). However, the most important function of the *cœur* is to transform man's wretchedness to greatness by ensuring his ability to receive faith: 'C'est le cœur qui sent Dieu, et non la raison: voilà ce que c'est que la foi. Dieu sensible au cœur, non à la raison' (Pascal 1991: 680). God's absolute otherness can only be apprehended through the heart, and not through reason alone: 'Qu'il y a loin de la connaissance de Dieu à l'aimer' (ibid.: 409). In other words, the heart is the faculty that remains open to that which transcends our fallen epistemological perspective. Hence the most quoted fragment: 'Le cœur a ses raisons que la raison ne connaît point' (ibid.: 680). This fragment has attracted countless readers to Pascal due to its rhetorical elegance and its indirect recognition of man as a complex psychological being. The heart

---

[18] This definition and the following presentation constitutes a simplification that none the less serves our purpose within the scope of the chapter. For more detailed discussions of the complexity of the heart see Sellier 1995: 125–39, Mesnard 1993: 167–78; Norman 1988: 38–44, who also refers to Jeanne Russier (1949) *La Foi selon Pascal*, and Jean Laporte (1950) *Le Cœur et la raison selon Pascal*.

invalidates a rational explanation of God, deeming it 'humaine et inutile pour le salut' (ibid.: 142). The religious experience challenges logical demonstration and argument: 'Les preuves de Dieu méta-physiques sont si éloignées du raisonnement des hommes et si impliquées, qu'elles frappent peu' (ibid.: 222). Herein lies the main dif-ference between Pascal and Descartes. Though recognizing the value of Descartes's attempt to prove God metaphysically, Pascal rejects the project as essentially useless: 'Descartes inutile et incertain' (ibid.: 445). Final redemption and grace do not rely upon a metaphysical knowledge of God: 'Quand un homme serait persuadé que les pro-portions des nombres sont des vérités immatérielles, éternelles et dépendantes d'une première vérité en qui elles subsistent et qu'on appelle Dieu, je ne le trouverais pas beaucoup avancé pour son salut' (ibid.: 690). The faith that can be explained remains sterile without the experience of *le cœur*. It is, however, important that Pascal under-lines the role of reason in matters of faith: 'Si on soumet tout à la rai-son, notre religion n'aura rien de mystérieux et de surnaturel. Si on choque les principes de la raison, notre religion sera absurde et ridicule' (ibid.: 204). Pascal affirms that 'la religion n'est point con-traire à la raison' (ibid.: 46) and also that there are 'Deux excès. Exclure la raison, n'admettre que la raison' (ibid.: 214). Reason acts on the principles that are comprehended only through the heart. It fol-lows that neither heart nor reason is self-sufficient—'the heart cannot know "toutes choses", and the reason cannot function without the principles which the heart furnishes it' (Norman 1988: 43).

Because it can know and love the inexplicable, the heart can receive the immediate which is beyond discourse. This presentation shows the heart as the faculty that has the potential to transcend fallen dis-course: 'Il est le siège de connaissances intimes, immédiates et non démontrables' (Sellier 1995: 134). It follows that there is an implicit association between the heart and the *silence éternel* that is God's lan-guage. It is this association that leads Melzer to the notion of the atex-tual heart. The conclusion is: 'We remain caught in the aporia in which neither God's presence nor his absence can be proven. Only the heart can pretend to transcend what our reason can never resolve' (Melzer 1986: 140). Melzer's reading is congruent with simple repeti-tion in that it produces a sense of the beyond, a non-symbolic princi-ple that transcends the aporia and that is the topos of silence outside language: 'The truth, then, must exist *outside* language, *outside* the *Pensées*' (ibid.: 137, my italics).

With the notion of the 'atextual heart' Melzer's astute analysis reaches a certain paralysis as there is nothing more to be said. The notion cannot be explicated further; it remains beyond the reach of thought and language. The aporia is transcended but thereby risks being just another 'dead end', providing no proper resolution to the impasse. With the 'atextual' heart Melzer's reading accepts Pascal's overt apologetic aim. I challenge the concept with the aim of showing that the apologetic value of the *Pensées* transcends the overt apologetic proceedings. According to the idea of the 'atextual heart' silence indirectly becomes the other or outside of discourse. In opposition to the 'atextual heart', fallen language becomes reinstated as the prison-house within which meaning can never be transparent. However, as I suggested above based on the letters of Barcos, fallen language, in its fallenness, is the potential mark of truth. We might imagine that in its lack of transparent signification, fallen language practises a certain *silence*. More precisely, fallen language is silent in the sense that it remains silent about the difference it always bestows. This is the silence that I associate with the indeterminacy of the silent *me* of *m'effraie* (Pascal 1991: 233). Melzer does not develop the potential infinite of fallen language, the suspended meaning, the disorder that can be order, the obscurity that is *sagesse*. In other words, she fails to see the potential for *edification* that Barcos perceived in fallen language, and, in her way, she opts for *contentment*, a closure to the analysis, a conclusion that is the atextual heart.

Melzer is obviously correct in observing that Pascal overtly posits the origin of truth outside of language. However, I believe the *Pensées* offer instances that are more radical. Closer readings of these instances reveal a language that actually precludes the beyond, or 'atextual heart', and that rather repeats the impasse of the aporia, remains in the aporia. It is in this constant play of in-between dynamics that there emerges a potential for literary silence and a shifted apologetic value. In the following I will consider some of these dynamics in the *Pensées* and show how they, by mutating from simple to complex repetition, potentially shift the silence of the 'atextual heart' into a silence that is closer to literary silence. The challenge is to read the *Pensées* while constantly questioning, even refusing, the notion of a beyond, and thereby enter into the mode of complex repetition. On a meta-level this implies staying within the vicious circle, within the aporia, rather than transcending it. In other words, the aim is to experience language as fallen, to see how language acts out its endless movement which ultimately questions its ability to signify, to create stable meaning. The observations by Marin and Barcos indicate that language might say the unsayable as it transforms from being productive of meaning into movements that eventually cease to signify, or at least challenge our limits of understanding. It is in this movement, which is unproductive of meaning, that language becomes *productive* of its own silence. In the following I will consider some general themes and more specific examples from the *Pensées* with the aim of uncovering such unproductive, yet productive, instances.

LES CONTRARIÉTÉS

Throughout the *Pensées* are repeated numerous descriptions of contradictions—*clair–obscur, figuratif–littéral, absence–presence, géométrie–finesse, raison–cœur*. Although different kinds of oppositions, these all form important dualistic *leitmotifs*—the *contrariétés*. Pascal sets up the contradictions and invites the reader to interact with them, to enter into the problematics they reveal. Contradictory affirmations are stated simultaneously, and the question is how, and if, they can be synthesized. My intention here is to consider some of these contradictions. I aim to show how, on an overt level, they can be understood as moments of simple repetitions, and then how a closer reading reveals a more radical movement that is complex repetition.

One of the most obvious examples is that discussed in the section called 'Contrariétés', namely *grandeur–misère*. These concepts are also treated in the separate sections, 'Misère' and 'Grandeur'. The concept of *misère* or wretchedness is developed by Pascal with various nuances and subtleties. The origin of man's wretchedness stems from the Fall: 'Nous naissons donc injustes. Car tout tend à soi: cela est contre tout ordre. . . . la pente vers soi est le commencement de tout désordre' (Pascal 1991: 680). This first designates the inclination to *amour propre* that makes man 'n'aimer que soi et de ne considérer que soi' (ibid.: 743). It also describes how, after the Fall, man is condemned to stay within the limits of his own perspective, to always come back to himself and not transcend his own epistemology. This *pente vers soi* is the essence of man's wretchedness, *tout désordre*, and the cause of other central concepts Pascal uses to describe our sinful nature such as *vanité, concupiscence, passions, inconstance*, etc. Man's potential to step out of his wretched state, that is, his *grandeur*, is linked to his ability to reflect and create a reflexive relationship to his self. Because he is a 'thinking animal' man might realize his own wretchedness: 'La grandeur de l'homme est grande en ce qu'il se connaît misérable. Un arbre ne se connaît pas misérable. C'est donc être misérable que de [se] connaître misérable, mais c'est être grand que de connaître qu'on est misérable' (ibid.: 146). *Grandeur* is linked to reflection and conscious thought: 'Toute notre dignité consiste donc en la pensée' (ibid.: 232). By consciously realizing his wretchedness, man achieves his greatness because he can turn towards God and be lifted above his sinful state. So the source of *grandeur* is in the *misère*: 'Grandeur de l'homme dans sa concupiscence même' (ibid.: 150) and 'La misère se concluant de la grandeur et la grandeur de la misère' (ibid.: 155).

This example of *contrariétés* leads to what at first seems to be an irreconcilable paradox: 'Quelle chimère est-ce donc que l'homme, quelle nouveauté, quel monstre, quel chaos, quel sujet de contradiction, quel prodige, juge de toutes choses, imbécile ver de terre, dépositaire du vrai, cloaque d'incertitude et d'erreur, gloire et rebut de l'univers' (Pascal 1991: 164). This strong fragment presents man as a living contradiction. Words like *monstre, chaos, cloaque* reveal Pascal's intention to shock and offend the reader and to make him into something unnatural—the opposite of our own self-image. The reader is presented with himself as both earthworm and bearer of potential truth, glory of the universe. Caught in this rotation of contradictory statements of truth, the reader is invited to seek a truth that can embrace both truths and hence lift the contradictions: 'N'y a-t-il point une vérité substantielle, voyant tant de choses vraies qui ne sont point la vérité même?' (ibid.: 680). Clearly this truth is God: 'Connaissez donc, superbe, quel paradoxe vous êtes à vous même! Humiliez vous, raison impuissante! Taisez-vous, nature imbécile! Apprenez que l'homme passe infiniment l'homme et entendez de votre Maître votre condition véritable que vous ignorez. Écoutez Dieu' (ibid.: 164) Pascal here first alludes to the paradox that reason cannot fathom and then introduces the solution: *Écoutez Dieu*. Only by turning to God can we resolve the paradox, as only God can embrace both sides of any truth and lift them up to a higher, transcendent truth: 'Ces extrémités se touchent et se réunissent à force de s'être éloignées, et se retrouvent en Dieu et en Dieu seulement' (ibid.: 230). God is the synthesis of the dialectic. Michon refers to this as the supernatural order, the order that transcends rational paradox: 'Le couple *bassesse/grandeur* relève de l'ordre strictement naturel: il ne trouve son explication et sa résolution que dans l'ordre surnaturel, où apparaît la notion de péché originel' (Michon 1996: 252). Michon points to the fact that Christianity, as a narrative, can explain the existence of the paradox (see also Wetsel 1981: 130–9). In the case of *grandeur–misère* the explanation is the Christian doctrine of original sin:

Car enfin, si l'homme n'avait jamais été corrompu, il jouirait dans son innocence et de la vérité et de la félicité avec assurance. Et si l'homme n'avait jamais été que corrompu, il n'aurait aucune idée ni de la vérité ni de la béatitude. Mais, malheureux que nous sommes, et plus que s'il n'y avait point de grandeur dans notre condition, nous avons une idée du bonheur et ne pouvons y arriver, nous sentons une image de la vérité et ne possédons que le mensonge, incapables d'ignorer absolument et de savoir certainement, tant il est manifeste que nous avons été dans un degré de la perfection dont nous sommes malheureusement déchus. (Pascal 1991: 164)

The story of the Fall accounts for the extent of our greatness and wretchedness. This permits Pascal to argue that only Christianity can synthesize the *contrariétés* that are basic to any understanding of man.

The conclusion is that where human reason reaches its own scandal, it must turn towards a principle that transcends its epistemological codes, that exists beyond our framework. The major persuasive aim of the *Pensées* is therefore not directly to describe God or even the truth of Christianity, but to make the reader accept the contradictions as irresolvable from the perspective of human understanding. This in turn becomes evidence that a different perspective is needed, namely a Christian perspective which places truth in God, in the non-symbolic. The third term of the dialectic, the synthesis or all-embracing truth, is consequently posited beyond the *Pensées*, beyond the text. We remember Melzer's 'atextual heart'. Language cannot make *sense* of the *contrariétés*, and the only resolution is therefore in silence, beyond language. This dialectic or gradation constitutes what we can define as Pascal's system of simple repetition. The *contrariétés* justify the apologetic discourse by enabling it to gesture towards God without talking about him. In other words this is the confident level of the text.

This confident level of the *Pensées* is reminiscent of the mystical tradition of *gradatio*, which imagines the process of conversion as those different stages through which human knowledge must progress (Force 1989: 242–5). The process is one in which different opinions succeed one another, each containing some truth: 'toute interprétation juste fût l'interprétation d'une interprétation fausse' (ibid.: 252). Finally this enables Pascal to 'humilier la raison humaine' (ibid.: 245) and lead it to the ultimate truth: God as a transcendent truth that embraces all interpretations and is larger than human reason. Pascal develops the traditional *gradatio* into what he calls the 'Renversement continuel du pour au contre'. This is described by Pascal as follows:

Nous avons donc montré que l'homme est vain par l'estime qu'il fait des choses qui ne sont pas essentielles. Et toutes ses opinions sont détruites.

Nous avons montré ensuite que toutes ces opinions sont très saines et qu'ainsi toutes ces vanités étaient très bien fondées, le peuple n'est pas si vain qu'on dit. Et ainsi nous avons détruit l'opinion qui détruisait celle du peuple.

Mais il faut détruire maintenant cette dernière proposition et montrer qu'il demeure toujours vrai que le peuple est vain, quoique ses opinions soient saines, parce qu'il n'en sent pas la vérité où elle est et que, la mettant où elle n'est pas, ses opinions sont toujours très fausses et très malsaines. (Pascal 1991: 127)

From one perspective it is true that *le peuple est vain*. However, from another perspective, people's or man's opinions do contain some elements of truth. Finally this second statement is cancelled out by a third claiming that although there might be some truth in opinions, the people do not know *where* this truth is. People are ignorant after all. Implied is a chain of reversals that ensues from a change of perspective: 'à la fin de chaque vérité, il faut ajouter qu'on se souvient de la vérité opposée' (ibid.: 479). The apologetic aim of the *renversement* is that 'la connaissance humaine s'élève graduellement vers le point de vue des chrétiens parfaits' (Force 1989: 252).

The *gradatio* or *renversement* implies a teleological process through which the interlocutor arrives at an understanding that implies conversion. However, from a different perspective, the actual process of the *renversement* questions the possibility of such a telos. Whereas the gradation leads to an overt production of the beyond, there is a coinciding movement that is somehow out of alignment with this production line, that happens simultaneously, but is different. As Melzer remarks: 'Theoretically, then, "the continual reversal of pro and con" continues infinitely' (Melzer 1986: 56). If it continues infinitely, this method risks creating a spiralling endless movement within which man's reasoning powers are locked, unable to transcend the movement. Suddenly there is no overt synthesis, merely a continuous in-between of different perspectives. As the telos evaporates, the process becomes more topological. The hierarchical dialectic collapses into a horizontal, endless back-and-forth that is unable to transcend itself into a synthesis. This movement has the potential to shift silence into literary silence.

The fragment that best plays out this non-teleological *renversement* is 163. The fragment figures a *Je* and a *lui*, who represents the reader:

> S'il se vante, je l'abaisse
> S'il s'abaisse, je le vante
> Et le contredis toujours
> Jusqu'à ce qu'il comprenne
> Qu'il est un monstre incompréhensible. (Pascal 1991: 163)

I want to show that this fragment holds within it the transformation from simple to complex repetition. The first three lines of the fragment stage a dialogue reminiscent of the Socratic dialectic. The thought interchange is between a first person and a third person. It is staged for the reader as exemplary. From the perspective of an imagined dialogue, the importance lies in always coming back to the third person with a contradictory statement, 'je le *contredis*'. This is still traditional *renversement*. The interlocutor must experience that his reason is insufficient as he attempts to interpret the different opinions, finding them all to be true from different perspectives. Involved in the experience of such a *renversement*, the reader will be baffled by the 'scandale pour la raison' (Mesnard 1993: 181). He will finally understand that he is a 'monstre incompréhensible', and implied is a turn towards God, beyond the dialogue. In other words the fragment gestures towards a silence *beyond* the actual formulation and its dialogic structure. The only potential synthesis this monster can have is in the silent realization of the 'atextual heart' and hence in faith and God. This is how the fragment behaves according to simple repetition.

However, the fragment also operates on another level. Whereas the beginning seems like an 'innocent' dialectic instance, the two last lines stage a more difficult scenario. *Comprendre* is juxtaposed to *incompréhensible*. We are asked to comprehend ourselves as incomprehensible. This presupposes a reflection that is intrinsic to the Cartesian view of man as a reflecting being. Man is a subject that can become his own object and thereby be sure, at least, of his existence. In the fragment the idea is that the comprehending subject can maintain the distance and superiority towards himself as incomprehensible object. *However, when we admit and realize that we are incomprehensible, we in fact lose our ability to further comprehend: the incomprehensible cannot perform the reflective*

operation of comprehension. In other words, the act of comprehending that
one is incomprehensible also affects the reflective ability of the subject
and precludes further reflection. Ultimately Pascal's formulation asks
us to sacrifice the superior, asymmetrical position of our subject self in
relation to the object self; it asks us to become incomprehensible. And
the moment we accept ourselves as incomprehensible, then we can no
longer relate to ourselves, no longer comprehend ourselves. Losing
the reflexive relation, the subject collapses into the object and reflection is an impossibility: the incomprehensible cannot comprehend
itself, cannot perform the reflexive operation that is comprehension,
cannot step outside of itself. This collapsed subject is distorted
and twisted. Herein lies the true monstrosity of the subject.
Incomprehension cancels the potential comprehension as it robs us of
our ability to reflect upon ourselves. This, I believe, is the powerful
dynamic of this five-line fragment.

   We can now appreciate that the implied realization leads to the disintegration and extinction of the humanity of the *lui*; he is revealed as
a *monstre*, a deformity created through human reasoning and dialectic.
This is because he loses the basis of his *grandeur*, namely his ability to
reflect. This suggests a complete reversal of Descartes's *cogito*.
Knowledge of one's own existence through thought here leads to a
certain disintegration: 'I comprehend therefore I am incomprehensible.' The fragment transforms and actually collapses into the unthinkable, the impossible. It incorporates a displacement of a perspective
that ultimately leads to a sense of breakdown. To be comprehended
as an incomprehensible monster can only take place in the perspective of the other. When this perspective is displaced and interiorized,
it indicates that the self must perish while remaining 'alive' through
the actual reflection.

   The fragment openly shows how simple repetition can reveal itself
as complex. On the level of simple repetition the fragment invites the
non-believer to realize how his own reasoning is insufficient, how he
is basically incomprehensible to himself, and thereby logically a crea-
ture of God. At this level the fragment suggests a double reflective
operation on the part of the reader: first one must realize one's own
limits as incomprehensible, and then, secondly, one must reflect one
step further to realize that the only possible solution to the monstrosity lies in God, outside the text. However, at the same time, the fragment reveals how this movement of simple repetition is precluded by
the same movement. The first reflective move is of course possible;

one can understand oneself as incomprehensible. But having internalized this understanding, one is unable to perform the second reflective or logical step because the incomprehensible cannot reflect, cannot realize even that the non-symbolic is beyond language. To accept that one is incomprehensible is also to sacrifice a further ability to reflect. It is hence a collapse that precludes the second movement of simple repetition. In other words, the production and stabilization of the beyond that is simple repetition is also the derailment, the destruction of this production. We are left with two incompatible meanings within the same fragment.

It now emerges that the fragment is basically aporetic. There is no final resolution. Both movements of simple and complex repetition are 'true'; the reader is both a reflecting being and a fallen monster that cannot perform this reflective move. This is a radical aporia in the sense that it cannot be transcended. To transcend it is to rely upon the reflective ability of the subject and thereby ignore the force of the incomprehensible monster, the forceful collapse of reflexivity. The fragment reveals a movement of language through which it becomes unruly and moves towards stating the impossible. Pascal's language, under the strain of saying the unsayable, stretches its own logic and moves towards the unknowable, the unsayable. Rhetoric here gives way to what Blanchot called *un centre d'illisibilité*—an unreadable topos where the literary transmits its silence. Through the actual language the 'atextual' heart emerges as a potential textual experience. The power of the apology operates through such aporetic language as language not merely gestures towards the beyond but re-enacts the experience of the beyond as its formulations become more than language.

The fragment enacts the dynamic of literary silence. It presents us with an aporetic statement that we cannot comprehend. More precisely, it describes a reality that does not correspond to any recognizable state. Through comprehension we find ourselves as incomprehensible and hence unable to further comprehend, yet we do continue comprehending. This is the movement of the implosion. The implosion has been defined as a double collapse. First it collapses our own relationship to ourselves, it implodes the ability of reflection. Secondly it collapses the relationship we entertain towards the text as interpreters. This is again related to the sacrifice that the implosion entails of reified language. The fragment stages both movements. First, as incomprehensible, the reader is asked to abandon any reflective ability; the incomprehensible cannot think or comprehend, but is locked in a state of immediacy. Secondly, the fragment, by staging us as incomprehensible, challenges our identity as thinking, interpreting readers. The reader is invited to collapse towards the text, to accept that the text is more than him or her, that it is not merely a passive object to be studied. The fragment itself becomes monstrous by suggesting that the text can transform the reader into an incomprehensible, unreflecting, immediate reader, a reader that can no longer interpret, but that still reads on. This 'monstrous language' is more than fallen language. Not only does it obviously not entertain a transparent relationship to any given reality, but it moves towards depicting a reality, a state that is fundamentally unthinkable.

Through this double collapse, this double sacrifice, we stand to gain a relationship to a language that is not reified, that is not telos-orientated, that does not strive to create stable meaning and agreement, but that floats, that says the unsayable and invites us to interact, through it, with this unsayable. To accept oneself as an incomprehensible monster is also to accept a suspended relationship to reified language, and be invited into a different relationship to a different language, a language that can relate literary silence. The meaning of this fragment is therefore not what it symbolizes or signifies, but its creation of the impossible, of Barcos's untranslatable 'sens suspendu', of movement, of play, back and forth, in between—the force of the radical aporia. This is the movement of literary silence. Reading the fragment we comprehend ourselves as incomprehensible monsters and we are therefore reading a language that can be called monstrous itself as it relates the unsayable, moves towards stating the unthinkable, the non-rational, and becomes its own silence.

In order to explore further the relationship between literary silence and the monstrous language, I will now consider further Pascal's observations on language, and particularly those addressing the *point fixe*.

LE POINT FIXE AND THE WAVE MOVEMENT

The *point fixe* on the one hand describes the dream of a stable location providing the *right* perspective, and on the other hand it defines the impossibility of fixing such a location. This impossibility influences language's ability to create stable, unchanging signification. The *point fixe* is therefore integral to fallen language, and to what has emerged as monstrous language, as it explains the lack of coincidence between language and the world. My intention is to explore the potential of this *point fixe*, that is not fixed, as far as literary silence is concerned.

Pascal approaches the *point fixe* in terms of a *milieu* which is the middle way between extremes: 'Deux infinis. Milieu. Quand on lit trop vite ou trop doucement, on n'entend rien' (Pascal 1991: 75). The right middle way is incorporated into Christianity through Christ's status as *mediator*: both man and God, both eternity and time, etc. (Michon 1996: 247–57; Force 1989: 167–84). It is also influenced by the climate ensuing from the astronomical discoveries of Kepler, in particular, that threatened man's sense of a centred position (Serres 1968: 647–810). The *point fixe* is 'le point central à partir duquel on peut comprendre l'ordre et le mouvement du monde' (ibid.: 676). Pascal compares it to viewing a painting: 'Ainsi les tableaux vus de trop loin et de trop près. Et il n'y a qu'un point indivisible qui soit le véritable lieu. Les autres sont trop près, trop loin, trop haut ou trop bas. La perspective l'assigne dans l'art de la peinture. Mais dans la vérité et dans la morale, qui l'assignera?' (Pascal 1991: 55). The fragment first asserts that there is one right point of perspective. However, this point is also described as *indivisible* and therefore infinitely small. In the words of Pierre Force, 'le jugement est incapable de percevoir isolément un infiniment petit' (Force 1989: 170). The essence of the *point fixe* is that it remains unfixable: 'Je ne puis juger de mon ouvrage en le faisant; il faut que je fasse comme les peintres, et que je m'en éloigne, mais non pas trop. De combien donc? Devinez' (Pascal 1991: 465). The only possible answer is a non-answer in the form of *Devinez*. In other words, the *point fixe* is not a calculated average, or 'simple' middle way: 'Le jugement juste n'est pas calcul de moyenne, mais plongé vers l'infini' (Force 1989: 172). As a disappearing infinity, the *point fixe* defies language—it can only be referred to as a *Devinez*. Because the location of the *point fixe* emerges as an infinitely unfixable point, it becomes a version of the non-symbolic; it can be experienced, but never directly stated. There is a parallel therefore between the *point fixe* and the synthesis of the *contrariétés*. It points towards a middle between the infinite *grandeur* and infinite *misère* that we are incapable of establishing without God: 'Ces extrémités se touchent et se réunissent à force de s'être éloignées, et se retrouvent en Dieu et en Dieu seulement' (Pascal 1991: 230). Only God, or more specifically Christ, as the mediator, can assign the fixed point. This leads to a possible understanding of the *point fixe* as simple repetition. By reaching the limits of the knowable the text indirectly refers to a knowledge, a truth that belongs to the non-symbolic, silent sphere of God. The *point fixe* represents a place that can only be beyond the text, beyond language, beyond history.

Pascal links this difficulty specifically to language: 'Le langage est pareil de tous côtés. Il faut avoir un point fixe, pour en juger' (Pascal 1991: 576). To be able to judge statements, a fixed point of reference is required. However, as we saw, to calculate such a point is impossible. This echoes the observation regarding the word *campagne* (ibid.: 99), showing that all it takes is a change of perspective for this word to change its relationship to any fixed reality , and hence lose its original meaning. 'A mesure qu'on s'approche'(ibid.) the word loses its meaning and dissolves into 'des maisons, des arbres, des tuiles, des feuilles, des herbes' (ibid.). Marin, in his analysis of the fragment, observes: 'Moving the point of view brings about a flux in the visible by which the appearances of being, so stable before the *fixed* eye that they acted as being itself, gradually fade away as appearances' (Marin 1975: 136). Marin seems to imply that due to its lack of a *point fixe* language risks opening towards a reality that is more fluid than fixed. So language, in order to signify a stable reality, relies upon a *point fixe* that is, however, defined as being indivisible and hence infinitely small. The indication is that language is doomed to a certain fluctuating state that again causes a fluctuating reality. This 'state of affairs' is echoed by the description 'C'est une sphère infinie dont le centre est partout, la circonférence nulle part' (Pascal 1991: 230). This is a typical example of language representing an unrepresentable reality. The formulation describes a reality that remains unfixed, an impossible locus. This is therefore again an example of language acting out its lack of a *point fixe* in relation to a thinkable reality. The *point fixe* takes on a double purpose: it is non-symbolic in that it defies language, and it simultaneously affects language's ability to signify any stable reality. Language then cannot signify the *point fixe* because it is always at the mercy of the indeterminate *point fixe*.

This view of language can be traced in the fragment 'Disproportion de l'homme'. The fragment addresses man's position between the infinitely small and the infinitely great, and his inability to grasp these realities:

Nous voguons sur un milieu vaste, toujours incertains et flottants, poussés d'un bout vers l'autre. Quelque terme où nous pensions nous attacher et nous affermir, il branle et nous quitte. Et si nous le suivons, il échappe à nos prises, il glisse et fuit d'une fuite éternelle. Rien ne s'arrête pour nous, c'est l'état qui nous est naturel et toutefois le plus contraire à notre inclination. Nous brûlons du désir de trouver une assiette ferme et une dernière base constante pour y édifier une tour qui s'élève à l'infini, mais tout notre fondement craque et la terre s'ouvre jusqu'aux abîmes. (Pascal 1991: 230)

The first sentence defines existence in terms of *un milieu vaste*. *Milieu* is an echo from fragment 75—a middle between the *deux infinis*. And here the *milieu* is defined as being vast—in other words this is a restatement of the indefinability of the *point fixe*. The formulation is almost a contradiction in terms: How can the middle way be vast? How can an average be vast? And how can the *centre* be *partout* and the *circonférence nulle part*? The closest language can come to signifying the *point fixe* is to create such instances that *practise* its indeterminacy. By stating these non-definable, infinite locations, language enacts the *point fixe* and its effect on language. Importantly the *milieu* is not only vast, it is also fluid: 'Nous voguons'. The idea of *voguer* and *flotter* and *poussés d'un bout vers l'autre* describes the effects of waves and of flux. And the element of water directly counteracts the concept of a fixed point. The wave movement is typically neither stable nor regular and as such constitutes one of the most complex movements. We recall that the wave movement also appeared in Kierkegaard's *Repetition* as the young man celebrated his own repetition. The flux of the wave was also identified by Bouhours in 1671 in his *Entretiens d'Ariste et d'Eugène* as a phenomenon of the *je ne sais quoi*, the inexplicable: 'N'en est-ce pas un [je ne sais quoi] aussi que le flux et reflux de la mer.' Returning to Pascal's fragment, reality is further described as 'slippery' ('il glisse'), never providing us with anything to hold on to. Any seeming stability is compared to the tower that reaches to infinity but that lacks any stable basis and hence merely disintegrates and reveals the infinite abyss. The reference to the tower recalls Babel and hence introduces a parallel to language. Not only reality, but the language we have to define this reality, is slippery. Language, as suggested above, is equally at the mercy of the indefinable *point fixe* and we are at its mercy as we attempt to create a stable reality.

From these observations the overt apologetic function and the corresponding movement of the fragment is clear. Due to the lack of a *point fixe* man is always floating in an unfixed existence. Realizing his own powerlessness, man should turn towards the beyond, to God. God is the only possible *point fixe*. However, a closer look at the grammatical structure of the fragment reveals another, simultaneous operation. The fragment suggests that man is subjected to language, powerless and *flottants* as we are *poussés d'un bout vers l'autre*. *Poussés* disempowers the subject *nous* and empowers the movement of the *milieu*. There is no *terme* to which we can attach ourselves. According to *Le Nouveau Petit Robert*, the first meaning of *terme* is the 'limite fixée dans l'espace'. However, it also refers to *word* as 'ce qui limite le sens'. *Terme* is therefore that which potentially can fix the *point fixe* by imposing limits. But according to the fragment there is no *terme* that can stabilize our reality. Against the disempowered *nous* the slippery *terme* is repeatedly presented as the agent, the subject of the sentence: 'il branle . . . il échappe . . . il glisse et fuit.' It is the *terme* that acts, and its action is never to remain still. The *nous* is designated as subject four times, but each time its subject status is demeaned. The first time, 'Nous voguons', the verb *voguer* indicates that the subject is not in control of its movement. The second time, 'nous pensions', the meaning is a negative: we might think we are attached to a word, but the word reasserts itself as subject and takes over in the *fuite éternelle*. The third time is comparable: 'et si nous le suivons' we are still not able to reassert any control. The last instance is again a devaluation of the will of the subject: 'Nous brûlons du désir'. In other words, we are powerless against the force of our desire. Grammatically the fragment repeatedly undermines the *nous* as active agent and leaves it forceless and exposed to the movement of the *terme*, as limit and word, which takes on subject status. The actual linguistic structure of the fragment acts out a language that takes control over man.

The result of such a vision is more seditious than the overt apologetic function implies. Simple repetition has again revealed itself as complex. Indeed if man is at the mercy of a language that always escapes him, then his power of thought is challenged as he is constantly overthrown by the waves of language. Also the relationship world–thought–language is radically questioned. If language, as the means by which we understand the world and think, is not in our control, but we in its, and it is always fleeing, then our ability to reflect is in fact undermined. The fragment, like the *monstre incompréhensible*, challenges and *implodes* the Cartesian *cogito*. The *cogito* presents an assertive first-person 'I' in control of language and thought. This is the same 'I' that can turn from the fluctuating world to the 'atextual' heart, the same 'I' that can comprehend being incomprehensible without necessarily becoming incomprehensible. In other words, it is the 'I' upon which the simple repetition of the apology depends, defined by his ability to reflect and think. However, this fragment radically challenges the supremacy of this 'I' by continuously devaluing the *nous* and placing it at the mercy of language. The thinking 'I' dissolves in the hands of an unruly, slippery, fleeing language that takes on the status of subjective agent and then offers no stability. The fragment is actually asking us to *think* (fathom) a subject that cannot think. Again we recognize the impossible reflexive stance presented in fragment 163. How can one think oneself as one that cannot think? The new unrealizable stance is: 'I think therefore I cannot think.' The fragment's overt apologetic aim collapses as the subject is reduced to an immediate state, caught in the playful, wavelike movements of a language that escapes control. Simple repetition becomes complex, and the aporetic dynamic again emerges. Language must be in our control for us to remain the reflective reader who can enter into the overt apologetic aim and turn towards the beyond. However, inherent in this operation is the movement that robs us of our reflective ability as it leaves us floating back and forth on the *milieu vaste* that is the operation of fallen or 'monstrous' language.

Like comprehending incomprehension, the unthinking, yet reading subject that emerges in this fragment is an impossibility. We cannot think this monster that we are asked to become, this disempowered *nous* at the mercy of the infinite movements of language. Again we recognize the potential for the implosion. The fragment challenges us to sacrifice our rational, or 'thinkable' relation to the reified, signifying language that is our most important tool, and rather give into a language that is waves beyond our control. Fragment 230 reveals how language, through its own fluctuating movements, creates a sense of the non-symbolic by ceasing to symbolize a stable reality. By gesturing towards the unthinkable, by collapsing our rational approach to language (it now 'controls' us), the fragment, as implosion, offers no beyond for us to turn to: it becomes infinite. It is through this transformation that the fragment plays out its apologetic value without referring to a beyond. Something *happens* within the language, grammatically and semantically, through slips and fluctuations, that relocates the sense of the unsayable into langage itself. The apologetic function of the text shifts as it no longer relies upon a beyond, but can become silent and strangely non-symbolic in itself.

But although meaning is no longer a beyond and no longer stable, this does not indicate that there is no meaning. Rather, meaning has shifted and now appears in the actual fluctuations and slips of language. We recall Barcos's and Marin's notion of the *sens suspendu*. Meaning is in the 'fallenness' of language, in its continual flux, in its lack of coincidence, its infinite monstrosity. We are here moving towards a closer understanding of literary silence. I propose that literary silence can be further developed in terms of waves and flux. Fragment 230 suggests an understanding of the infinite *point fixe* of language in terms of waves. When language becomes the unthinkable, it is fluctuating in relation to reality, and also in relation to the beyond. As we observed, fluctuating language cancelled the 'atextual' heart as language became infinite. Metaphorically we can imagine that as language becomes congruent with waves and flux, it floods into the 'land of the beyond', lifting the dualism between silence and language. Waves are congruent with the movement of complex repetition. It matters that waves cannot be measured as dualistic operations—they are their own movement. This again echoes play and force as movements that are self-sufficient. Whereas simple repetition relies on a repeated dualistic system, complex repetition can be imagined as waves that erase the dualism. Literary silence happens when language takes on the movement of waves.

It is important that Pascal actually offers a description of waves that fits our observations:

La nature agit par progrès, *itus et reditus*. Elle passe et revient, puis va plus loin, puis deux fois moins, puis plus que jamais, etc.

Le flux de la mer se fait ainsi, le soleil semble marcher ainsi:

(Pascal 1991: 636)

Pascal describes the movement of the sea, and sun, as non-regular. He privileges this movement against that of continuity and hence indirectly motivates complex repetition and our understanding of literary silence: 'L'éloquence continue ennuie. . . . La continuité dégoûte en tout' (ibid.). I think continuity can here be best understood as a certain linear progression opposed to a back-and-forth: 'La nature de l'homme n'est pas d'aller toujours. Elle a ses *allées et venues*' (ibid.: 61, my italics). There is a sense of a privileged back-and-forth. Fragment 636 is remarkable in that Pascal should chose to draw these movements, clearly feeling that they defy description.[19] This indicates that the wave movement, and I concentrate on that rather than the movement of the sun, somehow resists signification. Fragment 230 described fallen language in terms of waves, and fragment 636 *draws* waves. The *Pensées* consequently suggest a parallel between fallen language and the wave movement. When language plays out its lack of *point fixe*, when its ability to signify breaks down (i.e. when it becomes the *milieu vaste* of the *point fixe*, or when the 'centre est partout, la circonférence nulle part') then language can be understood as 'slippery' waves that cannot be pinned down. This is also the grounding for the implosion as we are drawn into a movement through which the unthinkable emerges. It is in this movement, this moment of non-signification, that literary silence emerges as the force of the unsayable, the flooded form of the silence of the beyond. As language becomes the unthinkable, it sacrifices, *implodes*, its purpose of signifying, and hence opens up the possibility of expressing the beyond through its non-sense. Fragments 230 and 636 together support an understanding of literary silence as a wavelike movement that is suspended in language, and that emerges in language's move towards the unthinkable.

We can conclude by referring back to Barcos and his image of the true meaning of the biblical language as the invisible traces left on water by God. These invisible traces are visible only in those instances when language, even while *continuing*, shifts to another plane where *movement is primary to meaning*. Language ceases to be a properly functioning signifying tool, indeed it becomes *un monstre incompréhensible* that is no longer proportionate with man, but takes on its own 'life' as it summons us to move topologically, around in the text, from move-

---

[19] For a discussion of different editions of the drawing of the *zigzag*, see Pierre Force, 'Itus et reditus, de l'impossible édition d'un zigzag' (Force 1988).

ment to movement, in a language that arises towards the end of thought and linearity. It is in such monstrous moments that language, no longer signifying, actually becomes the trace of God, *becomes silence*.

CONCLUSION

This reading of the *Pensées* can be summed up as the attempt to articulate the apologetic value of the text without referring to a 'beyond' that is outside the text. I have tried to show how the beyond, or the 'atextual' heart, can be relocated into the startling formulations of Pascal. In addition to gesturing towards the beyond, Pascal's language itself has the power to create the experience of the non-symbolic. It achieves this by performing shifts whereby the silence of the beyond becomes literary silence. In order to explore these shifts, I have attempted to remain in the aporia described by Melzer, rather than referring to the 'atextual' heart. In the aporetic instance the *Pensées* play out a language that can be described as a never-ending movement of back-and-forth that ultimately offers no synthesis, no sense of beyond. And as Pascal himself states: 'Notre nature est dans le mouvement, le repos entier est la mort' (Pascal 1991: 529).

Specifically I have considered the impossible *monstre incompréhensible* (ibid.: 163) and the thinking subject that cannot think (ibid.: 230). These are fragments that represent a view of man that robs him of his ability to reflect. The importance, however, lies not in a negative view of man but in the challenge these fragments offer to our rational relationship to ourselves and our language. Ultimately, we are invited to read and listen to representations of ourselves that undermine our ability to reflect upon ourselves through language. From this ensues a double operation. First, we are permitted to sacrifice our relationship to ourselves as it is defined through the subject–object constellation implied in the *cogito*. Secondly, we are permitted to sacrifice our relationship to language as 'bearer of meaning' as we are caught up in a language that presents what are to us unthinkable realities. These operations provide the grounds for the implosion that again is the potential for literary silence. As meaning breaks down, language becomes primarily a 'field' of movement. This movement has been compared to Pascal's descriptions and drawing of the wave movement (Pascal 1991: 230 and 636) as a sense of endless back-and-forth. Through these wave movements meaning becomes suspended in the movement of meaninglessness. The fragments in question are moments in the *Pensées* that offer us a potential release from reified, everyday language and open a clearing in which it is possible to enter into a different relationship with a different language.

Language ceases to signify as it evokes the unthinkable. No longer referring to a stable meaning, it becomes movements reminiscent of waves. In this movement language approaches silence. This is as close as we can come to a definition of literary silence in the *Pensées*. Like the created monster, language, originally created by a human rational endeavour, takes on a life of its own and comes back to 'haunt' its creator. As it becomes monstrous and hence no longer obedient, language no longer means, it moves. This is the surprising and engaging force of Pascal's formulations. Some might object that my analysis challenges the authorial intention of Pascal. I would argue back that Pascal overtly describes language as beyond the control of man, as slippery and fleeting. To pretend that language was stable would constitute the sin of pride as it pretends to transcend the sinful nature of language. I read Pascal's language as an endless performance of such slippages and hence as an endless flight away from itself and its overt apologetic function. And in this characteristic of language lies the more modern apologetic value of his project. Pascal's fragments, exactly because they enact an endless performance of slips and shifts, move towards saying the unsayable as they become movements— waves, silence.

5

LITERARY SILENCE IN ROUSSEAU'S
RÊVERIES

The desolation and fear that accompany the *silence éternel* in the *Pensées* reappears in a different guise in the confessional project of Rousseau. It is no longer the silence of a mute God, but of the mute and silent *others*. Remaining silent, the people surrounding Rousseau do not recognize and affirm the interiority of his self. This is the terrifying silence that leaves one abandoned, uncertain, and ultimately dead in the eyes of the world. It follows that one of the most famous and certainly most painful silences in the work of Rousseau is that which follows his public reading of the *Confessions*: 'J'achevai ainsi ma lecture, et tout le monde se tut' (Rousseau 1959*b*: 656).[1] Silence here bears the greatest sense of betrayal and misunderstanding. It incapacitates Rousseau's dream of reconciliation as it becomes the empty end of communication; the hopeless beginning of isolation. Starobinski, in his perceptive study *Jean-Jacques Rousseau: la transparence et l'obstacle*, remarks: 'Rousseau rencontre le *silence*, qui est l'obstacle ultime, le mystère d'inquiétude . . . la séparation absolue' (Starobinski 1971: 267–8). Silence is rejection.

But, as observed by Starobinski, the obstacle has the potential to become transparency. Silence is therefore not only dead; it is also a transparent, immediate medium that language can only dream of. The happiness of the 'matinée à l'anglaise' (*La Nouvelle Héloïse)* and the intense *joie* and *agitation* experienced with Madame Basile (*Confessions, ii*) are all preconditioned by the silence that makes words and signs superfluous. Silence becomes the medium of reconciliation, understanding, and immediate communication that language cannot offer: 'L'accueil idéal, le retour idéal se produisent en deçà ou au-delà du

---

[1] I am quoting the Pléiade edition (Rousseau: 1959*b*). The edition is based on Rousseau's original manuscript and reproduces all variations with regard to spelling and expressions. See 'Note sur l'établissement du text': xcvi–xcix.

langage' (Starobinski 1971: 165). Romantic and nostalgic on the one hand, and realistic and awful on the other, Rousseau's relationship to the notion of silence is double and complex.

The more romantic idea of silence is necessarily linked to Rousseau's notion of *origins*: *l'origine de l'inégalité, l'origine des langues.*[2] The state of the origin is of course famously romanticized. It is blissful, peaceful, harmonious, void of envy, jealousy, and more importantly, pre-linguistic or silent. This invented original state was one in which man did not posses discourse or articulated words. He moved around in a silence interrupted only by gestures and by *le cri de la nature.* Conditioned by this silence, man's original relation to the world was immediate and whole, unfractured by language and articulated words. Inscribed in Rousseau's world view, and in his writing, is therefore the dream of a pre-cultural topos of silence (see Chapter 1) as an immediate communion with nature, as unfractured knowledge, as a being in time that is not discontinued. An ideal takes shape in which words are superfluous and verbal expression is associated with a great unease.

This ideal of silence is coupled with a strong sense of nostalgia due to its being lost and impossible to regain. After the dawn of culture and its implied introduction of words and articulation, silence is reduced to the object of a certain hope, a desire for the impossible return to the origin. Merely by considering the extent of Rousseau's *œuvre* we are led to conclude that the silence of which he dreamt was not an option for him. If Rousseau had felt that retreat into silence would restore him to the origin, he surely would have opted not to write; but 'Rousseau ne parvient pas à se resigner au silence' (Starobinski 1971: 269). Incessant acts of articulation, Rousseau's texts indirectly reveal the impossibility of the romantic ideal of silence, yet display a continuous longing for it. But Rousseau's writing is also an attempt to overcome the dead and mute silence considered above. As such it is an act of articulation *against* silence in the name of reconciliation and mutual understanding. The dilemma, of course, is that this ideal reconciliation can only take place in silence. Rousseau must therefore write in order to break the silence that separates him from others; but he can only be reconciled with these others in silence. The

---

[2] Rousseau's preoccupation with origins is largely a result of a growing anthropological interest in the 18th century. Whereas the 17th century had generally been concerned with the religious and divine origins of man, the Enlightenment investigated natural history as a potential explicative source of man's contemporary condition.

result is an aporetic dilemma: the need for a silent beyond of plenitude and immediacy, and its parallel impossibility. The text is haunted by this aporetic dynamic, a dynamic that arguably underlies the sense of desperation throughout Rousseau's *œuvre*.

My intention is to consider how the *Rêveries du promeneur solitaire*, as part of his autobiographical corpus, reveals the movement of this yearning for a silence that must necessarily be written, yet resists words. Already it is possible to foreshadow the operation of simple repetition as that dynamic that stabilizes and indicates the immediate silence as a beyond. The immediacy of the self, because it is non-symbolic and silent, necessarily has its essence outside the text. My intention is to isolate some dynamics whereby the *Rêveries* refers the reader to this non-symbolic beyond. As we shall see, the dynamic of simple repetition in the text is largely based on dualisms. In order to move towards the movement of complex repetition it will therefore be necessary to reveal instances of instability in the dualistic system.

In order to understand the dynamic of simple repetition it is first of all necessary to gain a more nuanced understanding of the non-symbolic self. I shall attempt to delineate how an underlying view of the self runs throughout the *Rêveries* and how it determines the sense of the non-symbolic. Rousseau repeatedly posits this self in terms of a traditional silence that is the negative other of the text, something I will show becomes a dynamic of simple repetition. This analysis will focus on the dualistic couplings of inside–outside and subject–object. Having established these systems, I will move on to consider how these dualisms are also sites of instabilities that can be discussed in terms of a *flux continuel* that occupies an important place throughout the *Rêveries*. Again we shall see how complex repetition emerges in association with wave-like movements (see Chapter 4). I shall then consider how this complex repetition manifests itself in dynamics of literary silence. Finally, I will attempt to define a certain marker, a 'signifier', that embodies the complex repetition in the *Rêveries* and see how it can be traced throughout the text.

QUE SUIS-JE MOI-MÊME? A DELIMITATION OF THE NON-SYMBOLIC IN THE *RÊVERIES*

Started in 1777, the *Rêveries* is Rousseau's last autobiographical attempt to articulate his self. Following what he experienced as the misreadings of the *Confessions* and the 'divine' rejection of the *Dialogues*, symbolized by the closed altar at Notre Dame, Rousseau no longer writes to a reader but merely to himself: 'je n'écris mes rêveries que pour moi' (Rousseau 1959*a*: 1001).[3] Still, the challenge is the same, namely to discover and reveal the essence of the self: 'Mais moi, détaché d'eux et de tout, que suis-je moi-même?' (ibid.: 995). Implied is the shortcoming of his *Confessions*: 'le connois-toi toi-même du Temple de Delphes n'étoit pas une maxime si facile à suivre que je l'avois cru dans mes *Confessions*' (ibid.: 1024). So the question remains 'que suis-je?' and it is this reverberating echo that designates the non-symbolic or the unsayable in the *Rêveries*. The self, then, is the locus of the original silence, of the unsayable and the non-symbolic, and the longing of the *Rêveries* is to be reconciled with this silence of the self.

Although still asking 'que suis-je?' it is noteworthy that Rousseau does not consider self-knowledge as a problem in and for itself. As Starobinski remarks, quoting the first letter to Malherbes: 'Pour Jean-Jacques la connaissance de soi n'est pas un problème: c'est une donnée: "Passant ma vie avec moi, je dois me connaître" ' (Starobinski 1971: 216). Knowledge of the self is given; the problem lies in the act of articulation and in the act of transmitting it to an *understanding* audience. Inscribed in Rousseau's text is this drive for reconciliation: 'Être reconnu, pour Rousseau, ce sera essentiellement être justifié, être innocenté' (ibid.: 221). Reconciliation with the other, with God, with the self—all hinges upon the articulation of the self. This is the desperation of the *que suis-je?* in the *Rêveries*. It is the burning desire for transformation of the 'silent' self-knowledge, the feeling of the self that is exclusive to the 'I', into discourse and writing. So the question *que suis-je* is actually *que suis-je en écriture?* The silence of the self must be rediscovered, and hence potentially transformed, through writing. Briefly stated, Rousseau's autobiographical texts can be summed up as the ongoing attempt to articulate the silent immediacy of intuitive self-knowledge. And it is implied that the original silence that is the immediate and private self-knowledge will change through writing. Herein lies the interest of literary silence as a potential new 'practice' of an original silence.

More precisely the non-symbolic aspect of the self lies in what Rousseau designates as its almost divine or holy element. In *Émile*

---

[3] I am quoting the Pléiade edition (Rousseau 1959*a*). See n. 1 above.

Rousseau invokes conscience as the 'immortelle et céleste voix'. Described as heavenly and immortal, the self takes on the transcendence previously only attributable to God. It is, as Eric Blondel writes in his article 'La Vérité et le moi dans *Les Rêveries du promeneur solitaire*': '[la] voix qui est en moi, mais qui en moi dit quelque chose de transcendant sur le bien et le mal, donc sur la vérité morale, quelque chose, qui, comme la vérité, est immortelle et céleste, c'est-à-dire universellement et éternellement vrai et qui, quoique issu du moi, témoigne d'une vérité absolue et supérieure au moi' (Blondel 1997: 26). The *moi haïssable* of Pascal has now become the new seat of divine attributes, the proclaimer of Truth. This is witness to the general shift in the nature of the non-symbolic from God 'out there' to the self 'in here' (see Chapter 1). Consequently, issues of morality are internalized, released from the order of the divine, and inscribed in the order of the self. This transition can be traced also in the fourth promenade, the essay on lying. Rousseau here defines a lie not by its objective truth value, but according to the *intention* of the speaker, that is, by his interior motives: 'Dire faux n'est mentir que par l'intention de tromper, et l'intention même de tromper loin d'être toujours jointe avec celle de nuire a quelquefois un but tout contraire' (Rousseau 1959a: 1029). The inner voice, 'heavenly and immortal', is the topos of good, of right and wrong. This voice overrules that of abstract reasoning: 'Dans toutes les questions de morale difficiles comme celle-ci, je me suis toujours bien trouvé de les resoudre par le dictamen de ma conscience plustôt que par les lumiéres de ma raison' (ibid.: 1028).

As the self becomes the carrier of transcendence, the importance of knowing the inner self is raised as a new and pressing necessity. In other words there is an urgency to articulate the silence of the self, to state and explain and hence make available the secret feeling of the self. The question of self-knowledge, still sinful to Pascal, has become a question of morality. This perspective helps explain the urgency of Rousseau's project and tells us more about the nature of the non-symbolic in the *Rêveries*.

'Que suis-je?' is then the central question that sparks our investigation into literary silence in the *Rêveries*. Pronounced from the 'chaos incompréhensible' (Rousseau 1959a: 995) into which Rousseau says he is precipitated, unable even to 'comprendre où je suis' (ibid.), this question remains. Rousseau is struggling to establish his location, his *place* from which he can order his biographical narrative. He is 'sur la terre comme dans une planette étrangére où je serois tombé de celle que j'habitois' (ibid.: 999).[4] And he knows from experience that merely stating the facts of his life (as he did in the *Confessions*) will not articulate the silence that preconditions reconciliation. Changing 'tactics', he concludes to himself, 'je n'ai vu nulle maniére plus simple et plus sure d'executer cette entreprise que de tenir un regître fidelle de mes promenades solitaires et des rêveries qui les remplissent' (ibid.: 1002). But only a paragraph later he asks: 'comment en tenir un rêgistre fidelle?' (ibid.: 1003). The actual walks and reveries are to provide the key to answer the question 'que suis-je?' and hence be the locus of the unsayable (see Morrissey 1984: 153). However, Rousseau's second question, *comment en tenir un rêgistre fidelle*, unravels the derived solution to the problem and undermines even the 'plus simple et plus sure' method. This on the one hand indicates the complexity of a text that contradicts itself and moves away from itself, and on the other hand it warns us of the difficulty of the project undertaken. It testifies how the reverie risks slipping away from any faithful register, how the text itself is prone to fail as a transparent mimetic rendition. The reverie is a state 'qu'on cesseroit bientot de connoitre, en cessant tout à fait de le sentir' (ibid.: 1003). It is an immediate, non-linear contemplative state, a pure feeling of being: an original silence. To know it is to feel it. The challenge of the *Rêveries* is to articulate the silence and immediacy of this feeling and the notion of self that it promises.

This problematic recalls the descriptions of the Charmettes in the sixth book of the *Confessions*. These months spent with *Maman* are some of the happiest in Rousseau's life and it is this blissful absence of torment that he attempts to impart:

Comment ferai-je pour prolonger à mon gré ce récit si touchant et si simple; pour redire toujours les mêmes choses, et n'ennuyer pas plus mes lecteurs en les répétant que je ne m'ennuyois moi-même en les recommençant sans cesse? Encore si tout cela consistoit en faits, en actions, en paroles, je pourrois le décrire et le rendre, en quelque façon: mais comment dire ce qui n'étoit ni dit, ni fait, ni pensé même, mais gouté, mais senti, sans que je puisse énoncer d'autre objet de mon bonheur que ce sentiment même. (Rousseau 1959*b*: 225)

The serene joy of this period challenges articulation. And, as we know, this type of joy is the closest Rousseau gets to the 'state of nature', the

---

[4] For more on the importance of place and its relation to identity in the *Rêveries*, see Alain Grosrichard 1997: 29–47, and Éric Blondel 1997: 22–5.

origin, the non-symbolic. The fear is, of course, that the immediacy of his joy (he compares it to taste and sensation) will not survive the difference bestowed by language. The frustration equals that of the reverie: 'mais comment en ténir un rêgistre fidelle?' Marcel Raymond, in his much celebrated work *Jean-Jacques Rousseau: la quête de soi et la rêverie*, concludes with regard to the quoted passage: 'Nous sommes en deçà de toute pensée, là où le langage fait place au silence' (Raymond 1962: 214; see Morrissey 1984: 158). Raymond here fails to realize the complexity of Rousseau's relationship to silence as he seems to fall for the Dream of Silence (see Chapter 1) as poetic transcendence that can somehow conclude an analysis. He ignores how Rousseau's articulation, by incessantly approaching silence is also undermining it, transforming it, exactly because it does not 'fait place au silence'. Rather the text continues for another six books, and Rousseau, driven by the *Sehnsucht* for this silence, will continue writing until he dies.[5]

This continuation, or repetition, of writing leads us back to the actual question stated in the quoted passage on the Charmettes: how can a text repeat itself, how can it always restart, without repeating the same and boring the reader? *Redire, répéter, recommencer*—all are verbs that imply a temporal loop, a going-back-to. The movement of repetition is the repeated attempt to articulate that which is experienced as beyond words. Literature's attempt to articulate the unsayable or the experience of the non-symbolic is not content with stopping or ending. So it will *re*turn, *re*state, *re*commence, and *re*peat its attempt in a movement of revisitation and reinvention of language. This constant repetition is the general operation of simple repetition in Rousseau's autobiographical work: the constant attempt to give credibility and authenticity to that which exactly cannot be written. Rather than endings or mythical silences, we are dealing with repetition. And within this simple repetition, there is, as we have seen in the *Pensées*, also a more complex movement. Through these movements the original, negatively defined non-symbolic silence can shift and emerge as literary silence.

---

[5] Ann Hartle (1983: 18–21) draws attention to how Rousseau's writing frequently announces its own termination only to continue.

MAINTAINING THE SILENCE OF THE UNSAYABLE SELF:
THE DYNAMICS OF SIMPLE REPETITION

Many have noticed how Rousseau's writing operates with contradictions or dualisms. Gouhier, in his philosophical study *Les Méditations
métaphysiques de Jean-Jacques Rousseau*, remarks how 'La pensée de Jean-
Jacques Rousseau est, semble-t-il, spontanément dualiste. . . .
L'homme selon la nature est lui-même défini par des dualités'
(Gouhier 1970: 163). And Vosine, in his introduction to the Garnier-
Flammarion edition of the *Rêveries*, says about Rousseau: 'Il n'aime
guère les nuances, et pense volontiers au moyen de couples antithé-
tiques de concepts: relatif et absolu, apparence et réalité, vérité et
mensonge' (Voisine 1964: 23). Rousseau's presentation of selfhood is
ordered according to dualisms. Raymond remarks that in order to
analyse the behaviour and self of Jean-Jacques: 'il faudrait examiner
les structures profondes, c'est-à-dire les ambivalences affectives qui le
travaillent: amour–haine, orgueil–humilité, besoin d'innocence–
sentiment de culpabilité, etc. . . . et de marquer nettement ce rythme
binaire et la répétition de ce schéma psychique où s'inscrivent les variations de sa conduite et de ses états de sensibilité' (Raymond 1962: 27).
Rousseau criticism, particularly that which precedes or rejects the
deconstructionist readings initiated by the work of Derrida and de
Man, seems to have found a system in the dualistic patterns that could
seemingly account for the diversity and richness of the autobiographical texts.

My reading identifies the dualistic patterns as the means by which
Rousseau's text overtly indicates, places, and outlines the non-
symbolic self against the text. It can be coined the *confident* mode of the
text because it is the mode which can 'talk about' the non-symbolic by
indicating it negatively. The immediacy of the inner self remains
intact in opposition to the mediacy of the written self. Simple repetition in the *Rêveries* works in order to guarantee and stabilize the non-
symbolic self by repeatedly recognizing it and addressing it as that
which transcends the sayable. In order to define how this simple repetition operates in the *Rêveries* I shall focus on two underlying binary
oppositions, namely *être–paraître*, or inside–outside, and the dynamics
of subject–object.

Rousseau's autobiographical project presents and operates with a
sense of selfhood based on the notion of an inner self, an essence that

is unavailable to others who see only the exterior. The aim of the text is to make this interior accessible by externalizing it through writing. Exemplary in this regard is Rousseau's claim regarding his *Confessions*: 'J'ai dévoilé mon *intérieur*' (Rousseau 1959*b*: 5, my italics), and later on: 'L'objet propre de mes confessions est de faire connaître exactement mon *intérieur* dans toutes les situations de ma vie' (ibid.: 278, my italics). This dualistic opposition between *intérieur–extérieur*, *être–paraître* runs throughout Rousseau's work. Already in the *Discours sur les sciences et les arts* Rousseau remarks: 'Qu'il serait doux de vivre parmi nous, si la contenance extérieure était toujours l'image des dispositions du cœur'(Rousseau 1964: 7).[6] The theme goes back to the seventeenth century and is not original to Rousseau. By the 1750s it has become, in the words of Starobinski, 'assez répandu, assez vulgarisé, assez automatisé' (Starobinski 1971: 14). Gouhier claims that 'le thème des apparences mensongères est banal' (Gouhier 1970: 93). It is, however, exactly this banal aspect of the dualistic paradox that interests me. As a commonplace antithesis it is repeated, in various guises, throughout the *Rêveries* and becomes one of the most basic instances of simple repetition.

Descriptions of the self in terms of interior space are repeated throughout the *Rêveries* (the following examples are all from the 'Seconde Promenade'): 'je m'accoutumois . . . à chercher . . . au-dedans de moi', 'L'habitude de rentrer en moi-même', 'la source du vrai bonheur est en nous', 'délices internes', 'tresors que je portois en moi-même'. These examples show with what naturalness the self is presented in terms of an inner essence. The rhetoric of inside, *charme intérieur, penchant naturel, rempli des sentiments tendres, je me suffis à moi-même, la sérenité, la tranquillité, la paix, mon plus secret intérieur*, determines the characteristic lyrical mode of the *Rêveries*. The interior designates the subjective singularity of the self, a topos that can be visited as it becomes the seat of that which is *good*. The interiorization of morality complements the experience of the self as an inner sentiment.

The importance of inwardness is sustained in opposition to an idea of an exterior. The inside is predictably privileged at the cost of the outside which necessarily becomes potentially deceptive: 'Si les hommes s'obstinent à me voir tout autre que je ne suis . . . ce n'est pas moi qu'ils voyent ainsi' (Rousseau 1959*a*: 1058–9). In fact one can never *see* the other; one could do so, muses Rousseau, only if one

---

[6] I am quoting the Pléiade edition (Rousseau 1964).

possessed a magic wand that made men invisible, thereby 'voyant les hommes tels qu'ils sont' (ibid.: 1058). The outside becomes an obstacle that hinders knowledge of the real self: 'je *paroitrois* à mes contemporains méchant et féroce' (ibid.: 1008, my italics). Starobinski claims that 'Le souci de Rousseau commence donc par cette question: pourquoi le sentiment intérieur, immédiatement évident, ne trouve-t-il pas son écho dans une reconnaissance immédiatement accordée?' (Starobinski 1971: 218). The question is of course increasingly pressing as Rousseau feels himself so misunderstood by others who fail to grasp who he *really is*.

Furthermore, the incompatibility between inside and outside affects Rousseau's ability to read other people and situations: 'on ne me laisse pas voir les choses comme elles sont . . . il n'y a que mensonge et fausseté dans les démonstrations grimaciéres qu'on me prodigue' (Rousseau 1959a: 1056). Surrounded by *des mistéres* and *tant d'énigmes* (ibid.: 1009), and 'trainé dans la fange sans jamais savoir par qui ni pourquoi, plongé dans un abyme d'ignominie, enveloppé d'horribles ténébres' (ibid.: 1019), he asks himself, 'puis-je prendre une confiance éclairée en des apparences qui n'ont rien de solide . . . ?' (ibid.: 1020). Undoubtedly the inside–outside dualism fuels what is often referred to as Rousseau's increasing paranoia.[7] If appearances are deceptive, then his conspiracy theories and fear of persecution are justified. If the world is always other than its appearance, always untrustworthy, paranoia becomes the only means of survival.

As long as the opposition inside–outside persists, only the 'I' can know its self. This privileged bird's eye perspective has often been compared to that of God. Hartle, in her study *The Modern Self in Rousseau's Confessions*, says: 'Rousseau sees himself as God himself would see him: he sees himself precisely as he *is*' (Hartle 1983: 92). Gouhier observes: 'le regard de Dieu sur moi coïncide avec le regard de moi sur moi' (Gouhier 1970: 96). The established antithesis *être–paraître* has two main consequences that determine the registers of meaning of the *Rêveries*. First, Rousseau can align his privileged point of view with that of God. This validates his text; it is the only truthful account of his self, only he can know his self, because only he (besides God) has access to the inner self. Secondly, he can maintain the notion of an innocent inside that will not be revealed through appearance

---

[7] See e.g. Hartle's comments on the *Confessions*: 'Certainly, the apparent paranoia (especially obvious in Part Two) lends credence to this understanding of the work [as Rousseau's personal apology]' (Hartle 1983: 29).

and that has therefore remained unavailable to his contemporaries. Within this perspective the confessional project can almost be seen as an obligation: the obligation of self-knowledge, and of making this knowledge available to others. This preconditions Rousseau's justification for the self-obsessed aspect of the project. The self-portrait always bears a trace of shame at its own self-referentiality, its own indulgence in itself. De Man, in his article 'Autobiography as Defacement', observes: 'autobiography always looks slightly disreputable and self-indulgent in a way that may be symptomatic of its incompatibility with aesthetic values' (de Man 1979*a*: 919). Beaujour, in his study of the self-portrait, *Miroirs d'encre*, makes a similar claim: 'L'inquiétude et la culpabilité débordent assurément l'autoportrait' (Beaujour 1980: 17), one reason being that its 'discours ne s'addresse à un éventuel lecteur qu'en tant que celui-ci est placé en position de tiers exclu' (ibid.: 14). This trait is accentuated in the *Rêveries* when Rousseau rejects the reader, proclaiming that 'je n'écris mes rêveries que pour moi' (Rousseau 1959*a*: 1001).

The inside–outside dualism is also used to describe the actual reverie. Reverie is presented as the ultimate experience of interiority. It is the state in which '[on ne jouit] de rien d'extérieur à soi, de rien sinon de soi-même et de sa propre existence' (ibid.: 1047). Self-sufficient, the reverie is that state in which Rousseau is 'pleinement moi et à moi sans diversion' (ibid.: 1002). Reveries are designated as experiences of the plenitude of the inner self. This in turn explains why Rousseau chooses to describe the reveries as a means of finding out who he is.[8] The key to self-knowledge lies in descriptions of this state of self-sufficiency that is the reverie. In his article 'Le Sentiment de l'existence chez Rousseau', Georges Poulet remarks how the reverie

subsiste sous la forme d'une intériorisation graduelle de l'être, quand celui-ci, ayant doucement mais fermement rompu les liens qui le rattachaient au monde externe, se réduit à être une voix qui, du dedans, se fait entendre dans le silence: exemple parfait d'une conscience de soi dépouillée de tous les éléments adventices qui auraient pu en troubler l'unité. (Poulet 1978: 38)

Within the dichotomy inside–outside, the reverie becomes congruent with the experience of the inner, original non-symbolic essence of the self.

---

[8] For more on the development of the reverie as a topos of the interiority and essence of the self see Morrissey 1984; Bachelard 1960.

What emerges through this dualism, then, is a certain 'vocabulary' that permits a particular description of the self in terms of inwardness. It is a language that models and preconditions our self-understanding. Its specificity is not original to Rousseau, but rather anchored in what one might call a Western, modern world view. However, as Charles Taylor reminds us in his *Sources of the Self*: 'The localization [inside–outside] is not a universal one, which human beings recognize as a matter of course . . . Rather it is a function of a historically limited mode of self-interpretation' (Taylor 1989: 111). This points to the 'artificiality' of the dualism. I stress this as it reveals how Rousseau draws upon a commonplace dualism in order to place and stabilize the self and its identity.

It is clear now that Rousseau's autobiographical project is driven by the longing for a sense of self and identity that is unchangeable, fixed, and permanent. By localizing identity inside, Rousseau can posit the existence of this permanent self in opposition to a fickle and changing outside. In accordance with the system delineated above, it is now clear that writing is an *outward* manifestation, a version of the capricious outside. It is a system of signs that necessarily transforms and betrays the immediate inner self, which remains beyond (or before) the text. The dualism ensures that the self remains locked within and that any external view, and specifically the exteriorization caused by writing, would change and distort this interiority.

It is now possible to see how the dualism works as simple repetition. The stable and permanent self escapes articulation. To express the self is to exteriorize it and hence fragment and transform it. Rousseau's texts therefore rely upon the system to maintain the stable, interior self as being always beyond, always one step removed from the words of the text. The dualism kindles the desire or longing by positing the object of desire in opposition to writing, thereby ensuring that this object remains forever unavailable in language. The dualistic system inside–outside upholds the dream of an original silence, of the inner self, as the negative other of discourse which is nothing less than a treacherous exteriority of the self. Simple repetition is the ongoing writing that repeatedly maintains the dualism. Continued writing hence, paradoxically, stabilizes and defines the non-symbolic self as its other. This operation summarizes the basic aspect of simple repetition, namely that the sense of the beyond is born through and hence depends upon the writing. As such it is a dialectic operation: only writing can recognize that which cannot be written. It follows that the silence of the reverie and of the self only emerge as a negative result of the writing that defines them as non-symbolic. Writing preconditions and *creates* the non-symbolic self. To stop writing is therefore to lose the silence of the self.

The dualistic opposition inside–outside describes not only the self, but also the relationship between self and writing. Morrissey, in *La Rêverie jusqu'à Rousseau: recherches sur un topos littéraire*, concludes: 'Rousseau aura toujours besoin de dire son silence, de faire de son *dedans un dehors*' (Morrissey 1984: 159, my italics). Writing, as a version, or *the* version, of the exterior, negatively defines the self as non-symbolic interiority. In order to further explore simple repetition in the *Rêveries* it is therefore necessary to define the underlying dynamic that presupposes the text as biographical writing, as *exterior*. This underlying dynamic works according to a subject–object dualism, the second aspect of simple repetition in the *Rêveries*.

Rousseau's autobiographical venture, and particularly the *Rêveries*, recalls aspects of Descartes's *cogito*. In his study *L'Ordre du cœur*, Rodier observes: 'Nul ne peut lire la première rêverie du promeneur solitaire sans évoquer l'auteur du *Discours de la méthode* et de ses *Méditations métaphysiques*. Deux esprits qui, pour reprendre un mot de Novalis sur Rousseau, retrouvent "le chemin qui va vers l'intérieur"' (Rodier 1981: 137). We might also note in passing that Taylor situates the emergence of 'the language of inner/outer' (Taylor 1989: 143) in relation to Descartes. More precisely, the point of comparison is the quest for self-knowledge and a certainty of self-consciousness detached from the exterior world: 'De quoi jouit-on dans une pareille situation? De rien d'extérieur à soi' (Rousseau 1959a: 1047). In the words of Poulet: 'On dirait que chez Descartes comme chez Rousseau, dans l'effacement provisoire des réalités secondes, la conscience de soi surgit de façon presque semblable, comme une force positive détachée de tout lien avec le monde externe, s'ouvrant en quelque sorte sur une existence vierge, une existence sans antécédent' (Poulet 1978: 38). The quest for such a 'pure' *sentiment de l'existence* links the two authors.

Needless to say, the differences between the two thinkers accompany the similarities. As Poulet points out,[9] Descartes's operation presupposes a disengaged reason that is not related to any affection or emotion, whereas Rousseau seeks a sentiment of existence that is not

---

[9] In his article 'Le Sentiment de l'existence chez Rousseau et ses prédécesseurs', Poulet (1978) carefully traces the development from Descartes to Rousseau via the moralistes, Jansenism, Malebranche, Condillac, Saint-Lambert, etc.

derived from thinking, but rather based on the activity of feeling.[10] However, what interests me is the basic similarity between the *cogito* and Rousseau's venture, namely the autobiographical reflexive turn that makes the 'knower' also the object of knowledge. The following extract from the first walk underlines this reflexivity:

C'est dans cet état que je reprends la suite de *l'examen* sévère et sincére que j'appelai jadis mes *Confessions.* Je consacre mes derniers jours à *m'étudier moi-même* et à préparer d'avance le compte que je ne tarderai pas à rendre de moi. Livrons-nous tout entier à la douceur de *converser avec mon ame* puisqu'elle est la seule que les hommes ne puissent m'ôter. Si à force de *réfléchir sur mes dispositions intérieures* . . . (Rousseau 1959a: 999, my italics)

The vocabulary of examination, study, observation, reflection, and even conversation, indicates a split within the self as it has to study itself. Even grammatically the self is transformed into an object, hence splitting the 'I' and introducing a new distance.[11] Taylor summarizes: 'The modern sense is one in which the subject and object are separable entities. That is, in principle—though perhaps not in fact—one could exist without the other' (Taylor 1989: 188). Rousseau indirectly emphasizes this split by insisting that the *Rêveries* are written for and about himself: 'un solitaire qui réflechit s'occupe necessairement beaucoup de lui-même' (Rousseau 1959a: 1000). The 'I' becomes objectified into a 'me'—an exteriorized object—that is both the contents and the designator of the text. This is one of the basic traits of autobiographical writing.[12] Grosrichard, in his article 'Où suis-je?, Que suis-je?', observes: 'La dialectique de l'énoncé et de l'énonciation, où se trouve engagé le sujet parlant, redouble, recoupe et relance donc sans cesse celle du "moi" et du "je" ' (Grosrichard 1997: 33). This polarization or split fixes the subject–object dualism of the *Rêveries*. It now remains to be seen how this opposition functions as simple repetition.

The significance of the reflexivity of the first person, that is, the opposition subject–object, is related to the circumstances that coin-

---

[10] For a consideration of Descartes's relation to the reverie see Morrissey 1984: 45–7.

[11] Of course this split first person is dramatized more clearly in the *Dialogues*. However, as the continuation of this project, the *Rêveries* reveals traces of the same dualism.

[12] For more on the genre of autobiography see Jean Starobinski, *L'Œil vivant II: la relation critique* (1970); Philippe Lejeune, *Le Pacte autobiographique* (1975); Georges May, *L'Autobiographie* (1979); Serge Doubrovsky, *Autobiographiques: de Corneille à Sartre* (1988); George Gusdorf, *Auto-bio-graphie* (1991a) and *Les Écritures du moi* (1991b); Geneviève Idt *et al.*, *L'Écriture de soi* (1996). See also Paul de Man 'Autobiography as De-facement' (1979) and Michel Beaujour *Miroirs d'encre* (1980).

cide with Rousseau's writing of the *Rêveries*. The text opens with the following line: 'Me voici donc seul sur la terre, n'ayant plus de frere, de prochain, d'ami, de societé que moi-même' (Rousseau 1959*a*: 995). He is cut off from the world, and convinced no one will listen to his voice as he is completely excluded from Parisian society. Hence the importance of the initial question: 'Mais moi, *détaché d'eux et de tout*, que suis je moi-même?' (ibid.: 995, my italics). What becomes of the self when it loses its entire context, when no one is there to reflect its identity or affirm its being? One philosopher who has grasped and discussed exactly these dynamics of recognition is Hegel. He writes: 'Self-consciousness exists in and for itself when, and by the fact that, it so exists for another; that is it exists only in being acknowledged' (Hegel 1979: 111).[13] Self-certainty requires acknowledgement from the other.

It follows that Rousseau's sense of self is deeply threatened when society refuses to recognize him. And the threat becomes more urgent when one knows that following Rousseau's accident (as described in the *seconde promenade*) the rumour spread in Parisian society that he was dead. Rousseau even read his own obituary. The voice addressing us from the *Rêveries* is therefore what we might define as a 'dead voice' that defines itself as having passed from 'la vie à la mort' (Rousseau 1959*a*: 995), that the world has decided to 'enterrer tout vivant' (ibid.: 996), and whose destiny is 'fixée à jamais sans retour ici-bas' (ibid.: 997). The voice is dead, however, not because of the accident or the rumours, but because of its radical solitary state. The lack of recognition causes 'la mort de tout interest terrestre et temporel' (ibid.: 1000). As we know from Hegel's Master–Slave metaphor, the struggle for recognition is a life-and-death struggle, that is, life is at stake. This drives the desperate and painful longing for reconciliation and recognition that we recognize in Rousseau's work. Again, the question *que-suis-je?* takes on a new degree of radical urgency. In order to answer, and in order to 'survive', Rousseau is forced to become his own object so that he can give himself the recognition he requires.

The reflexive turn is the necessary move of self-recognition that ensures the existence of the self. It is this reflexive turn that also underlies the operation of simple repetition. As an object, Rousseau can

---

[13] A. L. Schibbye's article 'The Role of "Recognition" in the Resolution of a Specific Interpersonal Dilemma' (1993) specifically addresses recognition in interpersonal relationships. She summarizes the essence of the problem: 'The paradox is . . . that I need *the other* to gain autonomy and independence for *myself*.'

write about his self and hence ensure his existence. And, as I have said, the silent, inner self depends upon the exterior writing against which it is defined. Again it is through the writing of the *Rêveries* that the unsayable self is paradoxically maintained. Recreating itself, the voice is alive to us, and to itself, through the writing which 'doublera pour ainsi dire mon existence' (Rousseau 1959*a*: 1001). He inscribes himself as his own object and becomes other to himself: 'je vivrai decrepit avec moi dans un autre age, comme je vivrois avec un moins vieux ami' (ibid.: 1001). Writing 'I', he 'survives' as subject. Whereas the *cogito* bases the subject's certainty of being and consciousness in the act of thinking, Rousseau might be said to place it in the actual act of writing. This also explains why Rousseau, despite his disillusion and final dismissal of his readers, could not stop writing. Through writing he 'inscribes' himself as a subject by turning himself into an object that can be recognized. Rousseau's autobiographical writing and the underlying subject–object dynamic become means of self-preservation.

The subject–object dualism provides the second aspect of simple repetition. The inside–outside opposition repeatedly maintained the self as non-symbolic inside. By writing the 'outside', the inside came into negative relief and was guaranteed existence. The subject–object opposition underlies and preconditions this writing of the outside. It is the reflexive dynamic that enables self-reflection and hence auto-biographical writing. It follows that the subject–object dualism, on another level, also indicates the stability and 'survival' of the non-symbolic self. Within this system the survival of the self is anchored in a dualistic understanding where it only exists through recognition. As an 'ideology' it enables Rousseau to maintain himself as a subject self in face of the lacking recognition. Blondel remarks: 'Nous pourrions dire . . . que Rousseau, en cela encore très cartésien, poursuit et illustre dans *Les Rêveries* une enterprise de type critique, qui consiste à justifier devant la raison les prétentions d'un discours du sujet, du moi, du je à la vérité, à la vérité sur le moi, sur sa position, son identité ou son innocence' (Blondel 1997: 26).

Subject–object and inside–outside are two examples of repeated dualistic patterns that more or less explicitly order the text and its idea of selfhood. They underlie and justify the rhetoric of the interior self, the examination of this self, the deceptive appearance of others, the rational, thinking subject, and the limits of language and the text. We are dealing, then, with repetitions that *produce* a stable system in which the non-symbolic is maintained in opposition to the text, and the act of reading is indirectly seen as primarily a reflective process. Simple repetition is the repeated stabilization of these dualistic patterns. The result is a notion of the inner self defined in terms of an immediacy that remains unavailable to language and that is hence congruent with a traditional notion of silence. This is the double operation of simple repetition. To conclude, we can say that the main effect or 'product' of simple repetition in the *Rêveries* is to ensure the stability of the experience of self that runs throughout the text, always against the text. Starobinski, in his essay 'Rêverie et transmutation', argues that the actual writing about the reverie is a so-called second reverie that 'consiste donc à résorber la multiplicité et la discontinuité de l'expérience vécue, en inventant un discours unifiant au sein duquel tout viendrait se compenser et s'égaliser' (Starobinski 1971: 419). I would argue that this is the exact function of simple repetition and dualism, that is, to create a unifying discourse that orders the experience, the self, and hence reduces and absorbs the irreducible multiplicity of the lived moment. But, as Starobinski observes: 'le trouble conflictuel persiste sourdement à l'arrière plan' (ibid.: 424). It is this mute conflict of instability and multiplicity, this *something else*, that always accompanies simple repetition as its repeated instability. This mute conflict is also the emergence of complex repetition and the implosion. In the following I shall explore complex repetition and the dynamic of literary silence in terms of the flux and reflux of water that also runs throughout the *Rêveries*.

LE FLUX ET REFLUX: COMPLEX REPETITION IN THE *RÉVERIES*

It is worth noting that some view the actual reverie as a potential synthesis, an *Aufhebung* of the difference located in the dualism. The dualism is thought to be lifted and erased in a dialectical manner. Raymond claims that in the reverie 'l'extérieur (les mouvements de l'eau) et l'intérieur (ceux du *moi*) s'accordent et s'identifient' (Raymond 1962.: 147), or Rousseau finds himself 'au plus près du point (mystique) où s'abolit toute distinction du moi et de l'univers, du sujet et de l'objet' (ibid.: 218). Bachelard, in his study *La Poétique de la rêverie*, says that the *rêveur* is lost in a *dedans* that has no *dehors*: 'Le monde ne lui fait plus vis-à-vis. Le moi ne s'oppose plus au monde' (Bachelard 1960: 144). The assumption is that through the reverie inside and outside are suspended. The reverie arises as the erasure of all difference and hence the realization of the ideal silence that I delineated above. Rousseau imagines, for example, that reading the *Rêveries* later 'rappellera la douceur que je goute à les écrire' (Rousseau 1959*a*: 1001), the illusion being that the reverie and the actual writing of it will finally coincide, hence lifting the difference imposed by writing. Beaujour remarks: 'La Cinquième Rêverie est une tentative pour effacer et naturaliser l'acte d'écrire . . . [qui] apparaît sous couvert de dénégation' (Beaujour 1980: 152). To erase writing implies the restoration of the unity of the experience of dreaming, unsullied by difference or reflexivity. But the attempt to erase writing will, needless to say, necessarily fail. To introduce the reverie as the topos of no-difference is merely to introduce a new, different relationship, namely that between the reverie and the writing of it. Writing remains. As synthesizer of difference, the reverie is still written and hence still subject to the difference bestowed by writing. It is this difference, this relationship between writing and dreaming, that I shall consider closer.

Towards the end of the fifth walk Rousseau asks in regard to l'Île de St Pierre: 'En rêvant que j'y suis ne fais-je pas la même chose?' (Rousseau 1959*a*: 1049). In other words: 'is there no moment of complete coincidence between reminiscing/writing, and the lost moment?' Considering Rousseau's question, Melberg, in the chapter on Rousseau in *Theories of Mimesis*, observes: 'The question is rhetorical, but, if one had to answer, the answer would be "no": the difference is still there' (Melberg 1995: 121). To dream about a moment is not to live it, and to write about the reverie is not to experience it. However, this difference does not emerge as an either-or. Rather the two seem to cross over into one another as writing becomes dreaming and dreaming becomes writing: 'En voulant me rappeler tant de douces rêveries, au lieu de les décrire j'y retombois' (Rousseau 1959*a*: 1003). Writing about his reveries, Rousseau claims to fall back into them. However, to remain in the reverie is not an option. It does not restore presence or exempt him from writing. Such an outcome would imply that the reveries were self-sufficient as moments of plenitude and presence, and there would consequently be no need to write them down. As Derrida remarks with reference to Rousseau: 'La jouissance *elle-même*, sans symbole ni supplétif, celle que nous accorderait (à) la présence pure elle-même, si quelque chose de tel était possible, ne serait qu'un autre nom de la mort' (Derrida 1967*b*: 223). Pure presence is impossible to bear, and hence any understanding of it must be directed through an intermediary. Rousseau cannot survive according to a maxim like *I dream therefore I am*, and finds himself condemned to the strange *cogito*: *I write therefore I am*, or, *I write my reveries therefore I am*. Rousseau is caught in the dilemma of having to continue *writing* the reveries down in order to preserve a sense of the presence and self established through them. Writing, although it disrupts the utopia of the dream, becomes perversely necessary both to preserve the self and the reverie: 'Le supplément rend fou parce qu'il n'est ni la présence ni l'absence' (ibid.: 222). There seems to be no rest in either writing or dreaming; rather the two are continually spilling into each other, continually becoming each other to the point where there is no regularity, no either-or, in the dualism.

This is one example of simple repetition gaining in complexity. Whereas the text maintains and supports outside–inside and subject–object dichotomy, it seems to struggle to make equal sense of writing–dreaming. This is a first pointer towards *complex repetition*.

This different sense of repetition can be approached in light of the repeated concept of the *flux continuel*: 'Tout est dans un flux continuel sur la terre' (Rousseau 1959*a*: 1046) and 'Tout est sur la terre dans un flux continuel' (ibid.: 1085). Furthermore, the movement of the *flux continuel* is associated with the reverie and the water that inspires it: 'Le flux et le reflux de cette eau, son bruit continu mais renflé par intervalles frappant sans relache mon oreille et mes yeux' (ibid.: 1045). The mention of water echoes the importance of the wave movement in the *Pensées* and its link to literary silence. It remains to be seen whether the flux and reflux in the *Rêveries* reveals a similar movement.

Privileging the idea of the continual flux, Rousseau is privileging the wave movement,[14] and as we know the movements of fluids are some of the hardest to predict and calculate. Water, or waves, cannot be thought of as dualistic. A wave is not intermittently at pole A or B; it cannot be divided in two. To look at a wave is to lose it: it leaves itself behind and is always already in front of itself. This description of the wave movement also describes the movement of writing–dreaming. The reverie is always already lost, always here, but then gone. Like the wave movement, this relationship creates a movement that radically challenges dualism. As such the wave movement is potentially closer to complex repetition; neither operates according to dualistic patterns. On the contrary, they have the potential to flood dualism by

[14] For more on the flux and reflux see Melberg 1995: 125–9, and Tripet, *La Rêverie littéraire: essai sur Rousseau*, 1979: 118–28.

introducing instability. And as a non-dualistic movement waves provide a rich metaphor for thinking the movement of literary silence that arises in the interstices of the dualistic production of a non-symbolic beyond.

The element of the reverie is, not surprisingly, *water*. 'j'allois volontiers m'asseoir au bord du lac sur la gréve dans quelque azyle caché; là le bruit des vagues et l'agitation de l'eau fixant mes sens et chassant de mon ame toute autre agitation la plongeoient dans un réverie delicieuse' (Rousseau 1959*a*: 1045). The experience of water *plunges* Rousseau into the reverie: 'plongé dans mille reveries' (ibid.: 1044). Also in the *Confessions* he writes, 'J'ai toujours aimé l'eau passionnément, et sa vue me jette dans une rêverie delicieuse' (Rousseau 1959*b*: 642). The continual flux is associated with the intervals of the sound of the water and hence evokes a movement that takes place *in between*. The *flux continuel* is, as mentioned above, neither here nor there, but a tension between the two, a state of apprehension. There is, in fact, no regularity, no rhythm, to the movement of water. Waves against a shore might seem to lap at a constant rate; however, there is always an element of inconstancy. I emphasize this movement as its effects are linked to the non-symbolic self. Above I mentioned that the inner self was defined through the reverie as the utmost experience of interiority. By linking the reverie to water, the text cannot escape congruence between the self and the *flux continuel* of water that defines the reverie. The most intense experiences of reverie, and hence of immediate self-presence, are predominantly associated with and inspired by water. In other words, the sense of self cannot ignore this 'aquatic' movement that is irreducible to dualistic thought. What then happens when the self, defined dualistically according to inside–outside and subject–object, is caught up in the wave-movement of complex repetition? Rather than stable dualisms, the self risks being defined by a movement that will 'flood' the dualistic system. The imagery of water is incompatible with the inside–outside dichotomy. Defined by water, the inside becomes liquid, as does the outside, and without these demarcations the self becomes 'fluid'. The dualistic system that defined and ensured the interiority and the existence of the self-consciousness risks flooding, hence erasing the 'border' between outside–inside and subject–object that ensured a solid sense of ego. Thus the non-dualistic movement affects the sense of a stable, negative non-symbolic that was maintained through simple repetition, and thereby indicates the operation of complex repetition.

It is noteworthy that the *flux continuel* is used to describe two different phenomena. On the one hand it is the reverie itself, and on the other it is the instability of the exterior world. On the one hand it is the positive movement that ensures the delicious reverie, on the other it is the distracting movement that prevents peace and joy. The continual flux itself fluctuates. This is the movement that is associated with the self. Caught up in this complex repetition, the self can no longer be understood according to dualistic paradoxes.

Melberg reminds us that 'water is the element of dreams and forgetfulness' (Melberg 1995: 125) and that, whereas memory governed the autobiographical project, forgetfulness is the faculty of the reverie. This again leads him to conclude that 'the negative components of a *rêverie* (efface, forget, escape thinking) positively create a self that is self-sufficient in making its own world. The self gains itself by losing itself' (ibid.) Melberg's words echo those of Raymond, who claims: 'Parce qu'il a fait en soi le vide, le rêveur connaît la plénitude; c'est lorsqu'il s'est dépouillé de tout qu'il éprouve sa suffisance. S'étant oublié, il se retrouve' (Raymond 1962: 183). The analysis of Melberg and Raymond can be understood from the perspective of simple repetition. Underlying this is the idea that the self can be regained, that it is a stable unit, here decided by memory–forgetfulness and losing–gaining. However, if the self is associated with flux and reflux, it follows that it transcends dualistic understanding. Because wave movements are indicative of the non-dualistic movement of complex repetition, the self ultimately slips away from any stable, dualistic understanding. A self that is defined by water will continually slip away from its own definitions. Like water, it is in continual motion. It follows that such a 'fluid' cannot be regained because it defies containment and demarcations. If you pour a glass of water into water, your water cannot be recollected. This is how complex repetition challenges and affects the self.

Unlike the simple patterns, the complex repetition indicated by waves is not productive of any coherent register of meaning. Whereas simple repetitions of dualism determine the notion of the self, and the search for its essence, flux and reflux unravels the notion of an inner self and questions the possibility therefore of searching for it. Sterile and unproductive, it is a movement that has no meaning beyond its own movement. It is self-referential, always returning to itself. It moves with no aim, towards no telos. It cannot be explained from the point of view of linearity because it does not advance. As movement of water against the shore, it creates a different sort of time that is closer to topology than teleology. As stated in Chapter 4, the wave movement, because it escapes dualistic thought, is congruent with complex repetition. The wave movement can be understood as the actual, empty movement of repetition which resides in the 'now' and therefore is going nowhere as opposed to somewhere. It is therefore interesting to note that this recalls the original meaning of *rêverie*, which is the Middle Latin 'reexvagare' meaning to roam or to vagabond.[15] In other words, reverie is an unconstrained, unplanned roaming that has no transcendental purpose. Rousseau often repeats the verb *errer*: 'durant ces égaremens mon ame erre et plâne dans l'univers sur les ailes de l'imagination' (Rousseau 1959*a*: 1062), '[j]e n'ai ni dépense à faire ni peine à prendre pour errer nonchalamment d'herbe en herbe' (ibid.: 1068). It designates the movement of the reverie and the walk that inspires them. Like *flux et reflux*, *errer* is a topo-logical movement that has no defined direction. Coz and Jacob, in their 'Introduction' to *Rêveries sans fin*, remark: 'Tous les cheminements du rêveur, loin d'offrir une vérité fixe dans un temps et un lieu déterminés, choisissent au contraire d'imprimer sa pensée du sceau de l'errance' (Coz and Jacob 1997: 8). The reverie is a movement that is self-sufficient in that it merely refers to itself, to its own errancy, not to an exterior system of meaning. It is of course noteworthy that the *Rêveries* do not present a linear narrative. Beaujour recognizes this as a basic trait of the form: 'L'autoportrait se distingue de l'autobiogra-phie par l'*absence* d'un récit suivi . . . [il] tente de constituer sa cohérence grâce à un système de rappels, de reprises, de super-positions . . . de telle sorte que sa principale apparence est celle du dis-continu, de la juxtaposition anachronique, du montage, qui s'oppose à la syntagmatique d'une narration' (Beaujour 1980: 8–9). We also know that the episode reported in the second walk took place before the writing of the first walk.[16] Again, the text is arranged according to various topoi, the landscape of the walks. The (non-)organization of the text is itself an erring *promenade* that returns to *places*. There is con-gruence between the lapping of the *flux continuel* and the actual text itself.

---

[15] For a historical overview of the origin of the word see Morrissey 1984: 17–36 and Tripet 1979: 7–33.

[16] For more on the issue of exact chronology and dates see Henri Roddier's Introduction to the Classiques Garnier edition of *Rêveries du promeneur solitaire* (1960).

Unproductive of meaning, this repetition of the flux and reflux is what we might call 'empty' or hollow. It is not a repetition of something, but rather of nothing. Rousseau associates the state of the *rêverie* with 'le précieux *far niente*' (Rousseau 1959a: 1042), 'l'occupation déli-cieuse et necessaire d'un homme qui s'est dévoué à l'oisivité' (ibid.: 1042). The nothing is central to the reverie and to complex repetition. To do nothing is in itself an unproductive, topological repetition that merely refers back to its own movement. The movement of water corresponds to Kierkegaard's repetition and therefore to the movement of the moment. A wave is always a transition between a past and a future. Its movement is always in the actual 'now'. One cannot tell where it is coming from or where it is going as it leaves itself behind and arrives before itself: 'Tout est dans un flux continuel sur la terre . . . Toujours en avant ou en arriére de nous, elles rappellent le passé qui n'est plus ou previennent l'avenir qui souvent ne doit point être: il n'y a rien là de solide à quoi le cœur se puisse attacher' (ibid.: 1046). There is nothing solid in the movement of the waves because the movement is always already gone. It resides merely in the moment. The reverie is described as that state 'où le présent dure toujours sans neanmoins marquer sa durée et sans aucun trace de succession' (ibid.: 1046). The present lasts because there is no linearity, merely a series of 'nows'. This is also why there is no succession; the series of instants cannot be lined to form a linear time.

The self of the *Rêveries* is primarily associated with wave movements and also with errancy. Whereas an overt system repeatedly defined the self as inside versus outside and subject in relation to object, a simultanous operation emerges that destabilizes this notion of the self. The self is linked to movements that are non-dualistic, unproductive, and that correspond to the movement of repetition that is essentially always in the instant. By linking the self to these non-dualistic move-ments, the text explores the inherent instability of simple repetition (see Chapter 3). Dualistic repetition is also waves, also instability, also flux and reflux. This shift from simple to complex repetition is the dynamic of literary silence. It now remains to examine more precisely how this shift affects the notion of self and how it manifests itself in the details of the text.

LES ENTRAILLES PALPITANTS: THE RESURRECTION
OF THE DEAD BODY

As indicated above, the *flux continuel* that is complex repetition affects
the subject–object dualism according to which Rousseau sustains his
subjectivity. As we concluded above, it was his ability to recreate
himself as an object that enabled him to undertake the objective
examination of his self—a conversation with his soul. Writing was
seen as the means of ascertaining the certainty of self that Descartes
found in the *cogito*. What then happens when the subject–object dualism is caught in the *flux continuel*? Initially the guarantee of a certain
'survival', this dualism cannot falter without introducing the menace
of a 'death' caused by the lack of recognition. Let us reread the famous
passage describing Rousseau's awakening after the accident in the
second walk (the accident that initiated the rumour of Roussseau's
death):

La nuit s'avançoit. J'aperçus le ciel, quelques étoiles, et un peu de verdure.
Cette prémiére sensation fut un moment délicieux. Je ne me sentois encor
que par là. Je naissois dans cet instant à la vie, et il me sembloit que je rem-
plissois de ma legere existence tous les objets que j'appercevois. Tout entier
au moment présent je ne me souvenois de rien; je n'avois nulle notion distincte de mon individu, pas la moindre idée de ce qui me venoit d'arriver; je
ne savais ni qui j'étois ni où j'étois; je ne sentois ni mal, ni crainte, ni inquiétude. Je voyois couler mon sang comme j'aurois vu couler un ruisseau, sans
songer seulement que ce sang m'appartint en aucune sorte. (Rousseau 1959*a*:
1005)

Rousseau loses his orientation and experiences his self as floating and
non-localizable. He is completely distanced from himself as he sees his
own blood flowing. Observing his body like a foreign object, he seems
to experience his own death or transformation—'Je ne me sentois
encore que par là'. It is 'la mort de tout interest terrestre et temporel'
(ibid.: 1000). Beaujour calls this episode 'cette petite mort' (Beaujour
1980: 69), and clearly the incident introduces a rhetoric of death and
dying in relation to the reverie. The passage is important also in that
it reveals the necessity of distancing and sublimating the body. In fact,
the non-symbolic voice is born as the body loses its physicality: 'Je
naissois dans cet insant à la vie.' The reality of the body, the blood, is
sublimated and distanced. As blood turns into a *ruisseau*, its 'bloodi-
ness' and 'bodiness' is avoided and transformed into abstract images.

The self in the *Rêveries* arises as it witnesses the death of its real physical body.

The experiences of death and dying associated with the reverie are also linked more directly to the dynamics of the flux and reflux identified above. Complex repetition, because it destabilizes dualism, threatens to expel the self from the security of the subject–object constellation, and hence disrupts the stability of the written ego. There are textual indications that this 'liquefaction' is experienced as a 'dying'. Rousseau asks: 'Est-il tems au moment qu'il faut mourir d'apprendre comment on auroit dû vivre?' (Rousseau 1959a: 1011). Life seems sacrificed in the name of dying. He also says: 'Tout est fini pour moi sur la terre. On ne peut plus m'y faire ni bien ni mal. Il ne me reste plus rien à esperer ni à craindre en ce monde, et m'y voila tranquille au fond de l'abyme, pauvre mortel infortuné, mais impassible comme Dieu même' (ibid.: 999). This voice reaches us from the bottom of the abyss—the other side. Not unlike the accident, this describes a self completely distanced from its own body, a self that does not fear any sensation or any emotion because it can no longer feel. Rousseau effectively writes off his body: 'Mon corps n'est plus pour moi qu'un embarras, qu'un obstacle, et je m'en dégage d'avance autant que je puis' (ibid.: 1000). These passages testify to a voice that can only describe itself as dead through the writing that in turn sustains this same self. Physical death is linked to the survival of the speaking voice. It speaks as an oscillating voice, detached from its body, alive because it has physically died.

If we return to the above passage describing Rousseau's condition after the fall, it is revealing that blood turns into a brook or river: 'Je voyois couler mon sang comme j'aurois vu couler un ruisseau' (Rousseau 1959a: 1005). The image provides yet another image of water. This, by now, suggests that the physicality of the body can become a force of destabilization. The materiality of the body is not easily repressed or transformed. First of all the actual organic movements of the body defy dualism. The body consists largely of fluids and is hence largely in a state of continual flux, like water. The body does not operate according to intermittent poles A or B; its movements do not adhere to a dualistic pattern. So although we admire the various operations of the body for their beautiful efficacity (it works!), they cannot be reduced to dualism. It seems that the dualism that underlies the sublimation of the dead body and the speaking of the 'new' voice could be threatened by the *flux et reflux* of the body itself.

We may now observe how the physicality of the body resists sublimation, and what the effects of this resistance could be. I shall compare two passages that reveal this resurrection of the physicality of the dead body. In the seventh walk Rousseau compares the study of animals to that of plants. The descriptions of the study of animals is quite shocking in its insistence on the actual physicality of the dead carcasses:

Il faudra donc les étudier morts, les déchirer, les desosser, fouiller à loisir dans leurs entrailles palpitants! Quel appareil affreux qu'un amphitheatre anatomique: des cadavres puans, de baveuses et livides chairs, du sang, des intestins dégoutants, des squelettes affreux, des vapeurs pestilentielles! Ce n'est pas là, sur ma parole, que J.J. ira chercher ses amusemens. (Rousseau 1959*a*: 1068)

This is then proceeded by the following contrasting description:

Brillantes fleurs, email des près, ombrages frais, ruisseaux, bosquets, verdure, venez purifier mon imagination salie par tous ces hideux objets. Mon ame morte à tous les grands mouvemens ne peut plus s'affecter que par des objets sensibles. (ibid.: 1068)

The overt intention of the two passages is obvious. It corresponds to a vilification of the actual physicality of the body, and a beautification of a non-physical nature, that again corresponds to the reveries and to the non-symbolic, non-physical self.

The first description insists on the actual rot, disintegration, smell, etc. of dying bodies. Exclamation marks enhance the effect and the passage is in general at odds with the lyrical atmosphere of the *Rêveries*. For a text that is mostly associated with the beauty of the fifth walk, this passage seems not to belong. It is strange also that Rousseau would say that this is not where he finds his amusement when in fact the descriptions testify to a transgressional indulgence in putrescent description. The visual imagery of the passage is strengthened also by the reference to the actual *activity* of dissecting: 'fouiller à loisir dans leurs entrailles palpitants'. There is something wonderfully vivid about this passage. Stylistically the passage is opposed to the freshness and cleanliness of the plants. The description is largely figurative. It starts out with an adjective, *brillantes*, hence stressing the abstract quality of the description rather than the actual flower. It is followed by a metaphor, *email*, to describe the meadows, and then the metonymy *ombrage frais* to designate the trees. Then we again have water, *ruisseaux*, which we by now know is never as innocent as it might seem. *Bosquets* is then the only actual concrete detail, which is immediately followed by the abstract modifier, *verdure*. The passage seems to avoid the literal, the actual *body* of the flowers and meadows, and rather sublimates them into transcendent entities that are beyond rot and decay. Such, then, is the attempt to order the dualism body–spirit, dead–alive, base–sublime, concrete–abstract.

However, the artificiality of the opposition leaves cracks. Plants are of course also alive, like animals, and hence also capable of a rotting death. But by evoking the sterility of the plants (they have the power to 'purify') and by sublimating them into the abstract, Rousseau denies this aspect of plant life. We are left with paper-flowers. The plants, the designated healthy occupation, are as dead as the rotting bodies of the animals. In fact, the rotting bodies seem more alive in contrast to the second passage that is in fact far less vivid in its descriptions. Whereas the former evoked an actual activity, *étudier, déchirer, dessoser, fouiller*, this second passage is noticeably passive, and as such more evocative of death than the former, which in fact is wonderfully alive and rich in its vocabulary and structure. It is therefore not too surprising to read on in the latter passage and find 'mon ame morte'. This uncannily echoes the earlier 'Il faudra donc les étudier morts'. Which passage, then, is actually about dead material?

The comparison shows how Rousseau's opposition between the living spirit and the dead body wavers. It is as if his body catches up with him, as if the mortal body which is no more than 'un embarras' or 'un obstacle' of which 'je m'en dégage d'avance autant que je puis' (Rousseau 1959*a*: 1000), resurfaces and complicates the ordered world. In short, the body emerges as a force of destabilization, a rebel force, if one likes, that resists being repressed. The result, as has been shown by the above comparison, is a flux in the opposition dead–alive. The dead, repressed body resurfaces and seems more alive than the sublimated, non-symbolic self. We are left to wonder whether the voice that speaks is alive and the body merely a dead abstraction, or whether the body is actually alive and the voice itself lifeless.

As dead is also alive, and alive is dead, a radical aporia emerges. The finality of death makes it absolutely impossible to imagine a dead that is also alive. In the following I shall trace more precisely how the self defines itself as dead, and how, underlying this definition, the aporia plays its movement of back-and-forth. My aim is to see how this aporetic dynamic finds articulation, and how this articulation provides an example of literary silence in the *Rêveries*.

Rousseau says in the *Confessions*: 'je ne commençai de vivre que quand je me regardai comme un homme mort' (Rousseau 1959*b*: 228). Already it is clear that the writing subject is not dead or alive; rather, like God ('impassible comme Dieu'), it quivers. To become your own object is at once the potential recognition of your self as a subject, hence implying 'survival', and the positioning of your self as an object that can be claimed by everyone, hence the dispersion and 'killing' of the subject self. To write 'I' is at once a means of surviving and a parallel death. This echoes observations made regarding the autobiographical use of the first person. Eugène Vance, in 'Le Moi comme langage: saint Augustin et l'autobiographie', summarizes:

L'énoncé contenant un 'je' appartient, comme le dit Benveniste, à un type de discours qui inclut, aves ses signes, la personne qui les utilise. Pourtant, contrairement à tous les autres signes linguisitiques, le sujet du pronom 'je' ne peut être identifié que dans *l'acte* de parole au moment où il le profère. Le 'je' n'a pas d'existence, hormis l'instance de sa production dans le discours. . . . Il appartient à tout le monde et à personne. (Vance 1973: 163)

The first-person pronoun only designates a specific 'owner' in the act of pronunciation. Once written down it can be claimed by all. We are all entitled to the pronoun. Hence autobiographical writing always shifts dangerously between the personal and the communal. The effect is that the self, by inscribing its 'I', also 'kills' it by sacrificing its individuality. As Rousseau says: 'je fus bien surpris du nombre des choses de mon invention que je me rappellois avoir dites comme vrayes dans le même tems où, fier en moi-même de mon amour pour la vérité, je lui *sacrifiois* ma sureté, mes intérets, ma personne avec une impartialité dont je ne connois nul autre éxemple parmi les humains' (Rousseau 1959*a*: 1025, my italics). As Ann Hartle points out, 'Rousseau has sacrificed himself for the "truth", for the fiction that is truly useful. . . . The "personal", private Rousseau is sacrificed to the fictitious, public Rousseau' (Hartle 1983: 22–3). The truth that has demanded this sacrifice is the writing of fiction, the writing of his self.

So writing, though a means of inscribing the ego, also becomes the altar for its sacrifice. De Man, in his article on autobiography, evokes this paradoxical movement: 'Death is a displaced name for a linguistic predicament, and the restoration of mortality by autobiography (the prosopopeia of the voice and the name) deprives and disfigures to the precise extent that it restores' (de Man 1979: 930). This simultaneous deprivation and restoration of the self enacted by the *Rêveries* echoes Derrida's excellent observations on the supplement in *De la grammatologie*. Language is the

> dessaisissement spéculaire qui à la fois m'institue et me déconstitue . . . Elle opère comme une puissance morte au cœur de la parole vive . . . L'acte d'écrire serait essentiellement . . . le plus grand sacrifice visant à la plus grande réappropriation symbolique de la présence. De ce point de vue, Rousseau savait que la mort n'est pas le simple dehors de la vie. La mort par l'écriture inaugure aussi la vie. (Derrida 1967*b*: 204–5)

The subject–object dualism cannot be sustained against the powers of what we might call the continual flux of writing. As these movements interact, the dualism falters and a living dead 'I' addresses us.

The living dead is of course a non-rational concept. It is noteworthy therefore that this in-between state is preconditioned by literature itself. In the words of de Man: 'The dominant figure of the epitaphic or autobiographical discourse is . . . the prosopopeia, the fiction of the voice-from-beyond-the-grave' (de Man 1979: 927). In the literary text, and this is taken to an extreme in autobiography, the subject is obviously never present, but at the same time it can never die; it is 'silent as a picture, that is to say eternally deprived of voice and condemned to muteness' (ibid.: 930); a muteness or death that still speaks and is forever living. This fundamental challenge to the dualism finds articulation when Rousseau asks: 'J'étois fait pour vivre, et *je meurs* sans avoir vécu' (Rousseau 1959*a*: 1004, my italics). The self is here described as dying in the present tense. In other words, death has not *taken place*, rather it takes place now and now and now and now— a dizzying prospect. Indeed we can only stretch our imagination and try to conceive of a continual dying that never enters either the past or the future. This repetitive movement starts resembling the *flux continuel* that is neither here nor there—neither dead nor alive, neither past nor future. To die continuously can never be explained through dualism; it can never be grasped as a linear movement. It is a suspended (non-)present that never ends or starts. We are dealing here with a certain stopping that refuses to stop, a movement that is no movement. The parallel to Kierkegaard's moment is obvious. To think dying as an impossible present, a duration, takes the form of a certain repetition. Like the movement of repetition, the movement of *dying* is never in the past or the future, it always happens right now, a moment of transition from dead to alive. We have already seen how the text experiments with and destabilizes the opposition dead–alive. By presenting an articulation of a continued dying, the *Rêveries* pushes the experiment even further, perhaps as far as it can go.

The articulation 'je meurs' presents us with a state of consciousness that is unthinkable. Again this echoes Pascal's fragment 163 (see Chapter 4) that invites us to comprehend ourselves as incomprehensible. One cannot be comprehending and incomprehensible at the same time. Similarily, one cannot be dead and alive at the same time. The logic breaks down as we try to conceive of this unimaginable state that depends upon the impossible presupposition: 'I say: *I die*'. The speaking voice announces its continual dying. Again, the statement can best be described as aporetic. It invites us to interact with a voice that is not dead (it speaks), yet defines itself as dead (*je meurs*). To say *I die* is to occupy one of the most fundamental aporias. You cannot die and live to say it. The moment you die, you are no longer in possession of a voice that can testify to your experience. Only text can say 'I die'. To interact with this textual instance is to be presented with a collapsed or imploded reason. Reason cannot continue to operate in a state of continued dying. The maddening scenario stages a reason that repeatedly dies, or implodes, in every instant, yet remains alive—at least alive enough to say 'I die'. Incomprehensible monsters are not too far away.

Reading this statement the reader is invited to relate, through language, to an aporia that escapes all everyday language. To read this aporia is also to be invited to commit the sacrifice that I have defined in relation to the implosion. Reading this unthinkable statement and interacting with the aporetic dynamic, the reader is given the opportunity to implode his own rational control. This statement cannot be translated or summarized in everyday, reifying language. It leaves us speechless, without language, but still in relation to language, in relation to text. Silence arises as a literary experience. Creating the force of this collapse, this unsayable experience, the instance emerges as an implosion, as literary silence. Writing this, the text reveals its ability to bear that which the 'everyday individual', within reified language, cannot. Again, it says what we can only conceive of in silence. The dynamic of the *flux continuel* that is non-dualistic, non-linear, and non-rational becomes manifest in the text. The text achieves this by twisting language, by making it adapt to the impossible. The 'Je dis: *Je meurs*' haunting the *Rêveries* is an example of such a 'stretching' of language to say the unsayable or unthinkable. Language seems to sacrifice its own coherence and its everyday function, namely to make sense, in order to reach for the unsayable.

To sum up, the *Rêveries* reaches us as a text in which a dead voice, cut off from everyone, asks *que suis je moi-même?* In order to answer the question and to sustain his self, Rousseau inscribes his 'I' by recounting his countless reveries. However, these reveries are themselves moments of flux, of destabilization, and hence of a dissolution, and ultimately they are revealed as movements of dying. The only possible answer to this *que suis je moi-même?* is 'a continual dying'—'je meurs'. In other words, *que suis-je?*, because it is not an empirical question, cannot be answered by a positive. Inside–outside, subject–object remain sterile attempts at fixing the unfixable. The self of the *Rêverie* is a continual death that escapes a dualistic world view. It can therefore neither be lost nor regained. And so the rational systems of meaning produced by simple repetition reveal their limited scope. Their ability to produce closed systems of meaning crumble, as the complex repetition emerges as an aquatic movement of the *now*, a 'dying' that is non-rational, that has no beginning or end. This (non-)locus is the dynamic of literary silence. As dualism has faltered, the beyond has been challenged, and silence has forcibly shifted into articulation. The immediacy of the self emerges within the text as the text bears the aporia that everyday language cannot bear. Its practice is moments of logical 'breakdowns', moments of non-knowing. Relating to these moments we are caught up in the implosion and the force and play of literary silence. In order to read on we must either ignore the moment, reduce it by an analysis that is deaf to 'le trouble conflictuel [qui] persiste sourdement à l'arrière-plan' (Starobinski 1971: 424) or dare to 'listen' to and endure the turbulence of the aporetic *now* of dying without understanding or concluding it. This is the potential moment of the implosion—the sacrifice of rational mastery, of linear being in time and of reified, rational language—a bold move towards silence as literature's own.

THE HEART

In the Introduction I suggested that the dynamic of complex repetition could be identified by a marker, a signifier. It now seems obvious that such a marker would have to be associated with the *flux continuel* of water and errancy. It should have the symbolic impact to disempower dualisms such as inside–outside, subject–object, dead–alive, body–soul. And it is also likely that such a marker will somehow be associated with the body, seeing that the body has emerged as a topos of destabilization. I propose to consider the heart as the one bodily organ that could answer to the above description. The heart is first of all a producer of repetitive movements that are congruent with errancy and water. Its beating is essentially empty and self-referential. Like play, the movement of the heart is self-sufficient. And, like water, it might seem rhythmical in its movements, but in fact the heart beats at different rates and is non-rhythmical. Furthermore, the repetitive beating is not productive of meaning; it does not order any experience or produce a register of signification beyond its own movement. Its purpose is its movement. Like repetition, therefore, the movement of the heart has its essence in the 'now'. In every 'now' it plays with life and death—its stopping is its death, its continued beating the guarantee of further life.

But the heart has also given way to a myth that transcends its status as organ. It is the one organ whose movements are perceptible to us through sensations like hearing and feeling. This, it can be argued, has given rise to a symbolic investment that cannot equal any other part of the body. As a topos it has been released from its initial meaning and invested with other values. The heart has been 'torn' out of the body and displaced as a symbol. It has been purified of blood, of its status as muscle, of its palpitating movements and arisen as a symbolic heart. This is clearly relevant to the role played by the notion of 'heart' in the *Rêveries*: it is the one organ of the body that appears both in the physical body and in the sublimated and non-physical body. Finally the heart plays a role in regard to a more concrete understanding of silence. One of the two sounds that can be 'heard' in a silent chamber is the beating of the heart (see Chapter 1). At the risk of being banal, one might say that the heart becomes the 'sound of silence'.

The word *cœur* is used repeatedly throughout the *Rêveries*. In the 'Quatrième Promenade' alone it is used more than ten times. Some examples are 'tous les vœux de mon cœur', 'une horreur qui a dû garantir mon cœur de ce vice', 'l'instinct moral . . . a gardé jusqu'ici sa pureté dans mon cœur', 'je le ferois de tout mon cœur', 'mon cœur avoit bien senti le vide'. The heart seems to be used as a collective concept that designates what Rousseau experiences as the essence of his self. It remains adequately obscure and cryptic in that it does not actually elucidate the notion of self that Rousseau is trying to articulate. The question *que suis-je?* can poetically be answered by 'je suis mon cœur'. The answer gives us little, if any, more insight into the self. In its vagueness, the heart is clearly related to the text's underlying, unsayable sense of selfhood. The heart is transformed into the topos of the non-symbolic self. Here lies its potential link to literary silence.

As we have already seen, the main topos of the non-symbolic self is the wandering movements of the reverie. There seems therefore to be a potential congruence between the heart and the reverie as both are linked to the non-symbolic answer to *que suis-je?* Rousseau's reverie is, as Rodier claims in his philosophical study of the heart, 'la rêverie du cœur' (Rodier 1981: 143) or 'la rêverie cordiale' (ibid.: 145) in that it is closely related to the experience of the self of the *rêveur*. Rodier goes on to define the cordial reverie as a unifying, calm experience: 'Le pouvoir pacificateur du cœur pointe doucement dans cette absence de conflit qui donne à la rêverie cordial son aspect totalitaire' (ibid.: 143). For Rodier the heart emerges as that which ensures that the reverie subsists as an experience of wholeness and totality, hence lending a moment of presence to the self: 'Le cœur', he claims, 'opère le "rassemblement" de tout l'être' (ibid.: 142). The heart, due to its location, is traditionally thought to be the unifying point of head and body. The heart, like the reverie, is here understood as a locus of synthesis and *Aufhebung*, hence suggesting a stable and fixed self that can be identified and defined according to a simple dialectics of opposites and synthesis. But as we saw in relation to the reverie, to posit the heart as the locus of such a synthesis merely introduces new difference, namely that between writing and the heart. How can one write the non-symbolic heart? How does the notion of the 'heart' behave in the text?

Although Rousseau uses the concept of heart symbolically and metaphorically, it still bears traces of the body from which it is removed. Although a recognized and accepted symbol, the heart primarily remains a blood-pumping muscle. And it is as such that the heart most obviously repeats complex currents of flux and reflux. As suggested above, the heart has the interesting double function of on the one hand sublimating the body, that is, designating the self that Rousseau tries to tear away from its 'caduque envelope' (Rousseau 1959a: 1002), and on the other hand forcing the concrete physicality of the body to 'resurface'. This double movement appears as Rousseau imagines that even physical pain would be preferable to his torment: 'En m'arrachant des cris, peut-être, elle [la douleur physique] m'épargneroit des gémissements, et les déchiremens de mon corps suspendroient ceux de mon cœur' (ibid.: 997). The heart is posited as the abstract locus of feeling and sentiment, the carefully aligned opposite of the body whose cries and torment would erase those of the heart. However, the choice of the signifier and it being aligned parallel with the body recalls the organ quality of the heart and again threatens to undermine the careful opposition. It borders on confusion as we ask to what extent the physical pains of the body can be opposed to those of the heart. Furthermore, *déchirement*, which here obviously refers to the body, can also refer to moral tearing apart, translated as 'heart-rending'. It becomes uncertain what is being torn apart, what is physical and what is emotional suffering. As *corps* and *cœur* catch up with each other, the sublimated heart becomes 'contaminated' with the mortality and materiality of the body and its movements of complex repetition.

One of Rousseau's observations regarding the 'flux continuel sur la terre' concludes with, 'il n'y à rien là de solide à quoi le cœur se puisse attacher' (Rousseau 1959a: 1046). The world is the *flux continuel* that is here opposed to the heart. However, the non-rhythmical movements of the heart also suggest instability. The observation reveals itself as potentially reversible, thereby making the heart the unstable factor. If the heart is defined as constant errancy, it would struggle to attach itself to anything that is stable, even if the world were stable. In order to take this further, let us return to the symbolic significance of the heart and see how also this finally catches up with the complex repetitive movements of the organ. As a symbol of love, the heart is closely linked to desire. In the *Rêveries* the role of desire is to want, *to desire*, a full presence of the self, a moment of complete being without difference and without the 'flux continuel'. However, the definition of desire is that it can never be fulfilled. When desire is satisfied, it dies and is no longer desire. Desire consequently never stops, unless it is interrupted by death itself. As desire, the heart can never stop, can never be satisfied with any object. The rambling and wanderings of the heart can therefore be understood as the movement of desire that can never be satisfied with anything stable, 'rien de solide'. In fact, attaching itself to something solid would imply the death of the heart as it would imply the end of its movements. The object of desire in the *Rêveries* is of course the utopia of the reverie as pure, non-symbolic self-presence. However, as we now know, the reverie is in itself an ongoing movement that never ends. In other words, there is congruence between the topos of desire, the heart, and its object, the reverie. Rousseau observes: 'Le mouvement qui ne vient pas du dehors se fait alors au-dedans de nous' (ibid.: 1048). The original *flux continuel* that was water not only defines the reverie but also the topos of interiority, namely the heart. The *flux continuel* spills into the heart, and the heart takes on the complex repetition of waves hitting the shore.

The dynamic represented by the heart, together with the wave-like movement of the reverie, suggest that the answer to *que suis-je?* cannot be presented in a solid or stable form. Heart and reverie, the two main topoi of the non-symbolic self, are both floating and wandering, unable to provide a fixed answer. Accordingly the text, with its topological (non-)organization, re-enacts the self as waves, as spillage, as body fluids, materiality, desire, and heart beats. Furthermore, any solid or stable answer is contradictory as it would require that the movement of the heart stop and consequently the death of the self that articulates *que suis-je?* And, as we now know, this self is not capable of death as it is continuously dying: 'Je dis: *Je meurs*'. Finally we can see how the continuous dying corresponds to the beating movement represented by the heart, or more precisely, to each moment in the beating of the heart. The dying in the present tense corresponds to the moment *in between* when the heart repeats its beat. This moment is one of instability—it is the moment in which death can always happen. The floating, undefined state of *je meurs* exists only in this moment—a moment that of course happens all the time, but which we cannot relate to. Only the heart's constant beating and the waves' constant flux can maintain this movement that permits the constant dying. If the movement stopped, the self would die once and for all. In other words, the non-symbolic would perish. It seems that the non-symbolic self can only persist as long as it is caught in complex repetition, as long as it is literary silence. The non-symbolic self can only survive as a constant dying, a constant movement that is congruent with the reverie, the wave movement, and the beating heart. Paradoxically, it is as literary silence, as a constant dying, that the non-symbolic can survive.

To sum up, the *je meurs*, as the instance of literary silence, is linked to the dynamic of the beating heart. It follows that literary silence is also contingent upon this beating, this constant movement of repetition. If, so to speak, the heart were to stop beating, that is, if there was something 'de solide à quoi le cœur se puisse attacher', it would imply the end or 'death' of the text itself, the end of the attempt to articulate the non-symbolic. And this ending would automatically constitute a surrender to a traditional notion of silence as the end of the text, which in turn would mean the death of the non-symbolic self. Literary silence therefore arises out of the ongoing attempt to articulate the non-symbolic, the repeated relation towards the unsayable.

CONCLUSION

This chapter has focused first on how Rousseau's *Rêveries*, as a last attempt to articulate the immediate, inner self, relies on explicit and implicit dualisms to order and stabilize the experience of the self. In the context of literary silence these dualisms function as simple repetition. They order the text according to an inside and outside, and the self according to a subject–object split. The effects are a delineation and a 'survival' of a non-symbolic self that remains spun in traditional, negative silence. The text emerges in opposition to a beyond. This non-symbolic beyond is called the reverie. To write an account of the reveries is therefore to attempt to answer *que suis-je?* However, the reverie, due to its association with the *flux et reflux*, also emerges as a dynamic of destabilization. The beyond, posited as a negative whole unity, is revealed as dispersion, movement, and instability. This repetitive wave movement is non-regular and unproductive and hence recalls descriptions of complex repetition. It has the power to undo dualism and disrupt productive systems. The self, defined according to the reverie, is not a topos of plenitude, stability, and synthesis, but of a constant dissolving. And as the non-symbolic silence of the beyond dissolves, it can emerge in the text.

My intention has been to trace this wave movement and see how its effects come to articulation. The constant flux brought about a destabilization of the opposition dead–alive that, needless to say, was intended to ensure the survival of the self. The sublimated body, posited in congruence with the alive, non-symbolic self, emerges as dead, whereas the physical, dead carcass emerges as alive. It is this basic aporia which leads to the discussed instance of literary silence in the *Rêveries*, namely the unthinkable, radically impossible articulation: 'Je dis: *je meurs*'. A speaking voice testifying its constant dying addresses us from the text. An immediate, imploded, non-reflective consciousness occupies language. And language is necessarily transformed from stable bearer of meaning, from reified, useful tool of communication to waves, monstrosity, silence.

Finally, the heart has been explored as a potential marker for complex repetition. We can say that the dynamic of the heart becomes the dynamic of the text itself and its attempt at articulating the unsayable. The heart designates a movement that cannot arrive at a stable answer without stopping, just as the text can never arrive at a silence of plenitude and finality without stopping. And as I said in the Introduction, literary silence is not at the end of the text but rather traced throughout it. Literary silence is the 'heart', so to speak, of the text. Its dynamic arises through the endless repetitive movement towards articulation that makes the text advance. And this 'desire', one might say, to say the unsayable cannot be satisfied without causing the end of the text, the stopping of the heart: death. So the text continues. And its only possible continuation becomes one of constant dying. The heart has thereby revealed its potential as a marker for literary silence. The topos of the heart, as the desire for the non-symbolic, transforms this non-symbolic into literary silence through repeated beats. Its force is its beating, its inability to stop at anything solid. And in the words of Pascal, 'Notre nature est dans le mouvement, le repos entier est la mort' (Pascal 1991: 529).

INTERLUDE. FROM ROUSSEAU TO BECKETT: THE OPENING OF THE 'THIRD MODE' OF LANGUAGE

Qu'une moyenne étendue de mots, sous la compréhension du regard, se range en traits définitifs, avec quoi le silence.

Mallarmé, *Crise de vers* (1990)

TOWARDS A NEW APPROACH TO SILENCE

To move from Rousseau's pre-romantic *Rêveries* to Beckett's trilogy is to approach a fundamentally different context of thought. There is a need, consequently, to pause and consider this shift before moving on to Beckett. Such is the motivation behind this Interlude. The overall intention is to trace the shift in question and attempt to disentangle the relevant consequences for the exploration of literary silence in the trilogy. Emerging in the twentieth century, Beckett's intellectual, artistic and historical frameworks have undergone dramatic changes that in turn echo through his work and that clearly set him apart from both Pascal and Rousseau. With what can be called the turn into modernism, new vistas of thought opened up that were previously unavailable. More specifically, a preoccupation emerged regarding the dynamics of language itself. Increasingly language becomes a central object of literary and philosophical reflection, and the result is a raised level of awareness regarding the complexities of the symbolic mode. This seems to bring about a similar will to explore the dynamics of silence with renewed awareness. This reflective focus on silence also affects manners of thinking silence in relation to the literary or poetic expression. In the light of literary silence it is therefore the increased reflective awareness regarding silence that characterizes the shift from Rousseau to Beckett.

One writer in particular has been associated with an aware probing of the potential or role of silence in poetic expression, namely Stéphane Mallarmé. His poems stage explorations of silence that testify to the transition I am trying to delineate. Central is his recognition of crisis within the activity of poetics: 'La littérature ici subit une exquise crise' (Mallarmé 1990: 232). It is this *crise* that is both cause and effect of the new approach to poetic language and its relation to silence. As an introductory observation, Mallarmé's move can be summarized as an overt shift from simple to complex repetition. His poetic practice, and this is perhaps most obvious in *Un coup de dés*, bypasses simple repetition by precluding a negative silence. Silence is no longer congruent with an 'outside', but rather explored as a result of a spacing and a poetic expression that radically challenges more traditional parameters. Famously, the dream is of a 'poème tu, aux blancs', the white spaces on the page taking on a silencing effect within the poem itself (Mallarmé 1990: 247). The scattered appearance of language can make silence, as suggested in the epigraph: 'avec quoi le silence'. In Chapters 4 and 5 respectively, we have seen how Pascal and Rousseau overtly posit their non-symbolic topos *outside* their text, thereby maintaining the dualistic relation between silence and language. Mallarmé, however, is arguably one of the first to move towards an expression that does not relate to such an outside, and that therefore practises an *overt* move towards complex repetition. It is this move that is the focus of the Interlude.

Mallarmé, for example in *Crise de vers*, presents reflections regarding the shift in question. However, these reflections are in many ways responses to the dynamics instigated by the new poetic practice, and not primarily theoretical observations. More theoretical articulations have been reserved for secondary readings. And the impact of Mallarmé's exploration of silence has perhaps been best formulated by Blanchot in his readings of Mallarmé.[1] Blanchot's readings emerge as dialogues with both Mallarmé's practice and his commentary. From this 'double-dialogue', Blanchot is able to dislodge and pinpoint some theoretical implications that are relevant. In other words, Blanchot articulates the basis for thinking silence as a result of a writing that posits no outside, that bypasses simple repetition. My intention is to see how Blanchot reads Mallarmé in a manner that can be said to pass beyond Mallarmé, that reads Mallarmé against Mallarmé, that creates a reflexive dialogue that in turn makes available a framework for thinking this new, more overt turn towards

---

[1] For a thorough understanding of the relationship between Mallarmé and Blanchot and the notions of *Crise*, *Le Livre*, and literature, I refer to the thesis of Marius Wulfsberg, *Det litterære rommet, En studie i Stéphane Mallarmés and Maurice Blanchots forfatterskap* (2002) ('The Space of the Literary: A Study in the Writings of Stéphane Mallarmé and Maurice Blanchot'). Unfortunately the thesis is not yet translated, and hence only available to readers of Norwegian.

silence in Mallarmé's writing. Specifically I shall refer to Blanchot's readings of Mallarmé in *La Part du feu* (1949), *L'Espace littéraire* (1955), and *Le Livre à venir* (1959).

Blanchot finds in Mallarmé the basis and origin of the transition that will affect my readings of Beckett's trilogy. Beckett's texts emerge as witnesses to this reflexive turn towards silence as they also preclude traditional understandings of silence as a negative outside. To read the trilogy is to enter into an experiment that radically destabilizes the boundaries between text and the silent non-symbolic. This implies a difference in the behaviour of literary silence that again will affect my methodological approach. To foreshadow my conclusion: *the trilogy can no longer be analysed in terms of simple repetition.* There is no *overt* attempt to negatively define the non-symbolic beyond the text. As a method-ological tool, the dynamic of dualism *no longer works*. The encounter with the trilogy therefore creates a methodological hiatus as far as my readings are concerned. The intention with this Interlude is to con-front this hiatus and suggest a means of overcoming it. Referring to Blanchot's readings of Mallarmé, we shall see how they delineate the necessary, alternative mode of thinking silence in relation to the text. This will then provide a framework that is capable of indicating the workings of a 'non-dualistic' dynamic that changes the behaviour of literary silence.

MALLARMÉ'S *PAROLE BRUTE* AND *PAROLE ESSENTIELLE*

Through the *crise* mentioned above, and the activity of poetic writing, Mallarmé discerns and explores the power of a new language, a *poetic* language, that is irreducible to other experiences of language. Mallarmé says: 'J'ai senti des symptômes très inquiétants causés par le seul acte d'écrire' (quoted by Blanchot 1955: 37). It is exactly the dynamic of this *seul acte d'écrire* that Blanchot recognizes as the occa-sion that gives rise to a unique language. He describes it as a *situation extrême* in which the poet risks the pulsations of a language that defies the predictability associated with 'everyday' language. It is the dynamic of this almost extreme language that Blanchot approaches in his readings of Mallarmé and that he explores as literature's own (see Chapter 2).

Essentially, Mallarmé describes the sense of a poetic language based on what he recognizes as a dualistic opposition between two modes of language. However, it is precisely this dualistic ordering that Blanchot, in his reading of Mallarmé's poetic language, challenges. Instead of accepting the opposition, Blanchot shows how both modes bear traces of the poetic language. Simultaneously he shows that the dynamic of Mallarmé's poetic language remains irreducible to either mode. In other words, he approaches Mallarmé's poetic language by way of destabilizing the dualistic opposition that Mallarmé himself suggests. It is this act of destabilization that designates poetic language as a different mode of language. In Chapter 3 I suggested that Abraham's breaking of silence, as described by Kierkegaard, could be called a 'third mode' of language that was neither silence nor speaking. It is this sense of third mode that can be traced further through the writings of Blanchot and Mallarmé. Specifically, it is Blanchot's approach to this poetic language through Mallarmé's writing that I intend to delineate in the following. I propose that it can further inform literary silence and the new ways in which Beckett's texts 'practise' literary silence.

In *Crise de vers* Mallarmé famously recognizes the two kinds of language. He writes: 'Un désir indéniable à mon temps est de séparer comme en vue d'attributions différentes le double état de la parole, brut ou immédiat ici, là essentiel' (Mallarmé 1990: 250). Simply defined, the *parole brute* is a useful language that serves to signify the immediate reality or world of objects. In the words of Blanchot: 'il est d'usage usuel, utile' (Blanchot 1955: 39). It serves the purpose of communication: 'il sert d'abord à nous mettre en rapport avec les objets, parce qu'il est un outil dans un monde d'outils' (ibid.: 40). The *parole essentielle*, on the other hand, is that which represents those things that are absent. It reflects a reality that is not present, at hand: 'elle est toujours allusive, elle suggère, elle évoque' (ibid.: 38). It is a reflexive mode of language that does not refer directly to a world of objects. It is more complex in that it at once makes *present* the things referred to and makes them *absent*: 'Les mots, nous le savons, ont le pouvoir de faire disparaître les choses, de les faire apparaître en tant que disparus' (ibid.: 45). The thing is made absent because the signifier mediates and thereby *denies* its immediate presence. However, it is made present (in its absence) in that the word, by taking its place, *represents* it. Blanchot says: 'Elle est, par elle même imposante, elle s'impose, mais elle n'impose rien' (ibid.: 40). In the *parole essentielle* the word imposes itself as it takes the place of the thing. But it imposes *nothing* because the thing referred to is mediated and absent. Blanchot defines it as *la parole de la pensée*: 'Mais rendre absent "un fait de nature", le saisir par cette absence, le "transposer en sa presque disparition vibratoire" qu'est-ce donc? Essentiellement parler, mais, aussi, penser' (ibid.: 38–9). To think is to be once removed from the world that thought evokes. The language of thought is therefore reflective as it serves to represent the absent object.

Having recognized this dualism, Blanchot proceeds to reveal the complexities implied. First of all he observes that Mallarmé, when talking about this distinction, 'donne la même substance, rencontre, pour le définir, le même mot, qui est le silence' (Blanchot 1955: 38). The *parole brute* is simply 'de mettre dans la main d'autrui en silence une pièce de monnaie' (Mallarmé 1990: 250). The word is almost superfluous: it could be a coin; it is a mere exchange, and therefore silent. The word is quiet; it does not impose itself, as the immediate object pretends to efface it by its actual presence. Basically, what is primary is the immediate object, not the word. The *parole brute* is therefore 'Silencieuse . . . parce que nulle, pure absence de mots, pure échange' (Blanchot 1955: 38). However, the *parole essentielle* is also silent, but in a different way. It *silences* the immediate world by making it mediate and thereby absent, *silent*. The word here takes on all the value as the object it refers to is denied presence. This is the negative silence of a language that makes objects disappear as it gives primacy to the word. The *parole brute* silences the word, whereas the *parole essentielle* silences the world. But what is significant, and rather surprising, is that Mallarmé should describe both these modes as silent. This suggests that the distinction is less absolute.

Blanchot continues to reveal the instability of the opposition. First he remarks that 'la parole brute n'est nullement brute' (ibid.: 39). Although this mode of language pretends to signify a present, immediate world, 'ce qu'elle représente n'est pas présent' (ibid.). The guise of immediacy, says Blanchot, is always denied by the very general dynamic of *all* language. All language is reflective and *negating*—this describes its inherent dynamic. A word only works by negating the presence of the thing: 'La parole brute n'est ni brute ni immédiate. Mais elle donne l'illusion de l'être. Elle est extrêmement réfléchie, elle est lourde de l'histoire' (ibid.: 40). Essential is the ability of this language to create the illusion of immediacy. The *parole brute* actually dissimulates its own reflective and negating dynamic: 'La parole a en elle le moment qui la dissimule' (ibid.: 41). This language has 'la puissance par quoi la médiation (ce qui donc détruit l'immédiat) semble avoir la spontanéité, la fraîcheur, l'innocence de l'origine' (ibid.). To conclude Blanchot's point, the *parole brute* is as reflective and mediating as the *parole essentielle*. However, the former mode hides this dynamic by pretending to silence the word. Owing to this guise of immediacy, language serves as the tool of communicating in a world of present objects. Blanchot summarizes: 'Dans le langage du monde, le langage se tait comme être du langage et comme langage de l'être, silence grâce auquel les êtres parlent, en quoi aussi ils trouvent oubli et repos' (ibid.). In order to work, everyday language *silences* (hides or represses) its negative dynamic and thereby denies itself *as language*.

Compared to the *parole brute*, the *parole de la pensée* recognizes the separation between the world and itself as it constantly removes man from the world about which he speaks or thinks: 'la parole de la pensée, ce mouvement silencieux qui affirme, en l'homme, sa décision de n'être pas, de se séparer de l'être, et en rendant réelle cette séparation, de faire le monde, silence qui est le travail de la parole de la signification même' (Blanchot 1955: 41). The *parole de la pensée* recognizes the reflective and negating dynamic of language, the silence that is all signification. It does not simulate immediacy and it thereby displays itself as language. However, Blanchot also challenges the definition of this mode of language by claiming that the *parole de la pensée* is essentially comparable to everyday language: 'elle nous renvoie toujours au monde, elle nous montre le monde tantôt comme l'infini d'une tâche et le risque d'un travail, tantôt comme une position ferme où il nous est loisible de nous croire en lieu sûr' (ibid.: 41–2). Even the discourse of thought, argues Blanchot, stands in relation to a signified world. Although it recognizes its own negative and reflective dynamic, the *parole de la pensée* still signifies something outside itself, it still safeguards our relationship to the world, it is still a useful tool of communication.

BLANCHOT'S APPROACH TO POETIC LANGUAGE

Blanchot has unravelled and destabilized the dualism recognized by Mallarmé by showing how the *parole brute* and the *parole essentielle* both have traces of each other. The *parole brute*, despite its apparent immediacy, is still reflective, and the *parole essentielle*, despite its open negation of the immediate world, is still caught in a relationship to a real world. It is against this now unstable dualism that Blanchot moves towards a description of Mallarmé's poetic language. Both

Mallarmé's descriptions of this language and his poetic expression, says Blanchot, indicate a mode that is different from both the *parole brute* and the *parole essentielle*: 'La parole poétique ne s'oppose plus alors seulement au langage ordinaire, mais aussi bien au langage de la pensée' (Blanchot 1955: 42). Blanchot suggests that poetic language is a third mode: it relates to the dualism, but is irreducible to it. This is the radical insight that Blanchot derives from Mallarmé.

As the third mode, poetic language behaves according to different dynamics. Mallarmé makes a fundamental observation in a letter to Cazalis of 30 October 1864: 'J'ai enfin commencé mon *Hérodiade*. Avec terreur, car j'invente une langue qui doit nécessairement jaillir d'une poétique très nouvelle, que je pourrais définir en ces deux mots: *Peindre, non la chose, mais l'effet qu'elle produit*' (Mallarmé 1995: 206). Mallarmé describes a language that is free from the obligation to refer to a world of objects. It does not signify, it has no *use* value as a referential tool. It is a language not of things, but of effects. This, according to Blanchot, is 'la décision d'exclure les choses réelles et de refuser à la réalité sensible le droit à la désignation poétique. La poésie ne repond pas à l'appel des choses. Elle n'est pas déstinée à les préserver en les nommant (Blanchot 1959: 305). Blanchot here develops Mallarmé's recognition in *Crise de vers* of 'la merveille de transposer un fait de nature en sa presque disparition vibratoire' (Mallarmé 1990: 251). Poetry has no obligation towards objects. Drastically cut off from a world of objects, it has the power to make objects *disappear*. Released from the obligation to reflect and mediate objects as a useful tool of signification, poetic language can move towards the *effects* of things. More precisely, it is free to reveal the effects of a language that both the *parole brute* and the *parole essentielle* had to dissimulate in order to work. Because it is not a tool of communication, poetry can afford to reveal language as pure negation of the world. Poetic language is free to openly display and exhibit the intrinsic, negative dynamic that is at work in all language—the *disparition vibratoire*.

At liberty to negate the world, poetic language refers primarily to itself as language; words refer to words, not things: 'ils [les mots] s'allument de reflets réciproques comme une virtuelle traînée de feux sur de pierreries' (Mallarmé 1990: 246). Words instigate the play of reflections, the trail of fires. The description echoes the notion of play, which was described in Chapter 2 as a self-sufficient movement that indicated the dynamic of literary silence. In his essay 'Mallarmé',

Derrida further formulates the point: 'La pureté du signe ne se remarque qu'au point où le texte ne renvoyant qu'à lui-même, désignant son inscription et son fonctionnement tout en simulant de se référer sans retour à autre chose' (Derrida 1974: 370). Poetic language does not refer to the world—its words 'ne renvoient finalement qu'à leur propre *jeu*, n'en sortent jamais en vérité vers autre chose' (ibid.: 375, my italics). Because poetic language is no longer a tool it does not need to either pretend immediacy nor mediate that which is absent. It can, so to speak, afford to play. Consequently it can become a language that is empowered to release those inherent negating energies that have to be dissimulated in any useful language. We of course recognize this moment of release as the movement that has made room for literary silence as waves, as repeated heartbeats, as language moving towards the unsayable.

But before moving on, it is worth quoting from Beckett's *Molloy* to show how a comparable view of language emerges in the first novel of the trilogy:

Oui, les mots que j'entendais, et je les entendais très bien ayant l'oreille assez fine, je les entendais la première fois, et même encore la seconde, et souvent jusqu'à la troisième, comme *des sons purs, libres de toute signification* . . . Et cela explique pourquoi j'étais peu causeur, ce mal que j'avais à comprendre non seulement ce que les autres disaient, mais aussi ce que moi je leur disais à eux. Il est vrai qu'avec beaucoup de patience on finissait par s'entendre, mais s'entendre à quel sujet, je vous le demande, et pour quel résultat. (Beckett 1951*a*: 66, my italics)

In Molloy's world words do not directly mean anything; they are *sons purs*—'mere' language. Consequently Molloy's language is hardly useful—it can only just serve as means of the most basic communication. However, Molloy does not seem to see this as a sign of poverty in language. By insisting that it is a language that is *libre de toute signification* he rather underscores the potential freedom of this mode of discourse. The quotation indicates how the innovative, poetic view of language can be traced through the trilogy.

Poetic language is, importantly, also a spatial result. This is of course most obvious in *Un coup de dés*. This is 'Une constellation' that is 'veillant doutant roulant brillant et méditant' (Mallarmé 1945: 477). Blanchot describes this as *l'espace poétique*, a notion of space that challenges more traditional approaches to space. Blanchot summarizes and quotes Mallarmé: 'L'espace poétique, source et "*résultat*" du langage, n'est jamais à la manière d'une chose; mais toujours, *"il s'espace et se dissémine"* ' (Blanchot 1959: 321). Space is thought in terms of a result, rather than an object. Furthermore, it is a space that has the dynamic of a *scattering*, a *spreading*. We are invited to think of a space that spreads itself out or, even better, spaces itself out—*s'espace*. It is a space that is flexible and amorphous—that repeatedly changes. It defies measurement and localization: 'L'émotion poétique n'est donc pas un sentiment intérieur, une modification subjective, mais elle est un étrange dehors dans lequel nous sommes jetés en nous hors de nous' (ibid.). Blanchot's spatial description of *Un coup de dés* challenges our imagination and our ability to map out a space. The suggestion is that poetic emotions correspond to a space that cannot be localized within a subjective sense of self, nor identified as an opposing outside. Rather he approaches a strange exteriority that is *en nous hors de nous*.[2] Blanchot here points towards a space that is irreducible to the dualism inside–outside and that hence threatens and destabilizes the fixed boundary that largely arranges and determines our sense of self. Blanchot dissolves traditional and dualistic currencies of measurement and thereby instigates a flux that threatens (or promises) to leave us with minimal spatial bearings. Overall, the suggestion is that poetic language gives rise to a spatiality that challenges any mapping as it has no fixed or localizable points from which to start any orientation.

It is worth noting that in *Un coup de dés* Mallarmé describes 'Le lieu' as 'dans ces parages du *vague* en quoi toute réalité se dissout' (Mallarmé 1945: 475, my italics). The appearance here of waves and dissolving recalls the importance of wave movements in both the *Pensées* and the *Rêveries*. In addition, the *espace poétique* described by Blanchot echoes descriptions of the movement of waves—non-dualistic, non-measurable. A modern conceptualization hence finds a prehistory in these earlier works. What Blanchot articulates in his reading of Mallarmé, to the extent that this can be articulated, the earlier texts also moved in relation to, experimented with, and practised. Pascal, we might recall, found it necessary to draw this wave movement, thereby suggesting that its complexity posed a challenge to articulation. What matters in this context is that the wave movement, congruent with complex repetition, finds a more precise, con-

---

[2] The concept of exteriority dominates Foucault's article on Blanchot called 'La Pensée du dehors' (1996). Foucault argues that Blanchot's language points towards a sense of exteriority that is irreducible to the opposition inside–outside. It is such a sense of exteriority that Blanchot is evoking here.

scious conceptualization at the time of Beckett's writing of the trilogy. It is this, in particular, that will affect the dynamic of literary silence in these texts.

To sum up, Mallarmé's poetic space is paradoxically described by Blanchot in terms of movement—a fluctuating *flux et reflux*, a moving topos that cannot be represented spatially, but that language still creates. As he says, *Un coup de dés* stages a poetic sentence that 'ne se contente pas de se dérouler d'une manière linéaire; elle s'ouvre; par cette ouverture s'étagent, se dégagent, s'espacent et se resserrent, à des profondeurs de niveaux différents, d'autres mouvements de phrases, d'autres rythmes de parole' (Blanchot 1959: 321). The poetic sentence creates a space in which movements and rhythms *s'étagent, se dégagent, s'espacent,* and *se resserrent.* Blanchot's descriptions of *l'espace poétique* point towards a non-representational space. To borrow from Pascal, it emerges as 'une sphère infinie dont le centre est partout, la circonférence nulle part' (Pascal 1991: fr. 230). The suggestion is that poetic language, free from any obligation to objects, can represent realities that other modes of language cannot; it can become 'le mouvement silencieux des rapports' (Blanchot 1959: 320). Poetic language, because it does not aim to signify a known world, because it is free to play, can become movement, can become silence.

POETIC LANGUAGE AS MUSIC

It is clear that poetic space is linked to the dynamic of a poetic language that has severed its relationship with the world of objects. No longer evoking a fixed reality, poetic language gives rise to the fluctuating, immeasurable spatial configurations indicated above. Mallarmé describes this power of poetic language in *Crise de vers*: 'Je dis: une fleur! Et hors de l'oubli où ma voix relègue aucun contour, en tant que quelque chose d'autre que les calices sus, musicalement se lève, idée même et suave, l'absente de tous bouquets' (Mallarmé 1990: 251). Through the word 'flower' *something else* arises: the flower that is absent from any bouquet. Mallarmé suggests that poetic language has the power to create an unrepresentable flower, a flower that does not appear in the known world of objects, that is foreign to our register of any known, and even forgotten, flowers. This, then, is not the immediate flower, nor the reflected thought of a flower, but the radical absence of a flower. According to Blanchot, it is not the idealized

Platonic idea of a flower either: 'A l'absence réelle d'un object il ne substitue pas sa présence idéale' (Blanchot 1949: 38). Poetic language does not relate any conception of flower, ideal or real. The point Mallarmé is making, and that Blanchot develops, is that poetic language offers us the experience of a reality, a flower, that is unrelated to any sense of the normal signified. It presents 'une réalité plus évasive, qui se présente et s'évapore, qui s'entend et s'évanouit' (ibid.). Mallarmé moves towards this dynamic of poetic language by evoking music: this absent flower *se lève musicalement*. Using music to describe the effects of a language is to introduce a new dimension that is central to Mallarmé's poetic language.

Music is of course not primarily a means of signification, but rather a series of tones in relation. Clearly, this proves a useful image for poetic language as a language where words relate primarily to each other and not to an exterior set of signifieds.[3] However, it is significant that Mallarmé did not embrace a parallel between music and language that reduced poetic language to mere sound. He insists that the poetic flower *musicalement se lève, idée même et suave*. In other words, poetic language, described as music, moves *between* idea and sensation and can embrace both. Music describes this paradoxical ability. Importantly Mallarmé's notion that music gives rise to both idea and sensation is integral to a specific understanding of music. In a letter to Edmund Gosse dated 10 January 1893 Mallarmé insists, 'Employez Musique dans le sens grec, au fond signifiant Idée ou rythme entre des rapports' (Mallarmé 1995: 614). Describing poetic language as music, Mallarmé aims to underscore the importance of the idea and the rhythm that is in between, *entre des rapports*. Again we are reminded of play and force as inbetween dynamics of literary silence. It is worth noting also that rhythm is described not merely as a movement between two things or poles, but between *des rapports*, that is between relationships. This increases the complexity of the movement: music is the *relationship between relationships*. The movement emerges as a multiple mirroring that reflects in innumerable directions—a *virtuelle traînée de feux sur de pierreries*.

As music emerges primarily as movement, it follows that Mallarmé is not concerned with the actual phonetic rhythm created by words:

---

[3] Vladimir Jankélévitch, in his work *La Musique et l'ineffable*, develops an interesting contrast between music and prose exactly by pointing to music's lack of signification: 'la musique ne signifie rien' (Jankélévitch 1961: 19). Through this lack of signification music is closer to poetry than to the meaningful prose of dialogue and everyday language.

Je fais de la Musique, et appelle ainsi non celle qu'on peut tirer du rapprochement euphonique des mots, cette première condition va de soi; mais l'au-delà magiquement produit par certaines dispositions de la parole, où celle-ci ne reste qu'à l'état de moyen de communication matérielle avec le lecteur comme les touches du piano. Vraiment entre les lignes et au-dessus du regard cela se passe, en tout pureté, sans l'entremise de cordes à boyaux et de pistons comme à l'orchestre, qui est déjà industriel; mais c'est la même chose que l'orchestre, sauf que littérairement ou silencieusement. (Mallarmé 1995: 614)

Poetic language is like a silent orchestra (and I will return to this idea later) and therefore not to be reduced to sound. Words occupy the function of the *touches du piano* as the means of creating a music somewhere else—*entre les lignes et au-dessus du regard*. Mallarmé seeks to highlight the effect that results from the movement of these words— *Idée ou rythme entre des rapports*. Mallarmé uses music as a metaphor for poetic language that gives rise to the unrepresentable through its *movement*.

It is noteworthy that Baudelaire, in his dedication in *Le Spleen de Paris*, also evokes an image of poetry and music that primarily becomes a description of movement:

Quel est celui de nous qui n'a pas, dans ses jours d'ambition, rêvé le miracle d'une prose poétique, musicale sans rythme et sans rime, assez souple et assez heurtée pour s'adapter aux mouvements lyriques de l'âme, aux ondulations de la rêverie, aux soubresauts de la conscience? (Baudelaire 1972/1998: 20)

Baudelaire challenges a traditional understanding of music by evoking a music without rhythm and without rhyme. What is left is movement: *mouvements, ondulations, soubresauts*. Again we recognize the wave movements. Baudelaire provides a more deliberate and direct evocation of this flux and reflux as a movement specifically relevant to writing and to text.

Describing poetic language as a music that is both idea and sensation, that is primarily movement, Mallarmé opens the imagination to a language that has the power to create a flower that is different from any known or ordinary flower. The flower arises from an in-between rhythm of a language that has renounced stability and signification in order to approach a music that is not yet music. As such movement, such music *sans rythme et sans rime*, poetic language delivers the unthinkable that only exists in the moment of poetic language's unfolding— *l'absente de tous bouquets*.

POETIC LANGUAGE AND SILENCE

The dynamic of poetic language as music paradoxically also links it to silence. In his letter to Gosse (see above), Mallarmé compares poetic language to an orchestra that silently creates music. Implied is the suggestion that poetic language positively gives rise to a silent music that is primarily movement. With this paradox we are approaching the real impact of the innovation that Blanchot traces in the work of Mallarmé. In order to understand it further, it is necessary to consider Blanchot's comments on poetic language and silence.

As observed by Blanchot, Mallarmé describes the general negating dynamic of all language as a silence. However, this is a silence that is itself silenced in ordinary, useful language. The guise of immediacy that characterizes useful, everyday language, says Blanchot, relies upon a dissimulation of the inherent silence. Silence is imprisoned, hidden, almost taken hostage, to ensure the useful operation of language. Only poetic language, because it is not useful—merely the *sons libres de toute signification*—can release this silence, can become the expression *avec quoi le silence*. Blanchot further articulates the point: 'l'art ne reproduit pas les choses du monde, n'imite pas le "réel" . . . L'art semble alors le silence du monde, le silence ou la neutralisation de ce qu'il y a d'usuel et d'actuel dans le monde' (Blanchot 1955: 49–50). The suggestion seems to be that poetic language can be thought of as silence: 'Avec des mots, on peut faire du silence . . . Tout proférer, c'est aussi proférer le silence' (Blanchot 1949: 42–3). Blanchot goes on to say that poetic language is not the opposite of silence, but, 'au contraire, [il est] supposé par les mots, et comme leur parti pris' (ibid.: 42). Blanchot's observations here echo his descriptions of silence in 'Mort du dernier écrivain' (see Chapter 1). He approaches a view of silence and its relation to language that challenges any traditional view of silence and that moves towards a non-dualistic view of silence.

We are now better equipped to return to Mallarmé's own description of poetry as an orchestra, *sauf silencieusement* (see Mallarmé 1995: 614). Poetic language arises as the orchestra that silently orchestrates and releases the music that is inherent in the dynamic of language. And this music is silence. In poetic language the words, free from signification, become the instruments that release the movement that circulates in between and lets it become the *espace poétique* or *espace littéraire* that Blanchot so beautifully describes: 'Il n'est pas silencieux, car précisement *le silence en lui se parle*' (Blanchot 1955: 55, my italics). Blanchot points us towards the image of a silence that has the ability to address itself. It is active and reflexive—*il se parle*. Again Blanchot's comment challenges our imagination: How can silence speak *to itself*? The indication seems to be that poetic language *liberates* the silence that is inherent in all language and lets it speak to itself. Words only become the occasion, the silent orchestra, that release silence and lets it talk to itself and thereby become unimaginably audible. Shrinking from the world, from objects, and from meaning, poetic words becomes a leaf-thin *paravent*, a porous membrane through which silence speaks to itself. Again this is a different formulation of the dynamic described in 'Mort du dernier écrivain'—literature, or poetic language, safeguards silence and makes it paradoxically 'present'.

Based on Mallarmé's writings, Blanchot's work is arguably the first historical attempt to *critically formulate* a silence that is not dualistic, but that arises through language. And it is the fact that he is contemporary with this new approach to thinking silence in relation to language that sets Beckett apart from Rousseau and Pascal. Above I mentioned that the trilogy does not operate according to simple repetition and that there was a subsequent need to rethink my method and some of the major concepts. Blanchot's formulation of Mallarmé's poetic language indicates a textual mode that can account for this shift. Primarily it is question of texts that have no 'outside', no negative silence, but that instigate an internal movement of play, *entre des rapports*, giving rise to rhythm, to silence. As a final part of this Interlude I shall use the concept of poetic language and see how this can permit an understanding of a *poetic text* that in turn might point towards a slightly different methodological approach to literary silence in the trilogy.

THE POETIC TEXT: A THIRD MODE

Blanchot's descriptions of Mallarmé's poetic language reveal a mode of language that cannot be categorized in terms of traditional notions of either silence or language. It can therefore, as suggested above, be approached as a third mode of language. Most importantly, poetic language, as a third mode, slips away from a dualistic dynamic whereby it defines itself against a negative definition of a silent non-symbolic. Consequently, *Blanchot's definition of poetic language does not operate according to simple repetition.* Rather it offers a dramatically different view of textual behaviour than that which we located in both the *Pensées* and the *Rêveries*.

As I mentioned earlier, the notion of a third mode of language has already been explored in Chapter 3, in relation to Kierkegaard's *Fear and Trembling* and the description of Abraham. Abraham cannot speak as this would force him to explain in the ethical language of the others his prospect of sacrificing his son according to a silent summons from God. He must therefore be silent. However, there is one instance in which he finds himself obliged to speak in response to his son. Abraham here speaks, but, according to Kierkegaard, he does not speak the ethical language of others. In my reading of this, Abraham finds an expression that functions as a third option—it is neither language nor silence. It is a language that safeguards the silence because it is a *different* language—not silence, not talk. This suggests a parallel between Abraham's third option and poetic language. In Chapter 3, the third option was defined as complex repetition, a destabilization of productive dualisms. Complex repetition takes the form of an instant—it always happens 'now'. In every instant simple repetition is also always complex.

Both the *Pensées* and the *Rêveries* overtly instigate and maintain simple repetition and thereby sustain the dualism. Simple repetition is the means by which these texts affirm the existence of the non-symbolic of which they cannot write. And although the wave movement destabilizes the productive system of simple repetition, this is through slips, momentary 'floodings' and disruptions. In contrast, the poetic text, as a topos of poetic language, is never congruent with the dynamic of simple repetition. Based on the descriptions offered by Blanchot, poetic language gives rise to a textual mode that collapses any attempt to establish silence as its negative other. Its dynamic is rather one of a repeated lapse into complex repetition, a repeated wave-like flooding of the borders, a repeated breakdown of dualism. It is as such that the poetic text moves towards what can perhaps be described as a *repeated third mode.*

As mentioned above, the trilogy, because it does not overtly define itself in opposition to a decided non-symbolic (i.e. God or Self), defies simple repetition. This suggests that the trilogy behaves as a poetic text. To recall: poetic language produces a textual mode that produces a movement, a music, that is always *somewhere else*. It is, according to

Blanchot's description of *l'espace poétique*, 'en nous hors de nous', a place that resists dualistic thought. To foreshadow the relevance of this non-localizable exteriority for the reading of the trilogy, it is worth quoting *L'Innommable*: 'c'est peut-être ça que je sens, qu'il y a un dehors et un dedans et moi au milieu, c'est peut-être ça que je suis, la chose qui divise le monde en deux, d'une part le dehors, de l'autre le dedans' (Beckett 1953: 160). L'Innommable here suggests that his voice arises from a position that is neither inside nor outside—but *au milieu*. The voice from this middle ground addresses us from a place that is both outside and in between the dualism and that cannot be defined according to it. It is a voice that arises from an aporetic locus, neither inside nor outside, a place with no such borders. I quote this merely to indicate how the trilogy, especially towards the end, *overtly* defines itself against dualism and thereby encourages and invites me to approach it as a poetic text.

It is important to note how the poetic text produces a different relationship to what I define as the non-symbolic. The *Pensées* and *Rêveries* were attempts to express something ('God' and the 'Inner Self') that the texts nonetheless defined as inexpressible. They actively pointed to this notion of a non-symbolic outside the text's realm of expression. The non-symbolic has hence functioned as a label for that which is a negative opposite of the text, that which the text wants to express, but which it repeatedly must admit is non-symbolic in character and hence beyond the text's power of expression. The poetic text entertains a different relationship to the non-symbolic. The non-symbolic is no longer a beyond, as poetic language does not relate to any such notion of the beyond. One of the challenges posed by Beckett's trilogy will be exactly to see how I can talk about the non-symbolic. Where is the non-symbolic? How can it be described? How does it relate to the text?

CONCLUSION

We can conclude that poetic language undermines any relation to a stable, localizable, or definable non-symbolic. Rather, because it is the third mode, defying dualistic ordering, it has the effect of dissolving the non-symbolic. As the non-symbolic repeatedly dissolves and 'floods' the text, it potentially becomes literary silence. Finally poetic language emerges as a mode privileging literary silence.

It is now clear that Blanchot's reading of Mallarmé leads to a notion of textuality that is radically different from that which dominates both in the *Pensées* and in the *Rêveries*. Poetic language indicates a description of a textual mode that cannot be approached as simple repetition. The notion of the poetic text thereby provides us with a description of textual behaviour that might resolve the methodological hiatus referred to in the beginning of the Interlude. It is in this sense that the notion of the poetic text inspires my approach to Beckett's trilogy. Methodologically this implies that rather than establish a pattern of simple repetition, I will explore how the trilogy can be approached as a dynamic of repeated complex repetition. Finally, to the extent that the trilogy behaves as a poetic text, it will offer a potentially different practice of literary silence that might in turn adjust, nuance, and further inform my understanding of it.

6

LITERARY SILENCE IN BECKETT'S TRILOGY

> How could I write, sign, countersign performatively texts which 'respond' to Beckett? How could I avoid the platitude of academic language?
>
> Derrida 1992: 60

INTRODUCTION: THE DIFFICULTY OF READING BECKETT

The above comment is from an interview in which Derrida explains why he will not engage with Beckett's text in a critical way. Of course, this refusal indicates an insight into Beckett's work that is sharper, perhaps, than that of many lengthy analyses. Derrida's implied suggestion is that any critical discourse on Beckett would inevitably 'miss' the text. Commentaries on the trilogy leave a certain sense of surplus. Left is that which slips away from any philosophical or analytical meta-discourse, that which Derrida calls the 'signature': 'this remainder which remains when the thematics is exhausted' (Derrida 1992: 61). The indication is that Beckett's texts resist a critical response—that they are incongruous with critical discourse. This is the fundamental *difficulty* of any critical reading of the trilogy, namely to develop a critical framework that does not neutralize or 'dull' the actual effects of Beckett's text by naming them.

Within the framework of this project, this difficulty can be summarized as the text's resistance to simple repetition. There is no 'outside' to the text from which one can critically respond. As concluded in the Interlude, the trilogy does not relate actively to a negatively defined non-symbolic. The question 'what does this text try to express?' does not point to a defined answer that can be compared to Pascal's 'God' or Rousseau's 'Inner Self'. The difficulty here identified is that of reading the trilogy without positing a sense of the non-symbolic. Once the question 'what does this text try to express?' is answered, one enters the domain of academic meta-language. Too easily the text is defined as the attempt to point towards an inexpressible Meaning or

Truth by virtue of simple repetition. The text is consequently analysed in relation to something beyond it. This in turn ignores the possibility that the meaning of Beckett's text is somehow intrinsic to the text and does not relate to any negative topos of inexpressibility. Leslie Hill, in his significant study *Beckett's Fiction*, concludes by describing Beckett's work as 'a series of textual conundrums' (Hill 1990: 162), implying that there is no final 'answer' to Beckett's text, only more text, more riddles, more conundrums.

In the light of this it is noteworthy that a general tendency in Beckett criticism has exactly attempted to define Beckett's work in terms of what it struggles to express, positing meanings comparable to the non-symbolic God or Inner Self. And although I will summarize this tendency further on, some introductory observations can be made. Attempting to answer the question 'what does the trilogy struggle to express?' critics have produced answers evoking an existential sense of Being, a true essence of a unified Self, and a Silence that is beyond language (see e.g. Robinson 1969; Chambers 1965, 1971; Butler 1964; Kenner 1961; Esslin 1980; Baldwin 1981). Using such philosophical and metaphysical frameworks, the critics tend to order their readings according to dualistic patterns. Exemplary is the comment made by Ross Chambers in his article 'Déstruction des catégories du temps': 'Le dualisme chez Beckett entre le moi et le non-moi, entre le temps et l'absence de temps, entre l'essence et l'existence, appartient à une tradition déjà longue' (Chambers 1971: 92). The systematic ordering of the text in relation to a negative beyond reproduces simple repetition and easily oversees the potential of complex repetition. Seemingly oblivious of this risk, numerous critics define systems of simple repetition in the trilogy and thereby create a systematic analysis that 'works', but that ultimately fails to account for the dynamic of the text that is the 'signature'. The approach is perhaps philosophical, but it is not literary. Overall my intention is to read Beckett's trilogy first and foremost as a literary text, as a text that produces and relies upon the dynamics of poetic language as defined in the Interlude.

To ask what the text means, indirectly or directly, is to assume that the text operates according to a signifying dynamic that is ultimately comparable to useful, everyday language. However, as we saw in the Interlude, poetic language gives rise to a textual mode that behaves according to a different dynamic altogether. To recap, the poetic text resists any congruence with an external set of philosophically defined ideas as it does not relate to any knowable flower 'out there'. Reading the trilogy as a poetic text, I can hence trace an approach that does not risk imposing a grid of philosophical thought onto the text, that questions the overall value of the question 'what does it mean?' More precisely, I suggest that there is a development in the trilogy that moves towards the dynamic of the poetic text. Gradually, from *Molloy* to *L'Innommable*, the trilogy questions any traditional relation to the world of signified objects, meanings, or defined ideas and initiates a movement whereby it repeatedly refers back to itself. In this ongoing return to itself the trilogy approaches a poetic practice that is a rich reservoir of readers' experiences that seem to resist articulation.

There are examples of critics who are aware of the risk of 'overshooting' the trilogy, and who try to avoid it, thereby seeking to safeguard this 'signature'. Here a tendency is to conclude the analysis with a certain 'non-conclusion'. Bernard Pingau, in 'Le Langage iréel', describes Beckett's work: 'Voici des livres qui ne demandent pas à être "compris"' (Pingau 1971: 164). Similarly Maurice Nadeau, in 'De la parole au silence', concludes regarding Beckett, 'non seulement l'auteur n'a rien voulu dire, mais n'a effectivement rien dit' (Nadeau 1971: 161). These critics reveal an approach closer to my understanding of the trilogy. However, to conclude an interpretation of Beckett on such a note is effectively to renounce, as does Derrida, the possibility or purpose of any interpretative reading. Ultimately such a conclusion runs the risk of consigning Beckett's work to a certain private, privileged realm. To renounce further interpretation is to accept that the meaning of Beckett's text is restricted to the moment of reading, and furthermore that any attempt at critical meta-language is doomed to transform this experience of the text.[1]

In the wake of such 'anti-conclusions' comes the privileging of the actual *experience* of reading Beckett's text. Is it not this sense of an irreducible, immediate, indeed silent experience that Derrida evokes with the concept of 'signature'? It seems that it is this experience of reading Beckett that Derrida fears losing by venturing a critical reading of the author. Similarly, it is this experience that others seek to safeguard by concluding their analysis with a non-conclusion, a refusal to

[1] These observations potentially invite a larger discussion. Are we to take the refusals (in the manner of Derrida) to read Beckett with us as an indication that the key to Beckett's text is exclusive to the actual reading of it? Is there no locus from which we can talk about the text in a critical way? And would not such a suggestion indirectly challenge the general practice of literary criticism? My intention is not to enter into this larger discussion, but merely to suggest it as an implication of a certain approach.

further describe or analyse the text. Although such an approach avoids the philosophical temptation to define the non-symbolic, it runs into an impasse where there is nothing further to say. The exploration of literary silence encompasses the attempt to move beyond this impasse and say something about the literary experience of reading the trilogy. Attempting to describe literary silence, I seek to 'test' the fragility of the experience, to talk about it without losing it. More precisely, I propose to take the unarticulated experience of reading the trilogy as my hypothesis, thereby making it my intention to explore which textual dynamics actually create this experience. So to explore literary silence in the trilogy is to develop a more nuanced understanding of how Beckett's text *works*, how its effects are achieved, and to focus on the mode or the dynamic that is created by the trilogy.

To sum up, my intention is to consider the trilogy as a development towards the poetic text, a text in which *le silence se parle*. Blanchot's definition of poetic language provides a framework that allows me to walk the thin line between the approach that relates Beckett's text to philosophical meta-discourse and that which rejects further analysis in the name of the immediate experience of reading. It is, in short, a description of textual behaviour that 'fits' Beckett's texts and that enables me to formulate the dynamic in trilogy that is literary silence.

The chapter will be divided into seven sections. A first section will consider examples of critical readings that approach Beckett's text as the yearning to express something unsayable and that name this sense of a non-symbolic. The intention is to show how these critical approaches read the trilogy as an instance of simple repetition, thereby not accounting for the potential impact of the poetic text. In a second section I will turn to the trilogy and consider how the repetition of the actual word 'silence' indicates the complex status of silence in the trilogy. In fact, the trilogy seems to practise its own 'programme' of silence that is irreducible to the status of silence in most critical commentaries. In a third section I will use these observations to move towards a further understanding of the dynamics in the trilogy that make it congruent with a poetic text. The question is how to describe or conceptualize the reading of the trilogy as a poetic text. Important here are Beckett's own descriptions of art in 'Three Dialogues'. These will, in turn, provide the initial description of literary silence in the texts. I will then use this understanding of literary silence to show more specifically how the trilogy practises literary silence and how this practice differs from the two earlier texts. In the two last sections I will show how there is a sense of an impersonal voice that is indicated throughout the trilogy, but that only takes on its final shape in *L'Innommable*. This voice will be explored as a certain repetitive, intense, or concentrated speaking of literary silence itself.

'NAMING' THE NON-SYMBOLIC: A TENDENCY TOWARDS SIMPLE REPETITION IN BECKETT CRITICISM

Above I listed some tendencies that characterize a lot of Beckett criticism, especially in the late 1960s and early 1970s. Collectively this might be coined the tendency to see Beckett's work as the yearning to express some sense of authentic, timeless Being or Self that lies beyond words.[2] Ruby Cohn, in *Back to Beckett*, writes: 'Beckett cuts through the circumstantial detail of fiction down to the "I" who tries to talk about himself' (Cohn 1973: 79). In a similar vein Michael Robinson, in *The Long Sonata of the Dead*, writes about Molloy: ' He would prefer to remain silent for silence would mean that he had reunited himself with his own identity' (Robinson 1969: 148), or later, 'Molloy senses that in being born he has been excluded from an ideally timeless existence' (ibid.: 167). Ross Chambers in 'Beckett's Brinkmanship' sees the self in Beckett as 'dimensionless, [it] exists outside the world of space and time and is by definition unattainable within the world' (Chambers 1965: 152); it seeks the dimension beyond time, 'an absolute permanent instant, occurring outside of time, in the atemporality of stopped time' (ibid.: 161). The tendency, then, is to regard the struggle in Beckett's work as a struggle to attain this sense of a beyond—a timeless, permanent self. Martin Esslin, in *The Theatre of the Absurd*, concludes that Beckett's work reveals the author's 'sense of the tragic difficulty of becoming aware of one's own self in the merciless process of renovation and destruction that occurs with change in time' (Esslin 1980: 70).[3]

---

[2] Let me make it clear that my intention is not to discredit the work of the cited critics. I think it goes without saying that 'deep existential anguish' (Esslin 1980: 30) plays an important role in Beckett's texts and Beckett studies. My intention is therefore not to dispute the validity of these contributions but merely to point to the overwhelming tendency to read Beckett in terms of simple repetition and its limitations regarding the exploration of literary silence.

[3] See also Esslin's later article 'What Beckett teaches me: His Minimalist Approach to Ethics', where he describes Beckett's work: 'His œuvre is a unique record of this rigorous self-observation and self-exploration of his own consciousness, of his own emotional and intellectual landscape' (1993: 19).

Already it is apparent that these critics are responding to the question 'what does the trilogy try to express?' by positing a non-symbolic answer.

Many of these approaches rely, directly or indirectly, on philosophy or philosophical discourses.[4] And they thereby risk what Simon Critchley, in his work *Very Little . . . Almost Nothing* refers to as an 'over-shooting' of the text:

> the peculiar resistance of Beckett's work to philosophical interpretation lies, I think, in the fact that his texts continually seem to pull the rug from under the feet of the philosopher by showing themselves to be conscious of the pos-sibility of such interpretation; or, better, such interpretations seem to lag behind the text which they are trying to interpret; or, better still, such inter-pretations seem to lag behind their object by saying too much: something essential to Beckett's language is lost by overshooting the text and ascending into the stratosphere of metalanguage. (Critchley 1997: 141)

Indirectly referring to Derrida's concern (see above), Critchley raises the problems involved in any philosophical reading of Beckett. Philosophical in this context seems to imply dualistic. A notion that is essentially non-symbolic is negatively defined against the text; the text can reach towards this essence, this authentic Being, but remains in negative opposition to it. Cohn says: 'Through the words with which Beckett endows Molloy, he attempts to penetrate to depths that have not before been penetrated by words' (Cohn 1973: 85). The truth of Beckett's text is posited in the unexplored 'depths' that language must penetrate: 'la meilleure chose que nous puissions faire est de nous approcher graduellement de cette essence impossible à atteindre' (Chambers 1971: 97). Such a view approaches Beckett's text in terms of a dualistic relation: the text versus the inexpressible non-symbolic.

The assumption underlying most of these critical observations is that the self in Beckett's work is caught in a hopeless, endless struggle to obtain a sense of true, essential and united Selfhood. Beckett's self 'existe en dehors du monde de l'espace et du temps, et est, par défin-ition, impossible à atteindre dans ce monde' (Chambers 1971: 94–5;

---

[4] Numerous critics rely on an Heideggerian conceptual framework, highlighting the importance of authenticity of Being. Critchley calls our attention to Lance St John Butler, *Samuel Beckett and Meaning of Being* (1964). Others specifically refer to Heidegger's notion of *Geworfenheit*. For a list of such works, see Genetti 1992: 37 n. The philosophical readings can also tend towards a Cartesian understanding of Beckett, one example being Hugh Kenner, *Samuel Beckett: A Critical Study* (1961). Hill provides more examples of Cartesian-inspired interpretations (and defines himself against it) in a lengthy footnote (see Hill 1990: 173 n. 15).

see also Robinson 1969: 17–18). Ultimately it is language that separates the self from its ideal fulfilment. As Olga Bernal says in her study *Langage et fiction dans le roman de Beckett*, 'Et si ce personnage [de Beckett] constate à chaque instant qu'il est indicible et impensable, c'est qu'une telle condition est contraire à la nature du langage' (Bernal 1969: 142). Caught in this impasse, the dream becomes a new language beyond time and space, culminating finally in 'the silence of eternal self-possession' (Chambers 1965: 155–6). So Beckett's characters are doomed to fail in their quest for essential Selfhood as they are trapped in language.

According to Shira Wolosky's book *Language Mysticism: The Negative Way of Language in Eliot, Beckett and Celan*: 'This reading, in which Beckett is seen as desperately pursuing an idea of self as pure essence, yet always being defeated in his attempts to achieve it, is almost universally accepted as applicable to all of Beckett's work' (Wolosky 1995: 72). What Wolosky identifies in most of the critical literature on Beckett is exactly the ordering of a dualistic system which places a non-symbolic idea of a pure Self, Being or Essence in opposition to fragmented discourse. As Chambers says: 'le problème reste celui de définir l'indéfinissable, de nommer l'innommable, de fixer le centre d'une circonférence hors du temps et de l'espace avec un instrument temporel et spatial' (Chambers 1971: 96). And Esslin describes Beckett's theatre as the 'attempt to reduce the gap between the limitations of language and the intuition of being, the sense of the human situation he seeks to express in spite of his strong feeling that words are inadequate to formulate it' (Esslin 1980: 86). In short, the critical tendency is to set up a system of simple repetition where the true object of Beckett's language lies beyond it.

It follows that these critical accounts also define Beckett's struggle to express in terms of failure. Robinson says of *L'Innommable*: 'Nowhere in Beckett is the tragic incapacity of language so clearly illustrated' (Robinson 1969: 201). The self that dreams of finally coinciding with itself is locked within language. The theme is repeated in a more recent revision in James Acheson's *Samuel Beckett's Artistic Theory and Practice*, which devotes a chapter to the trilogy and the general frustration of a failed language (Acheson 1997: 96–140). Again language is seen to miss the sense of self that precedes articulation. Wolosky sums up what she defines as the general, accepted view: 'The "true" self, essential and interior, beyond time, space, and extension, is also beyond any representation. It is beyond language, which through discursive formulation can only raise a barrier to knowledge and access to the true inner self. Such defeat of language forms the central thesis in study after study of Beckett' (Wolosky 1995: 82).[5] When the Self is defined as Truth, it follows that language becomes inadequate. The scenario is not wholly unlike that which marked the *Rêveries* and the dream of a Silence that safeguarded the immediacy of the self beyond articulation. In other words, there is a general tendency in Beckett criticism not to take into account the shift that I delineated in the Interlude. It follows that these responses to Beckett rely on an implicit framework that is restrictive and even insufficient for the exploration of literary silence.

A first indication of the limits of this framework in the context of literary silence is revealed as the critical accounts almost unanimously fail to pass beyond a first-degree understanding of silence (see Robinson 1969; Chambers 1965; Coe 1964; Baldwin 1981; Hesla 1971). Silence is repeatedly described as the only possible (non-)expression of the self. Silence is hence generally imagined as a telos to be reached, a final end or release from language. As José Carnero-González says in his article 'Silence in Beckett: *The Unnamable*—A Hinge Work' : 'the Trilogy represents the gradual progress towards silence as the negation of all.' (Carnero-González 1993: 209). Silence remains the other of language, an object that can be pointed to, and the dualistic opposition prevails. Michael Robinson sees the trilogy as 'attempts to speak the name which will resolve the particulars in a silence where one need speak no more' (Robinson 1969: 169). Olga Bernal's analysis also tends to operate with a silence that is in opposition to the text: 'L'œuvre de Beckett est sans cesse au bord du silence et de l'origine de la parole' (Bernal 1969: 196). Silence surrounds the text as its negative other. We can conclude that the interpretative urge to name the non-symbolic in dualistic opposition to the text implies a traditional understanding of silence. Silence remains the other of language—oil remains separate from water. It follows that in order to explore literary silence in the trilogy. I must resist the urge to define Beckett's texts in opposition to a defined and circumscribed non-symbolic.

Wolosky's approach to Beckett discusses the above-quoted philosophical readings and finally rejects them: 'in rushing to condemn

---

[5] For further citations from critical works exemplifying this trend see Wolosky 1995: 82–5.

language as inadequate, these critics are endorsing a notion of reality, truth, and selfhood that Beckett's work disputes' (Wolosky 1995: 83). Wolosky argues that, although Beckett's texts might seem to operate according to a negative dynamic that corresponds to negative theology (ibid.: 91–132), the 'use of negative tradition is finally ironic' (ibid.: 134). Wolosky thereby questions the privileged sense of what she calls the 'inexpressibility topos' (ibid.: 269) in Beckett's work. It follows that her approach to silence is more subtle. Although she still claims that 'the other world is figured, both in tradition and in Beckett, by silence' (ibid.: 123), she recognizes that this silence is not the end of speech: 'His [Beckett's] ongoing stream of words contests rather than culminates in silence' (ibid.).

Wolosky's work represents a more recent trend in Beckett criticism that rejects the existentialist or phenomenological readings of Beckett. Thomas Trezise, in his study *Into the Breach*, observes that 'Beckett's prose signals the exhaustion or failure of phenomenology itself' (Trezise 1990: 5). Trezise's attempt to move beyond such philosophical readings leads him to read Beckett in reference to more 'anti-philosophical' French thinkers. Trezise is representative of the contemporary tendency to read Beckett in the context of such thinkers as Derrida, Deleuze, Guattari, Levinas, and Foucault (see Uhlmann 1999; Begam 1996; Connor 1988). Anthony Uhlmann, for example, in his *Beckett and Poststructuralism*, observes: 'If the works of Beckett and philosophers such as Deleuze, Foucault, Serres, Derrida and Levinas have numerous striking points of intersections, then it is partly because they have encountered or existed within the same non-discursive milieu' (Uhlmann 1999: 34). Importantly, most of these studies avoid analysing Beckett in terms of simple repetition. Steven Connor's work, especially, is noteworthy for its original development of repetition in the trilogy.[6] However, many of these more recent commentaries still get caught in what Critchley describes as the 'network of philosophical illusions' or the 'innumerable philosophical red herrings' (Critchley 1997: 142–3). Although these readings reject more traditional philosophical approaches, they are still concerned to

---

[6] Connor discusses repetition in the trilogy referring specifically to theories of repetition by Deleuze and Derrida. He shows how the trilogy stages a repetition of difference rather than sameness, hence rejecting any sense of a privileged original. The attempt to fix the self as original and autonomous is hence unravelled as a dispersing play of repetition and simulacra (see Connor 1988: 44–88).

understand Beckett in relation to other thinkers.[7] Although the frame of reference changes, the risk remains that the experience of reading is sidestepped.

It is noteworthy that the analyses that avoid reproducing a dynamic of simple repetition similarly do not profess an idealized version of first-degree silence. In fact, they show little or no thematic interest in silence. When silence is mentioned, it is most often in terms of paradox. Trezise quotes *Malone meurt* and writes: 'not even Malone escapes "the voice of that silence" . . . that compels Moran, Molloy and the Unnamable to speak, if only in order to silence that voice by telling the impossible history of silence itself' (Trezise 1990: 63). Such a response captures the way in which Beckett's texts 'play' with and stage silence as a paradoxical topos, but it does not offer any further analysis. So despite such remarks on silence, it remains that these more recent readings of Beckett are generally not interested in exploring silence further. Silence remains silenced.

The critical responses to Beckett discussed so far have operated within frameworks that have arguably produced the philosophical meta-discourses of the kind Derrida warns against. The experience of reading Beckett's text slips away from the commentary and remains a blind spot. The approaches can schematically be divided into two. The first group takes as its starting point existential and phenomenological philosophy and discovers in Beckett's text a quest for Selfhood, Being, or a Truth that remains inexpressible. The second group focuses on the parallels between the French post-structuralist thinkers and Beckett's texts. Overall, it seems that these responses to Beckett attempt either to define what Beckett's texts struggle, and ultimately fail, to express, or to place them in dialogue with various philosophical trends. In short, the text is generally approached in dualistic opposition to something else. Consequently, the commentaries considered so far have not moved beyond a first-degree understanding of silence. By opposing language to a privileged, non-symbolic Truth, the dualistic system is established that leads to a view of silence as the other of language. Also the more recent, post-structuralist approaches do not succeed in developing a different framework that would permit new approaches to silence. Perhaps it is symptomatic that they refrain from talking about silence, as if they fear that there is no way of doing so

---

[7] Uhlmann (1999), for example, reads *Molloy* in relation to Foucault's work on surveillance, *Discipline and Punish* whereas Begam (1996) relies heavily on Derrida's concepts of *différance* and *écriture*.

without reproducing the dualism. This indicates the challenge of my reading.

If Beckett's work does not lend itself to philosophical speculation, it does, as suggested above, lend itself to reading. My aim is therefore to see what notion of silence meets the reader of these texts. As a first move I suggest that we turn to the texts themselves and discover what notion of silence they enact. The trilogy uses the word silence to perform dynamics that eventually cause the word itself to slip away from a traditional, dualistic understanding. This development within the trilogy recalls Blanchot's approach to poetic language as a language that cannot entertain a dualistic relationship with silence. I will approach silence in the trilogy not by creating a theoretical understanding of silence but rather by considering concrete mentions of the word 'silence' and thereby discover what the trilogy itself says about silence.

THE BEHAVIOUR OF SILENCE IN THE TRILOGY: TOWARDS THE POETIC TEXT

A first observation indicates that Beckett's trilogy, compared to the *Pensées* and the *Rêveries*, has a far higher frequency of repetitions of the actual word 'silence'. The word is repeated often enough to create a certain echo throughout the text. This in turn explains the tendency of critics to focus on silence and use it in their critical discourse (see above). In fact, towards the end of *L'Innommable* the word 'silence' is repeated more than ten times over the last three pages. My overall intention is to consider how the word is used and conclude what this usage tells us about the 'state of silence' in the trilogy. I should underline that my intention is not to analyse what the different mentions of silence *mean*; rather it is to describe the general *behaviour* of the word 'silence' and consider the nature of the textual dynamic it instigates.

The word silence seems to evoke different associations throughout the three texts. Molloy says: 'Ramener le silence, c'est le rôle des objets' (Beckett 1951a: 16). Molloy posits silence in congruence with objects and thereby indirectly suggests that silence is related to the immediate presence of objects that are not mediated by language. The observation invites a comparison with the silence of Mallarmé's *parole brute*: a silent word that gives primacy to the object. However, the quotation also suggests that the act of naming an object can never grasp this same object; the object remains silent (see Hill 1990: 71). The brief, seemingly casual observation lends itself to numerous possible interpretations regarding the role and status of objects, the relationship of objects to language, the relationship of naming objects to silence, the meaning of *ramener le silence*, etc. In other words, silence is not objectified or limited to a conventional understanding. However, Molloy also uses silence in a more conventional or recognizable manner: 'Car cette nuit là . . . quand j'essaie d'y penser je ne trouve rien, pas de nuit proprement dit, seulement Molloy dans le fossé, et un parfait silence' (Beckett 1951*a*: 36). Silence describes the night and is as such recognizable. However, it is also the replacement of the night *proprement dit*, indicating that silence can function where a more literal signification fails. Silence in *Molloy* is also the traditional absence of noise: 'Un instant de silence, comme lorsque le chef d'orchestre frappe sur son pupitre, lève les bras, avant le fracas des colles' (ibid.: 18). Silence is here an interval between noise. A last noteworthy silence in *Molloy* takes the form of an almost ironic romantic notion. In the description of the first landscape where Molloy will see A and B, Molloy concludes: 'dans d'immenses champs des vaches mâchaient, couchées et debout, dans le silence du soir' (ibid.: 9). The observation is followed by 'J'invente peut-être un peu, j'embellis peut-être' (ibid.). *Le silence du soir* is put into question as a possible reality and taken as a romantic, commonplace topos, the result of invention and embellishment, a blurring of facts. Already in *Molloy* we recognize numerous different uses of the word silence that are irreducible to any one definition.

The frequent mentions of silence continue in *Malone meurt*. Again there are mentions that correspond to a more traditional understanding of silence as the absence of noise: 'Le silence en effet est tel par moments que la terre semble être sans habitants' (Beckett 1951*b*: 131). But there are also mentions that forewarn of a less straightforward understanding of silence. As he reflects on the night outside his window, Malone says: 'C'étaient des choses qui étaient à peine, à la limite du silence et de la nuit, et qui bientôt cessaient' (ibid.: 54). Here objects are verging on silence as they somehow cease to be. Objects no longer bring silence; they disappear into it. We can here draw a parallel with the silence of the *parole essentielle* in which the world is silenced through the difference of language. The observation not only points back to the one in *Molloy*, it also questions it and causes uncertainty. This uncertain state of silence is enhanced as Moran reflects: 'Alors c'est le silence dont, averti, je me contenterai de dire qu'il n'a rien de, comment dire, rien de négatif peut-être' (ibid.: 78). One senses here an increasing hesitation regarding silence, apparent in the interruption *comment dire* and the *peut-être*. It appears that the description of silence is not self-evident but rather requires some effort on the part of Malone. Another mention introduces yet different connotations: 'ce faible bruit de grève aérienne qu'est mon silence' (ibid.). Silence is here defined as almost personal (*mon silence*) and it is characterized by *bruit*.

In *L'Innommable* silence emerges in its ultimate strangeness: 'Ce silence qu'ils ont toujours dans la bouche' (Beckett 1953: 149) or 'Entendre trop mal pour pouvoir parler, c'est ça mon silence' (ibid.: 178). These mentions of silence complete and affirm the tendency that has been foreshadowed in *Molloy* and *Malone meurt*: a constant repetition of the word 'silence' accompanied by its increasingly slippery meaning. The use of the word 'silence' resists conventional understanding and challenges any familiarity we might have established with the term. Silence is repeatedly associated with murmuring noises: 'Car il y a de longs silences, de loin en loin, de vrais armistices, pendant lesquels je les entends murmurer' (ibid.: 139). Silence as whispers or murmurs constitutes a leitmotif: 'Mais il y a de longs silences aussi, de loin en très loin, très très loin, pendant lesquels, n'entendant plus rien, je ne dis plus rien. C'est à dire qu'en prêtant l'oreille j'entends chuchoter' (ibid.: 108). This silence permeated by whispers underscores how silence resists being fixed conventionally as the absence of noise. It also recalls Blanchot's description of the raw silence in 'Mort du dernier écrivain' as 'le vide qui parle, un murmure léger' (Blanchot 1959: 297). The silence that L'Innommable hears is similarily populated by nameless whispers. I shall return to possible implications of this parallel later. L'Innommable further dramatizes the indeterminate status of silence as he rambles: 'ce n'est pas le vrai silence, elle dit que ce n'est pas le vrai silence, que dire du vrai silence, je ne sais pas, que je ne le connais pas, qu'il n'y en a pas, qu'il y en a peut-être, oui, qu'il y en a peut-être, quelque part, je ne le saurai jamais' (Beckett 1953: 203). Silence arises as unfixed and undefined: *je ne le saurai jamais*.

The trilogy offers a profusion of the word 'silence'. However, this repetition does not have the effect of stabilizing the term. Rather it scatters and destabilizes it.[8] It seems impossible to conclude what silence

---

[8] For more general observations regarding repetition as difference see Connor 1988 and Hill 1990: 59–78.

means or points towards as no general interpretation could account for all the different references. Once one meaning is seemingly established, there comes a countermove that sets it afloat again. This is the development of the trilogy, from *Molloy* where the concept showed small tremors, to *Malone meurt* where it shook off the last guise of the already shaky familiarity, to *L'Innommable* where any sense of silence as one might define it dissolves. In short, the trilogy, as a unit, develops an open play with the concept that overtly refuses to fix its meaning. Seen together the repetition of the signifier 'silence' throughout the trilogy does not function as *parole brute* or *parole essentielle*. In other words, 'silence' behaves neither as a useful sign for an immediately present object nor as a reflection of an absent phenomenon. Rather the use of the word silence seems to release the signifier from any sense of an objectified, accepted notion of silence. This is a first indication of how the trilogy stages poetic language and emerges as a poetic text.

For a more concrete example of this poetic silence, Malone's words on silence are relevant:

Mais au fond de l'ombre c'était le silence, celui de la poussière et des choses qui ne bougeraient jamais, s'il ne dépendait que d'elles. Et du réveil qu'il ne voyait pas le tic-tac était comme la voix du silence qui lui aussi, comme l'ombre, vaincrait un jour. Et alors tout serait silencieux et noir et les choses seraient à leur place pour toujours enfin. (Beckett 1951*b*: 48)

Silence is the silence of shadow, of dust and stillness, it is the voice that one day will take over and make everything dark and silent and give order to things. This is no longer a silence reducible to the absence of language. It is what one might call an 'overvalued' silence. By virtue of its repetition it is highly valued. However, through this same repetition the word's meaning, and hence its value, becomes questionable and slippery. And as suggested above it is this repeated slipperiness that indicates the dynamic of the trilogy as a poetic text. The dynamic of the poetic text is a result of the way in which the text practises itself, the way it *behaves*. It is also noteworthy that the description quoted above is spatial, thereby recalling Blanchot's notion of poetic language and its unrepresentable spatiality. From the pits of a shadow, to a voice, to voice like a shadow that awakens to take over one day, the silence described by Malone behaves spatially in a manner comparable to Blanchot's *espace poétique* (see Interlude). Released from any definable understanding, it reaches towards other dimensions, towards a space that refuses to be mapped spatially, towards the space of the poetic text.

Tracing silence in the trilogy is to discover a fluctuating topos that indicates how the trilogy behaves poetically. The word 'silence' practises a dynamic that is released from the dynamic of signification and that exercises this newly won freedom to produce other dynamics. The behaviour of the word 'silence' in the trilogy creates a movement that is comparable to the wave movement discussed in relation to both Pascal and Rousseau. Whereas both in the *Pensées* and the *Rêveries* the wave movement, the *flux et reflux*, was directly described and hence played an important symbolic role, Beckett's text does not so much provide direct references to waves. Rather, the behaviour of silence creates a movement that is comparable to the wave movement earlier described. Perhaps we can say that to read the trilogy is also to be carried along by this wave-like fluctucation. Earlier the wave movement has been identified as a marker of literary silence in that it causes the destabilization of the dualism that ensures silence as the negative other of the text. It is exactly such a wave movement that Beckett's text creates in direct relation to the status of the word 'silence'. I draw attention to this parallel only to indicate how Beckett's texts openly practise the dynamic that I have so far associated with literary silence, and how, therefore, his work seems somehow 'closer' to literary silence.

It is necessary now to show more closely the dynamic of the trilogy as a poetic text. I will therefore consider one last example of how the word 'silence' performs the shift from everyday, useful language to poetic language.

Towards the end of the trilogy there is an increasing sense of silence as a potential relief or redemption: 'Tout se résoudra, tard dans la soirée, il n'y aura plus personne, le silence redescendra' (Beckett 1953: 123). Silence seems to be associated with the dream of certain end or *termination*: 'ce sera le silence, c'est peut-être une chute, trouver la porte, ouvrir la porte, tomber, dans le silence, ce ne sera pas moi' (ibid.: 209); or 'et le silence redescendra sur nous tous, se posera, comme sur l'arène, après les massacres, le sable en poussière' (ibid.: 148). These quotes point to a stable notion of silence that can be read as a conventional absence of noise or the end of language. This use of the word 'silence' arguably functions as everyday language. It is such instances that inspire the critical tendency to focus on a traditional silence and to approach the trilogy as *parole de la pensée*.

But again the trilogy instigates a parallel dynamic that repeatedly destabilizes any such dualistic understanding of silence as termination of language. L'Innommable claims: 'le silence une fois rompu ne sera jamais plus entier. Il n'y a donc pas d'espoir? Mais bien sûr que non' (Beckett 1953: 132). In other words, there might once have been a silence, but it is now lost forever. Again a new dimension is introduced that questions any simple, straightforward definition of silence. Whereas many critics refer only to a silence that is the telos at the end of language, the trilogy here admits the existence only of a lost silence that once was. And as for silence as a final release or end to discourse, the texts openly question the possibility even of any kind of termination: 'c'est la fin qui commence, on se tait, c'est la fin, ce n'en est pas une, on recommence' (ibid.: 179). In such endless restarting, termination is never final and the beginning is never the actual beginning. Consequently silence is irreducible to ends or beginnings: 'le silence, la fin, le commencement, le recommencement, comment dire' (ibid.: 211). Leslie Hill grasps the movement: 'In Beckett's writing, the end of speech, that is to say, both the object of speech and the falling silent of speech, cannot be separated from the movement of speech itself' (Hill 1990: 82). Silence is not an object outside speech.[9] Language seems to be the state from which there is no escape. At the cost of a romanticized telos of silence, the trilogy produces endless writing against silence, repeatedly fighting it off. Beckett's continuous writing is a constant refusal to fix or define silence. Only through more writing can the destabilization that I have described take place. Writing is the necessary fluctuation that wards off any frozen or fixed stabilization of silence.

The reluctance to define silence might also throw light on L'Innommable's repeated and despairing attempt to talk about silence: 'Le silence, un mot sur le silence, sous le silence, ça c'est le pire, parler du silence' (Beckett 1953: 197); 'quelques mots sur le silence . . . quelques mots sur le silence' (ibid.: 199). There is very little, if anything, to be said about silence; it cannot be talked about because is slips away from any

---

[9] It is worth referring briefly to Deleuze's reading of Beckett entitled 'L'Épuisé' (1992) that appeared as an appendix to a French edition of Beckett's pieces for television, *Quad*. Briefly stated, Deleueze recognizes the pieces for television as a specific mode of language (*langue III*) that is finally rid of language and words, and that can hence attain a different silence. In other words, Deleuze envisages the absence of language in the name of the image as a potential realization of silence. I here agree with Critchley who, although appreciating the essay as a valuable commentary on the pieces for television, wonders whether 'Deleuze significantly underestimates the fateful necessity of language in Beckett' (Critchley 1997: 153). He concludes: 'Although Beckett's protagonists desire to be done with words, to be finally silent, such silence is impossible, unattainable' (ibid.).

attempt at definition. Or rather, through the ongoing attempt to talk about silence (L'Innommable does not after all stop to do so), the destabilization is acted out. The trilogy creates a constant back-and-forth movement, a play of words, described by Mallarmé as 'reflets réciproques comme une virtuelle traînée de feux sur de pierreries' (Mallarmé 1990: 246). In a return towards itself, this language refers only to the movement it practises which can be thought of as a repeated undoing of its own meaning, as multiple and mirroring reflections. The word 'silence' reveals itself as playful, productive of play in the Gadamerian sense of self-sufficient movement that is always in between, and in the Derridean sense of *jeu*, productive only of more difference, more play. In other words, the movement in question prepares for literary silence. Furthermore, the unstable movement also recalls Mallarmé's descriptions of poetic language as music. As the word shrinks from the world and from its purpose as useful signifier, it shifts into a music that gives rise to new ideas and sensations. Through this dynamic arises a silence that is like the flower—*l'absente de tous bouquets*: 'ce sera le silence, c'est peut-être une chute, trouver la porte, ouvrir la porte, tomber dans le silence, ce ne sera pas moi, je resterai ici, ou là' (Beckett 1953: 209). *Ici, ou là*—silence moves, creating a space that refuses coincidence with itself.

THE PRODUCTION OF MEANINGLESSNESS

The analysis of silence in the trilogy shoes how the texts tend to undermine any straightforward signification. There is no shared community of meaning that Beckett's readers can take shelter in. We recognize this breach between the text and a knowable world of objects or meanings as integral to the poetic text. According to Blanchot's understanding, poetic language makes realities disappear rather than mediates them. That the trilogy has echoes of Blanchot's thought is revealed as Malone himself remarks: 'mes notes ont une fâcheuse tendance, je l'ai compris enfin, de faire disparaître tout ce qui est censé en faire l'objet' (Beckett 1951*b*: 143). Malone keeps losing his things (his stick, his pencil) and here suggests that writing is related to this constant disappearing. Indirectly, he affirms writing's power to make the objects of which it is supposed to speak evaporate. In a similar manner, 'silence' disappeared as a defined notion and gave way to a new movement, a new silence. The trilogy behaves as a poetic text

by challenging the signifying dynamics of everyday language that
guarantee reference to shared meaning.[10]

Such a non-operational language also dominates amidst the characters in the trilogy. In the Interlude I mentioned the example from
Molloy where Molloy recounts that his language is no longer *useful*.
This problem is portrayed in the famous incident with the police officer where Molloy cannot make himself understood, nor understand
the police officer (see Beckett 1951*a*: 29). He informs us: 'J'ai si peu
l'habitude qu'on me demande quelque chose que lorsqu'on me
demande quelque chose je mets du temps à savoir quoi' (ibid.: 27).
Beckett's characters repeatedly evoke this sense of estrangement from
the everyday language of the others. Malone cannot understand his
visitor (see Beckett 1951*b*: 159) and Molloy understands Lousse's
parrot better than he understands her (Beckett 1951*a*: 49). To Beckett's
characters the everyday, useful language of the others becomes inop-
erative: 'Je ne sais pas ce qu'ils veulent. Je le dis, mais je ne le sais pas.
Moi j'émets des sons, de mieux en mieux il me semble' (Beckett 1953:
110–11). L'Innommable speaks the words of the others, but they are
merely sounds to him: 'ce sont des mots qu'on m'a appris, sans bien
me faire voir le sens' (ibid.: 201), or 'ce sont des mots blanches' (ibid.:
202). Words are neutralized as they are released from meaning.
However, the characters still write in this language of the others,
because, says L'Innommable, 'je n'ai que leur langage à eux' (ibid.:
65). L'Innommable sees no alternative but the everyday language of
the others: 'J'ai à parler, n'ayant rien à dire, rien que les paroles des
autres' (ibid.: 46). The solution is to create, within this everyday language of the others, a different language that does not obey the same
rules, that does not *mean* in the same way. This parallels the dynamic

[10] Barbara Trieloff's article '"Babel of Silence": Beckett's Post-Trilogy Prose
Articulated' (1990) describes Beckett's post-trilogy language as 'semantically fluid',
'Meaning . . . continually dissolves'. Her argument focuses on how this moves Beckett's
language towards other 'sense-making patterns', focusing on sound and materiality. But
despite her insistence on meaning dissolving in the text, she concludes that 'meaning . . . lies
in the relationship between the text and the interpreter' (Trieloff 1990: 95) and thereby
relocates and restores the stability of meaning by referring to reader-response theory. J. E.
Dearlove, in her book *Accommodating the Chaos: Samuel Beckett's Nonrelational Art* (1982), makes
a related point. She discusses Beckett's work as an art that explores a non-transparent
relationship to a non-ordered or chaotic reality. However, it becomes clear that this 'non-
relation' still relates to a sense of the beyond that Beckett's language seeks to evoke: 'Beckett
uses the limitations of language and literature to *capture the essence of the void* by implication
and exclusion' (Dearlove 1982: 127, my italics). There is still talk of an *essence* beyond the text,
a non-symbolic that risks restricting Dearlove's reading to patterns of simple repetition.

of the poetic text: namely to use the word 'flower' (or 'silence') in order to produce an unknown flower (or silence). It also recalls literary silence as a transformation of a normal, signifying language into something else—a different, non-symbolic dynamic.

Let us consider one example that performs such an operation within normal language, stretching it towards literary silence. The example, often quoted, is from *Molloy*—the beginning and end of Moran's report. The beginning starts by Moran observing: 'Il est minuit. La pluie fouette les vitres' (Beckett 1951*a*: 125) and ends by Moran repeating this observation while transforming it through negation: 'Il est minuit. La pluie fouette les vitres. Il n'était pas minuit. Il ne pleuvait pas' (ibid.: 239). Clearly the example, like that of 'silence', challenges the stability of signification by undermining itself and questioning to what extent we can 'trust' the narrative that has taken place between these two observations. It performs a destabilization of its own meaning as a multitude of unanswerable questions arise: is this the same voice? Was it raining then or now? Or never? Are we back at the beginning or at some sense of end? The meaning is no longer clear as the dynamic of signification is set afloat.

The choice of midnight and window pane also deserve closer attention. The words give associations to transitions and borders. Midnight is of course the magical stroke that turns princesses into chamber maids and carriages into pumpkins. It is a topos of displacements and transformations. The window pane is an almost invisible, but very tangible, border between an inside and an outside. These words only emphasize how the two passages signal a certain crossing of a border, from stable meaning to instable language, from order to disorder. In fact, the passages themselves are borders, like windows and midnight, that are in between, producing a change, a transition.

The quoted text can be called poetic because it is not primarily concerned to communicate anything specific about either 'minuit', 'pluie', or 'vitres'. Rather, it is concerned to practise an *effect* and it is this effect that matters. Cancelling each other out, the two sentences initiate a movement that affects the entire second part of *Molloy*. The example reveals how the trilogy, as poetic language, does not aim primarily to signify. However, the trilogy, as a poetic text, should not be reduced to an instance of non-signification or complete meaninglessness. Blanchot's description of the poetic language does not rob it of its power to *mean*, but merely its power to be a useful means of communication. Poetic language brings into question the dynamic of meaning altogether. So if the poetic text resists a fixed relation to the world of objects, its effects are none the less linked to a mode of meaning. The example of 'silence' showed a text that constantly dismantles the word's meaning in order to give rise to a different movement a different silence. Critchley indirectly touches on these issues as he discusses the meaning of meaninglessness in Beckett's work:

> It is not true to say that Beckett's work is meaningless as if meaninglessness were a fact that did not need to be conceptually communicated; rather it is a question of establishing the *meaning of meaninglessness*, making a meaning out of the refusal of meaning that the work performs without that refusal of meaning becoming a meaning. (Critchley 1997: 151)

Rather than seeing Beckett's texts as meaningless, Critchley sees meaninglessness as an accomplishment of the text. In other words, it *means its constant operation of meaninglessness*. And in order to perform this operation, the text relies on repeated instances of meaning that then unravel, unwork or 'un-mean' themselves.

The trilogy initiates series of such instances of un-meaning. It is reductive therefore to say that the trilogy means *something*. Oblivious to this, commentators none the less produce topoi of meaning (see above) that are insensitive to the production of meaninglessness. The challenge hence remains to describe how Beckett's fiction repeatedly produces text that is neither meaningless, nor means something. It is, as I observed in relation to the behaviour of the word 'silence', a repeated complex repetition. But how can one conceptualize such a repeated complex repetition? How can I talk about, and here we again confront the problem delineated at the beginning of the chapter, the constant production of meaninglessness? It never stands still; its constant movement evades any attempt to be pinned down by analysis. Finally: how can I approach this third mode that is also potentially literary silence?

Beckett himself has provided a key to this question in 'Three Dialogues'. He here defines the preference of art as 'The expression that there is nothing to express' (Beckett 1965: 103).[11] It is this sense of an 'expression that there is nothing to express' that I want to move towards as a marker of literary silence in the trilogy.

---

[11] Almost all critics refer to this by now famous artist's credo (see e.g. Wolosky 1995; Acheson 1997; Dearlove 1982). But despite the various approaches, the general tendency is to define this nothing as a negative 'Nothing' and thereby risk adopting the framework of simple repetition.

First of all we must ask what it means to express nothing. Whenever we speak in a meaningful, communicative manner, we are saying something. To express nothing one would have to be silent. So when Beckett suggests that a text can become the expression of nothing he is also suggesting an experiment with the ability of a text to move towards a non-symbolic mode, to say the silence of nothing. The challenge faced by the trilogy is, as stated earlier, not to express the non-symbolic Self or God, but to repeatedly express nothing. Nothing emerges as a new and different sense of the non-symbolic. This nothing must not be mistaken for an objectified Nothing that stands in opposition to a Something. This would again imply an underlying dualism. Rather it is *no thing*, that is, not an object. To express nothing is to create a movement that cannot be reduced to some thing, that resists reification. No thing cannot be pointed to or defined because it slips away from any objectified measurements. It should be underlined that the preference of art is 'the *expression* that there is nothing to express', and hence the movement of no thing must arise out of an expression. Nothing is therefore not congruent with the end of expression. Rather nothing is intertwined with and dependent upon expression. It is this sense of an expression of no thing that is the non-symbolic towards which the trilogy moves.

TOWARDS THE EXPRESSION THAT THERE IS NO THING TO EXPRESS

This expression of nothing can be exemplified by returning to the example in *Molloy*. The production of meaninglessness that arises between the first last sentence of Moran's story cannot be summarized or paraphrased. This resistance to summary and paraphrase characterizes the expression of nothing. (Whenever I say *something* this can be translated and summarized.) So although it is impossible to say nothing in everyday language, Beckett's text, as a poetic text, suggests a shift from a signifying operation towards the expression of an *unsayable* no thing. Specifically, it is the poetic language that achieves this expression. The flower, absent from all bouquets, is not an object, not a flower, but primarily an *effect*. This effect has been described as music, as movement, as unrepresentable space. And the common factor is a resistance to objectification. The effect or (non-)meaning of poetic language cannot be reified because it is no thing. And to become the expression of nothing is to become the textual expression of the unsayable, to experiment with the limits of everyday language. The example from *Molloy* is therefore a first indication of how literary silence operates in the trilogy.

The example from *Molloy* reveals the dynamic of the poetic text, and the corresponding expression of nothing, as a slip away from a more dominant mode. The overall story of Molloy and Moran can still, to a certain degree, be summarized. It is therefore still largely a text about some thing. The nature of the two sentences, although it affects the whole, is primarily a slip. However, I suggest that the trilogy moves towards a more radical expression of nothing. As we move to *L'Innommable*, there seems to be an increased urgency or more intense dynamic taking place. It becomes harder and harder to summarize the story of the trilogy. The question arises as to how this mode can be seen as a move towards a *repeated* expression of nothing, or, more precisely: can the expression of nothing last? Can it become the dominant mode? And what are the consequences for literary silence? Can literary silence, as a weak dynamic, become the dominant mode? I shall address these issues by first looking at the dynamic of the repeated 'now', and secondly by identifying the aporetic dynamic of *L'Innommable*.

For the expression of nothing to arise as an expression that lasts, the text must repeatedly ensure that the signifying operation of language, the normal mode of language, is destabilized. There must, so to speak, be no chance of the signifying, meaningful operation being rein-stalled. The poetic mode must 'take over'. This conditions the expression of nothing. The quest for a constant expression of nothing can be traced in L'Innommable's questions 'Where now? When now? Who now?' The questions challenge the basic parameters of any meaningful language, namely a speaking subject in a time and a place.[12] To leave these questions unanswered is to indicate a voice that seeks to be liberated from the confines of symbolic language—that can say no thing, speak from no where, be no one, yet speak. In other words, a voice that becomes the constant expression of nothing.

The move towards an expression of nothing can be approached as a temporal process. Meaningful, everyday language is linked to the voice of a subject in linear time—a story always unfolds in time.[13]

---

[12] See Angela Moorjani's article 'Beckett's Devious Deictics' (1990) and Genetti 1992.

[13] Linguistically this corresponds to the diachronic aspect of all language structure. As Saussure has said in his *Course in General Linguistics*, 'The signifier, being auditory, is unfolded solely in time from which it gets the following characteristics: (a) it represents a span, and (b) the span is measurable in a single dimension; it is a line.' (Quoted from Rivkin and Ryan 1998: 80).

However, linear time is of course a series of instants that are strung together. These instants are synthesized and 'erased' in the experience of succession. We cannot live with awareness of every *now* as this would paralyse our ability to reflect and create meaningful sentences. However, as we have seen, the movement of complex repetition arises as an effect of the instant. As Kierkegaard's understanding of repetition revealed, every *now* is a potential destabilization, an in-between state (see Chapter 3). And literary silence, both in the *Rêveries* and in the *Pensées*, has been linked to this instant and the ensuing deformation of the subject. Only in the instant can the incomprehensible monster comprehend itself. And, as I said in Chapter 5, only in the instant can a voice testify *je meurs*. Only in the instant can the implosion take place because to occupy or to think the instant is to experience a collapse of rational reflection. Linear time, by definition, involves reflection. And the minute one regains reflection, the incomprehensible monsters and the continued dying become non-rational, impossible states. My suggestion is that the expression of nothing must somehow pervert linear time and bring the instant into relief, and hence destabilize or dissolve the reflecting, speaking subject.

A first indication of how this mode emerges is provided by L'Innommable, as he describes his state as a constant arrival of instants:

c'est chaque instant qui est le pire, ça se passe dans le temps, les secondes passent, les unes après les autres, saccadées, ça ne coule pas, elles ne passent pas, elles arrivent, pan, paf, pan, paf, vous rentrent dedans, rebondissent, ne bougent plus, quand on ne sait plus quoi dire on parle du temps, des secondes, il y en a qui les ajoutent les unes aux autres pour en faire une vie, moi je ne peux pas, chacune est la première, non, la seconde, ou la troisième, j'ai trois secondes, et encore, pas tous les jours. (Beckett 1953: 181)

Rather than a flow of time, the voice here describes a staccato, divided, interrupted time. L'Innommable experiences time as an endless repetition of separated instants that arrive but that do not create duration. Genetti, in his work *Les Figures du temps dans l'œuvre de Samuel Beckett*, calls it 'un assemblage brut d'instants décousus qui nie toute continuité' (Genetti 1992: 44). In other words, the instants cannot be linked together to make linear time. It is noteworthy that L'Innommable, at the mercy of the repeated instants, cannot perform the operation that seamlessly sews together these instants to a measurable or linear time: 'je ne comprends rien à la durée, je ne peux pas

en parler' (Beckett 1953: 201). L'Innommable is exiled in the time of
the repeated instants. No meta-view is possible as he cannot 'step out'
of the series of instants and make them components of duration. Lost
is therefore any linear narrative, and in its place arises a mode that
repeatedly returns to the instant, that moves, yet goes nowhere. We
could say that this mode is topological rather than teleological. It
keeps returning to itself rather than move towards something.

To be caught in the constant arrival of instants is to renounce the
possibility of meaningful language. Every attempt to create meaningful language, a narrative, is caught in the interruptive arrival of the
next instant. The movement that tries to point towards a meaning is
constantly punctuated and returned to the movement of language
itself. Trapped in the instant, there is no sense of past or future, merely
the now, and there is therefore no possible narrative. One could say
that the privilege of the instant is such a dissolution of meaning. The
dynamic of the instant is therefore closely related to the dynamic of
the expression of nothing. The only possible point of reference is in
the now, and this now is also *no thing*. The instant cannot be measured
because it is always already over, it cannot be grasped or pointed
towards because it is not an object. To express nothing is possible,
even inevitable, when one writes from the perspective of the 'now'.

Finally, it appears that literary silence, as the constant expression of
nothing, is congruent with a repeated arrival of the instant. To return
to Rousseau's statement *je meurs*, it is now clearer how this statement
can only be acceptable within a similar experience of time. In linear
time the statement becomes absolutely meaningless: one is either
dead or alive. Only in the repetition of the instant can one testify to a
constant dying.

Returning to the questions at the beginning of *L'Innommable*, we can
now see how they suggest an enactment of this movement. The three
questions are linked by the repetition of *maintenant*. In other words,
they are all concerned with temporality. And if we stress this 'now', a
different reading appears, suggesting a new dynamic. If I ask 'Qui
maintenant?', and emphasize the 'maintenant', the primary issue at
stake is suddenly temporal. The moment I attempt to answer 'Who
now?', the *now* has passed and the appropriate answer is no longer
relevant. The point is that time, 'that double-headed monster'
(Beckett 1965: 11), always affects the status of the person: 'we are other,
no longer what we were' (ibid.: 13). The following imagined exchange
might help underscore my point:

A. 'Qui maintenant?'
B. 'Molloy'
A. 'Non. Qui *maintenant?*'
B. 'Molloy'
A. 'Non, qui *maintenant?*' Etc.

In his essay on Proust Beckett develops the idea that time irreversibly changes us so that we are never the same. Time is therefore not a 'milestone that has been passed, but . . . irremediably part of us' (ibid.: 13). Clearly the questions in *L'Innommable* evoke this problem of inconstant selfhood (see Wolosky 1995: 71–5). But they push the argument to its extreme by suggesting that the self is, radically speaking, *never* the same—from instant to instant it changes, or at least it can potentially change. Each instant must therefore ask the question again. Uncertainty takes over as any certainty dissolves at the mercy of the always arriving instant. And that is what is important for my analysis, namely that it is the *maintenant* that initiates this problem of selfhood, and in fact takes over the problem of defining the self. By evoking the instant the question rejects any stable answer and rather reproduces itself endlessly into a series of instants. In other words, the only answer to 'Who *now?*' is 'Who *now?*', 'Who *now?*', etc. Any attempt to reflect and answer is caught in the arrival of the new *maintenant*. The questions reproduce the state described by L'Innommable in which seconds arrive almost like bullets, *pan, paf, pan, paf,* interrupting any duration. Read in this manner, the three questions create a dynamic, a movement that is the repeated return to and arrival of the instant. No answer can satisfy these questions, and we are left with a potentially infinite propelling of more instants.

Because no synthesis, no final answer is possible the questions in fact veil an aporetic dynamic. To interact with the questions in this way is to repeat *who now, who now, who now, who now, who now* . . . Like the aporia the questions invite a participation in a repetitive movement that offers no resolution. The dynamic dramatizes, in a compressed manner, the trilogy's indecisive relationship to time, to endings and beginnings. The voice that speaks in *L'Innommable* is a voice that constantly endures this aporia, that speaks, so to say, from inside the aporia.[14] It is therefore a voice that can be defined in terms

---

[14] For more concrete observation regarding the aporia in Beckett's work, see Hill 1990. Hill is less concerned with how the text creates aporetic dynamics, and more concerned with how the aporia undoes dualisms and posited differences in a resulting play of

of implosion. First of all, this involves the implosion of meaningful, reified language. As I showed above, to be constantly caught in the
instant is to sacrifice any potential relationship to a linear language.
Reified language dissolves and poetic language arises as the constant
expression of nothing. To read to this voice is therefore to read a constant expression of no thing. Secondly, the dynamic of the instant
causes an implosion in the reflective self. To only exist in the instant is
to have no possible reflection. To relate only to the repetition of *nows*
is to renounce any relation to linear time, to language and oneself as
reflecting individual. There is, so to speak, no time to reflect—in every
instant it is time to start again.

L'Innommable emerges as a voice that testifies to the experience of
the instant, to an experience that cannot be thought, that escapes consciousness, but that defines all experience and that is therefore not
congruent with an unconscious state. To speak from within this arrival
of the instant is to speak a voice that is in between, not conscious, not
unconscious, not able to speak, yet not silent. Again, it speaks a state
of consciousness that is unthinkable, the *monstre incompréhensible*, the *je
meurs*.

Listening to the questions, the reader is invited to participate in the
implosion testified by L'Innommable. More precisely the questions
encourage the reader to relate to a repeated arrival of instants: who
now, who *now*, who *now*... The questions have the effect of bringing
into relief the actual instants, unravelling the seam that invisibly binds
them together, and thereby sacrificing linear time for the discontinuous, interrupted arrival of instants. Interacting with the questions one
is permitted a participation in non-linear time, and hence the questions stage the potential implosion, also for the reader. One might
imagine that there is no *exit* from this repeated instant. To exit the
endless questioning is to adopt a reflective attitude and fall back into
linear time, and hence to create the expression of *something*.
Succumbing to the aporia, the reader is allowed a momentary loss of
and release from linear time, and he or she is invited to occupy a language that expresses nothing, and to abandon reflection, to roam
from moment to moment. This is the invitation, the potential, of the
aporetic dynamic created by the questions.

The questions allow us to approach an experience that we cannot
think or express, but that is still mediated, expressed through the text.

indifference. Whereas Hill points out direct evocations of aporias, my aim is to focus more
on how the trilogy indirectly stages aporias, without overtly recognizing them as such.

This is the textual expression of nothing—no thing, no thought, no reflection. The state described by L'Innommable and evoked by the questions can be compared to Blanchot's description of *l'espace poétique* as *en nous hors de nous*. The *en nous hors de nous* was related to Blanchot's concept of a radical *exteriority* as a state that is non-localizable and that is irreducible to dualistic ordering or spatial mapping. Similarly the endless repetition of instants—*now, now, now, now*—that disseminate and scatter, undermining linearity, suggest a space that is always on the move, always already further through these repeated instants. No dualistic thought can order this space, there is no inside or outside or up and down, because there is no reflection—merely 'nows'. To be in it is to abandon rational control and succumb to the whirlwind of repeated collapsing of thought and meaningful language. As language, the questions become the expression that there is nothing to express, an expression that defies description and that is essentially the expression of the *unsayable*. In the poetic space that arises, language is, as I said in the Interlude, merely a porous membrane through which *le silence se parle*. The questions, because they are the poetic expression of nothing, liberate the energy of language's inherent silence (see Interlude) and lets it relate to itself in the movement created by the repeated instants. The questions are hence an instance of literary silence.

It seems that the experience of reading the trilogy is potentially also non-symbolic. Sharing in the movements expressed by the voice, the reader can be riveted to a place of no time, no reflection, and no defined location. It is an experience therefore that resists summary and analysis. This might explain why Beckett's texts repel philosophical readings and why Derrida, through his refusal to reply academically to Beckett, reveals himself as one of the most sensitive readers of these texts.

So far we can conclude that the expression of nothing, no thing, is possible through the aporetic dynamic of the instant. The aporia creates a repetitive movement that cannot be synthesized and that hence cannot advance. This aporetic repetition causes the instant to stand out in relief and disrupt linearity. Before continuing, I would like to return to the observation 'the expression that there is nothing to express' and suggest that this, like the questions, veils an aporetic dynamic that also appears in the trilogy.

It is possible to imagine two different understandings of the observation from 'Three Dialogues'. First one can say 'there is *nothing* to express'. Emphasizing the nothing, this reading advocates a silencing of any further expression. There is nothing to say—writing might as well stop as there is no point in continuing. However, it is also possible to say 'there is nothing to *express*'. To emphasize the *express* implies that it is necessary to continue the expression, the writing. Nothing thereby becomes a result of continued expression and not stopped expression. Express *nothing*, or *express* nothing. The expression of nothing requires that one stops and that one continues. Both are necessary. A more familiar aporia takes form for those who know the trilogy. The trilogy constantly evokes an obligation to continue paralleled with the impossibility of such continuation. L'Innommable says: 'Je ne vais pas pouvoir continuer en tout cas. Mais je dois continuer. Je vais continuer' (Beckett 1953: 177). This repetitive impasse runs throughout the trilogy like a seemingly hopeless echo: 'impossible de m'arrêter, impossible de continuer, mais je dois continuer, je vais donc continuer' (ibid.: 180).

The impasse reaches a climax at the end of *L'Innommable* where the dream of silence is constantly overtaken and blurred by the obligation to continue: 'ça va être moi, ça va être le silence, là où je suis, je ne sais pas, je ne le saurai jamais, dans le silence on ne sait pas, il faut continuer, je ne peux pas continuer, je vais continuer' (Beckett 1953: 213). Already it is clear that this dynamic is aporetic—to continue is not an option, nor is to be silent. The result of this aporia is an expression that does not go anywhere, but that is not standing still. As Molloy says: 'ma progression m'obligeait à m'arrêter de plus en plus souvent, c'était le seul moyen de progresser, m'arrêter' (Beckett 1951*a*: 105). It is noteworthy also that Molloy, after leaving Lousse, finds himself in a passageway: 'Le passage était sans issue, donc pas un vrai passage mais plutôt une impasse' (ibid.: 81).

I suggest that this aporetic mode is congruent with the *expression* of nothing and the expression of *nothing*. In every instant, every 'now' the voice, and the text, can either stop or continue (like Rousseau can either die or remain alive). Every 'now' repeats the aporia. Again this disrupts linear continuity. Once one enters a linear experience of time, the voice must 'choose' either to stop or continue (like Rousseau must be either dead or alive, not dying). *But in the instant it can occupy the aporia.* The instant gains in relief as every attempt to go on is caught in the obligation to stop and express *nothing*. And every attempt to stop is caught in the obligation to continue and *express* nothing. And, as we have seen above, when the instant gains in relief it implodes meaningful language and reflection and thereby becomes the expression of no thing. This basic aporia therefore produces the dynamic of literary silence.

Only in *L'Innommable* does this aporetic mode takes on its final form, or non-form; or, even better, its final movement that is perpetual but that is going nowhere. The language of L'Innommable emerges as a series of interruptions, scattering repetitions, open contradictions, a never-ending, dizzying flow of words. There is no end because 'La recherche du moyen de faire cesser les choses, taire sa voix, est ce qui permet au discours de se poursuivre' (Beckett 1953: 21). To end is to continue. In fact, to attempt to end is what enables continuation. The predicament produces the expression that can best be described as *back and forth* or *in between*:

Ces choses que je dis, que je vais dire, si je peux, ne sont plus, ou pas encore, ou ne furent jamais, ou ne seront jamais, ou si elles furent, ou si elles sont, ou si elles seront, ne furent pas ici, ne sont pas ici, ne seront pas ici, mais ailleurs. Mais moi je suis ici. Je suis donc obligé d'ajouter encore ceci. Moi que voici, moi qui suis ici, qui ne peux pas parler, ne peux pas penser, et qui dois parler, donc penser peut-être un peu, ne le peux seulement par rapport à moi qui suis ici, à ici où je suis, mais le peux un peu, suffisamment, je ne sais pas comment, il ne s'agit pas de cela, par rapport à moi qui fus ailleurs, qui serai ailleurs, et à ces endroits où je fus, je serai. (Beckett 1953: 25)

This quotation indicates the behaviour of the language that arises out of the aporetic obligation to continue when continuation is impossible, to say no thing with words that still mean some thing. It is a movement where each comma signals a reversal, a cancellation of that which preceded it, yet still a moving on. Reading the passage, we are engaged in a movement where each observation hits us like a moment—*pan, paf.* The reader is hence given no chance to construct a linear narrative and any attempt to summarize this passage would fail. The observation *il ne s'agit pas de cela* questions what precedes it and sets it afloat. But then comes an echo of what was stated earlier *par rapport à moi* that seems to say that *il s'agit encore de cela*. The effect is to question the *il ne s'agit pas de cela* and in turn set it afloat. So the meaning of the passage dissolves into movement. It is a dynamic that is locked, yet that moves. Any attempt to advance in a linear mode is imploded, interrupted. Constantly returning to itself and to the instant, the passage enacts a constant unravelling of the meaning that colours the words. This is the movement that conditions the expression that there is nothing to express. The things he is going to say are not, or not yet, or never were. In other words, there is no teleological progression towards a meaning, rather a constant back-and-forth—a topological movement that traverses, to and fro, endlessly spinning the space that is spatially unrepresentable: 'Allées et venues incessantes, atmosphère de bazar' (ibid.: 9).

It is worth noting that Critchley, in reference to *L'Innommable*, talks about the 'syntax of weakness'—'an endlessly proliferating and self-undoing series of sayings and unsayings' (Critchley 1997: 168). The observation echoes the description of literary silence as a weak dynamic. At stake is a mode that rejects the strength of reflection, observation, measurement, and linearity through repeated punctuations, repeated slips. It is weak because it practises a repeated deflection away from the impetus to create argumentative and meaningful statements. It uses the aporia to repeatedly implode and cancel any attempt to 'step' out towards a stable outside from where a linear, meaningful narrative could be formed. In *L'Innommable* there is no alternative to the syntax of weakness. That is to say, *the weak mode* persists. It reveals its paradoxical strength through its refusal to let any rational, linear, seemingly transparent mode of language reassert itself. As an extreme potential of poetic language, the syntax of weakness unfolds as a discontinuous and disruptive mode that, in every instant, returns to itself and destabilizes any outside, any beyond, any meaning. It is a mode that repeatedly wards off reified and dualistic language, that repeatedly unravels the apparently seamless duration of linear time into fragmented instants. With this force, or rather this weak-force, the syntax of weakness becomes a mode of poetic language that does not end. This in turn points to an alternative understanding of literary silence as a weak mode that can none the less persist.

To conclude we can say that the expression that there is nothing to express emerges in its most extreme form in *L'Innommable* as an aporetic dynamic that can be described as the persisting, even 'strong', weak dynamic. As a result of this observation we are approaching a view of literary silence as a mode that is no longer a slip, but rather a repetitive, discontinuous, intensified mode that can persist. The result is an uncanny, discontinuous, yet 'continuous' expression of nothing. *L'Innommable* thereby offers a different understanding of literary silence as a dynamic that arises through the intensified, repetitive performance of a poetic language and that does not end. In order to grasp this movement of literary silence more closely, I shall focus on the actual voice that addresses us from *L'Innommable* and see how this voice can itself be approached as the speaking of literary silence.

THE VOICE OF LITERARY SILENCE

The analysis above recognized literary silence as the 'expression that there is nothing to express', an expression that arises from the trilogy's aporetic obligation to continue versus the impossibility to continue, the obligation to *express* nothing versus the obligation to express *nothing*. Out of this in-between arises a voice that is irreducible to everyday language but that still relies upon everyday language. This voice, in other words, can be approached as the topos itself of literary silence in the trilogy, and therefore demands closer description. What is the nature of this voice? What does it reveal about literary silence? Where does it come from? L'Innommable's answers are more enigmatic than enlightening: 'je suis une grande boule parlante, parlant de choses qui n'existent pas ou qui existent peut-être' (Beckett 1953: 31). Already it is clear that this is not a voice like others. Of all commentaries it is Blanchot's essay on Beckett, 'Où maintenant? Qui maintenant?' (1959), that treats this question with the most care. Who speaks and from where asks Blanchot: 'Quel est ce vide qui se fait parole?' (Blanchot 1959: 287). It is a voice, suggests Blanchot, that is 'un être sans être qui ne peut ni vivre ni mourir, ni cesser ni commencer' (ibid.: 290). First of all it is a being without being that is neither alive nor dead. It cannot stop or start. It defies traditional description. We are reminded of Rousseau's *je meurs*. Of course the title, *Malone meurt*, echoes this dying in the present tense, and, as we shall see, the dynamic of an impossible dying runs throughout *L'Innommable*.

The expression of nothing arises as a move towards a speaking that is released from reflection. Indicative are L'Innommable's words following the questions at the beginning of the text: 'Dire je. Sans le penser' (Beckett 1953: 7). L'Innommable evokes a voice that speaks, but that does not think what it speaks. Imagined is a language that is free from reflection and therefore possibly free of any first person, to say 'I' without thinking this 'I'. It is noteworthy that the observation follows directly after the questions analysed above. With their cloaked dynamic of the repeated *maintenant* and the repeated collapse the questions evoke the non-reflective voice that can *dire je sans le penser*. The trilogy repeatedly indicates such a radical notion of selfhood, or even better, of a dispossessed selfhood: 'Oui, il m'arrivait d'oublier non seulement qui j'étais, mais que j'étais, d'oublier d'être' (Beckett 1951*a*: 64–5). Whereas speaking is usually a guarantee of one's existence, we are here relating to a voice that testifies the *forgetting* of its own being. Malone observes: 'Perdre connaissance, pour moi, c'était perdre peu de chose' (Beckett 1951*b*: 14.) Malone does not exist because he is conscious of it, he exists in the vacuum left by the absence of this consciousness. He is not conscious nor unconscious, merely voice.

This impossible temporality of the voice is evoked by Blanchot's description of the voice as one that 'ne peut ni vivre ni mourir'. Malone says: 'La possibilité ne m'échappe pas non plus bien sûr, quelque décevante qu'elle soit, que je sois d'ores et déjà mort et que tout continue à peu près comme par le passé' (Beckett 1951*b*: 75). Molloy says about life: 'elle est finie et elle dure à la fois, mais par quel temps du verbe exprimer cela?' (Beckett 1951*a*: 47). We are referred to an experience that resists linear representation. Temporality emerges as the non-symbolic. Further on Malone remarks: 'je pourrais me croire déjà mort' (Beckett 1951*b*: 15) and 'C'est vague, la vie et la mort' (ibid.: 83). Molloy says: 'Mais c'est seulement depuis que je ne vis plus que je pense' (Beckett 1951*a*: 32). These observations set afloat the most absolute limit of all, namely the one that separates being alive from being dead. And as this limit fluctuates we are presented with a continual dying that never enters either the past or the future, that occupies an impossible time.

So far we can conclude that the voice in *L'Innommable* speaks from an absence of time, a dying without death, a reflection without an 'I'. This is what defines it. It is a voice that repels parameters that dominate everyday language and rational thought. It is therefore absurdly logical that the voice be neither dead nor alive, but *dying*. Only from the moment of dying can it 'Dire je. Sans le penser'. The moment of death emerges as one of dispossession of subjectivity. To die continuously is to lose one's subjectivity every instant. The voice in *L'Innommable* can be described as performing a repeated shedding of subjectivity, of any 'I'. Its voice arises from a place where this 'I' is meaningless, where the notion of the subject itself is repeatedly dissolved in every instant, leaving nothing but a neutral, empty, non-reflective voice: 'je n'ai pas à réfléchir, ni avant, ni après, je n'ai qu'à ouvrir la bouche pour qu'elle témoigne de ma vieille histoire et du long silence qui m'a rendu muet' (Beckett 1951*b*: 103). A mute voice, testifying silence, arises out of the collapsed reflection—a mouth that opens to release this different language: 'Non, je ne dois pas essayer de penser. Dire simplement ce qu'il en est, c'est préférable' (Beckett 1953: 21). The voice emerges, free-floating, unattached, a stream of words, no 'I'. And it is this voice that preconditions poetic language's ability to say no thing. Because as long as language is produced by an 'I', it is saying something. The trilogy's move towards the expression that there is nothing to express introduces an 'emptying' of the first-person pronoun, a destabilization of, even an unthinkable, repetitive death of the thinking subject.[15] Because a voice that has no 'I', that has no defined place, can become the expression of no thing. This dispossessed voice itself becomes the voicing of the non-symbolic, the voicing of a silence that is literary.

The force of this voice is linked to what emerges as its impossible origin. L'Innommable says: 'C'est moi qui écris, moi qui ne puis lever la main de mon genou. C'est moi qui pense, juste assez pour écrire, moi dont la tête est loin' (Beckett 1953: 24). L'Innommable indicates that his voice, his writing, arise out of an unthinkable situation. It is a writing that comes from no hand. But from where, then? His body, he has observed, is 'incapable du moindre mouvement', yet he can write? Similarly Malone writes: 'Je crois que j'ai encore dormi. J'ai beau tâtonner, je ne trouve plus mon cahier. Mais j'ai toujours mon crayon à la main' (Beckett 1951*b*: 57). The phrase poses the question: how can this be written down in the present tense? He has got the crayon in his hand, but is it writing, and if so, on what? If the *cahier* is lost, how can this writing be recorded alongside the rest of the writing? But how can it be recorded like this if it were not written down? Malone also observes that he can no longer move: 'Ramène tes mains. Je ne peux pas' (ibid.: 183). What we get is a voice that denies its own capacity to write. Yet writes.

To take Beckett's, or rather the voice's, words seriously is to be faced with a writing that arises from an impossible act—a writing that emerges from arms that are paralysed, from a head that is absent, on a pad that is absent. There is no satisfactory explanation to this. Writing cannot take shape on a lost notebook, yet we read this writing, recorded as the notebook is missing. The observations recall the

---

[15] Without going into detail it is worth noting that the next step in this shedding of the subject comes in *Comment c'est* where there is no subject at all. However, it is *L'Innommable* that reveals the *process* of shedding, of dispossessing the subject.

instances of literary silence in Pascal and Rousseau. It is a writing that challenges imagination, the writing of the unrepresentable. These descriptions are instances of literary silence. The voice describes its own origin by positing an impossible thought through language, a thought that in fact undermines any explanation. I write and I cannot lift my arms towards the paper. *Il pleuvait. Il ne pleuvait pas.* We cannot think or rationally explain the origin of this writing that constantly questions itself, unworks itself, and sets itself afloat.

It is this question of origin that Blanchot explores. His exploration leads him to indicate the presence of 'une parole neutre' that exists independently of any expression: 'Là, la parole ne parle pas, elle est, en elle rien ne commence, rien ne se dit, mais elle est toujours à nouveau et toujours recommence' (Blanchot 1959: 294). Blanchot suggests the ongoing talking of a voice that is irreducible to interiority, that is impersonal, but that repeatedly continues. The description recalls the observations on poetic language: 'La parole poétique n'est plus parole d'une personne: en elle, personne ne parle et ce qui parle n'est personne, mais il semble que la parole seule se parle' (Blanchot 1955: 42). This describes the voice in the trilogy and suggests that it approaches the poetic voice itself. As I have already suggested, L'Innommable's voice also recalls Blanchot's descriptions in 'Mort du dernier écrivain'. Here literature was defined as the voice that dared enter into dialogue with the nameless speaking—the raw silence—and give it an expression. Literature arises as the writing that recognizes and hears this silence and transforms it into an expression that we can all share. Like the silence in *L'Innommable* this raw silence was characterized by a vague noise, whispers, and murmurs. As the poetic voice itself, the voice of L'Innommable stands in a constant relationship to this silence, and the constant flow of words emerges as a sort of oracle that gives voice to this silence.

But there is no sense of peace to this expression. It is an expression that is both necessary and impossible. And, writes Blanchot, the voice is 'le mouvement qui, à mesure que l'œuvre cherche à s'accomplir, la ramène vers ce point où elle est à l'épreuve de l'impossibilité' (Blanchot 1959: 294). The only origin of this voice of silence is that which makes it impossible for this voice to exist in the first place: it arises out of, against, in relation to its own aporetic impossibility. Released from its own subjectivity, this is a voice that cannot exist, yet must, that cannot continue, yet must, that cannot be silence, yet is.

In order to maintain itself as such a dispossessed, empty expression of nothing, the voice must perform an ongoing implosion of the rational parameters of space, time, and language. What I mean is that this voice, as the speaking of literary silence, must somehow create its own 'milieu' where rational thought never gets the upper hand. Let us consider a longer example:

Je ne me sens pas une bouche, je ne me sens pas une tête, est-ce que je me sens une oreille, répondez franchement, si je me sens une oreille, eh bien non, tant pis, je ne me sens pas une oreille non plus, ce que ça va mal, cherchez bien, je dois sentir quelque chose, oui, je sens quelque chose, je ne sais pas ce que c'est, je ne sais pas ce que je sens, dites-moi ce que je sens, je vous dirai qui je suis, ils me diront qui je suis, je ne comprendrai pas, mais ce sera dit, ils auront dit, qui je suis, et moi je l'aurai entendu, sans oreille je l'aurai entendu, et je l'aurai dit, sans bouche je l'aurai dit, je l'aurai entendu hors de moi, puis aussitôt dans moi, c'est peut-être ça que je sens, qu'il y a un dehors et un dedans et moi au milieu, c'est peut-être ça que je suis, la chose qui divise le monde en deux, d'une part le dehors, de l'autre dedans, ça peut être mince comme une lame, je ne suis ni d'un côté ni de l'autre, je suis au milieu. (Beckett 1953: 160)

This is a voice that cannot identify itself according to the usual points of physical orientation. It feels no physical presence, no body. The only thing this voice can identify itself as is a *milieu* that is neither inside nor outside, but rather irreducible to the dualism. I referred to this passage in the Interlude saying that this voice identifies its own origin in terms of a radical exteriority that is comparable to Blanchot's description of the poetic space as *en nous hors de nous*. In other words, the voice slips away from any dualism. Its impossible origin is indeed this unthinkable *milieu*. And now we can see that this *milieu* is the only possible existence for the voice. From the *milieu* the voice can hear and interact with the movement of raw silence; it can give it its appropriate expression—the expression of nothing, and become what emerges as a sort of poetic speaking, a speaking of silence. If the voice were to be either inside or outside, it would re-enter the domain of dualism and reflection and linearity would get the upper hand. The expression of nothing would be lost. The suggestion is that the voice requires its aporetic, impossible origin in order to uphold the syntax of weakness, and that, in turn, the origin conditions the syntax of weakness. The nameless origin, the *milieu* without exit, emerges as that impossible place that conditions the dynamic of literary silence in the trilogy, and especially in *L'Innommable*, as a non-ending dynamic of repetitive, playful return to itself.

We can now suggest a different understanding of the obligation to continue versus the impossibility to continue that characterizes the voice. There is a certain inexplicable urgency to this aporia that leaves many readers uneasy. But now there is a sense that the existence of the voice, and of literary silence, indeed depends upon remaining in the aporia. The aporia performs a repetitive implosion of rational thought and the voice requires thought to be imploded and suspended in order to maintain itself as the aporetic impossibility it is. From this perspective the voice emerges as strangely fragile. If the voice either stops or continues, it opts for an exit out of the *milieu*, thereby losing the expression of nothing for everyday language. And as everyday language, the voice would be either dead or alive, either meaningful or meaningless, either silent or speaking, and hence no longer *in-between*. In order to remain the expression of no thing, in order to remain the expression of literary silence, the voice depends upon the aporetic dynamic. This is its fragility or its *weakness*. This struggle gives a different beauty to the intense urgency of L'Innommable's voice: 'ils se taisent, un à un, et la voix continue, ce n'est pas la leur, ils n'ont jamais été là, il n'y a jamais eu personne, personne que vous, jamais eu que vous, vous parlant de vous, le souffle manque, c'est presque la fin, le souffle s'arrête, c'est la fin, ce n'en est pas un, je m'entends appeler, ça recommence' (Beckett 1953: 180). Such is the attempt to let the raw silence of nothing speak, to guard the expression of nothing and to make it last. And it is the persistence of this fragile voice, of its constant resistance to give in to everyday language, that emerges through the trilogy.

To protect this poetic voice and give it free rein is also to release literary silence beyond the bounds of the momentary slip that has so far defined it. In both the *Pensées* and the *Rêveries* literary silence emerged as *centres d'illisibilité*. In the trilogy, however, this centre seems to have become a surface. The voice of literary silence has, so to speak, taken over. Through the *milieu* and the aporetic dynamic the weak dynamic is maintained. Linearity and reflection is repeatedly imploded, meaningful language is repeatedly undone, and in the vacuum the poetic voice rambles on.

The dynamic of the voice has now been defined as a repeated dying of the 'I' and a repeated return to its own aporetic, impossible origin. The movement is one that precludes any stable 'outside' because it performs a non-ending, disruptive return to itself. The consequence is, as I have mentioned earlier, that the trilogy does not relate to a stable non-symbolic outside itself. A different sense of the non-symbolic emerges. The trilogy only relates to itself, to its own movements, its own unworking—its own potential to become the non-symbolic. Shedding the 'I', the voice in *L'Innommable* moves towards becoming the repeated expression of the non-symbolic no thing. In order to achieve this, the text is constantly undoing itself in the manners delineated above. In other words, any attempt to refer to the non-symbolic beyond is also imploded, and consequently the non-symbolic expression of nothing arises as the text relates to itself. The non-symbolic is no longer the negative other of language: it is language itself. In the *Pensées* language was about God, in the *Rêveries* language was about the Self. And in the trilogy language is about itself, round and about itself, its own movements, like waves, non-dualistic, non-linear, constant repetition.

CONCLUSION

Beckett's trilogy has revealed a different version of literary silence compared to Rousseau's *Rêveries* and Pascal's *Pensées*. It has given rise to a voice that can be identified as the speaking of literary silence itself. This nameless, or 'I'-less, voice arises, from the *milieu*, as the persistent staging of poetic language, the expression that there is nothing to express. Literary silence arises in the trilogy as an aporetic, impossible, 'empty' speaking that has no end, and that yet must end. It testifies to an increasingly intense occupation of the locus of the impossible, and it also invites the reader to enter into this experience without exit. Reading the voice in *L'Innommable*, one is permitted to read a language that only returns to itself, that refers to no outside, that implodes any attempt to reflect, that invites you, in every instant, to roam its topological wandering from moment to moment, from reversal to reversal, reflection to deflection, in and out of movements that are here and now. To participate in this movement is to experience the repeated implosion of the 'strong', reflective, reified, linear language, to be suspended from its rational, argumentative, and teleological drive. It is a voice that, through its syntax of weakness, releases the silence of poetic language, again, and again, and again—in every now. The voice in the trilogy emerges as an amorphous, porous membrane that, ceasing to behave like everyday language, releases silence and lets it speak to itself. This prepares for the boldest, most compelling, and beautiful description of literary silence: 'les mots sont là, quelque part, sans faire le moindre bruit, je ne sais pas ça non plus, les mots qui tombent, on ne sait pas où, on ne sait pas d'où, gouttes de silence à travers le silence' (Beckett 1953: 159). The words of this voice make no noise; they fall like drops of silence through silence. In this voice silence relates to itself like drops of water through water. And in this unthinkable, unmappable space, silence speaks to itself. This is the voice of literary silence.

CONCLUSION

My discovery was not significant, and yet it was curious, for I had discovered that there simply is no repetition and had verified it by having it repeated in every possible way.

Kierkegaard 1983*a*: 171

To conclude the exploration of literary silence is, in itself, not unproblematic. The question seems inevitable: how can I *conclude* the exploration of literary silence? To conclude is to condense developed ideas, to *repeat*, to provide a final statement. It presents itself as the end of a teleological, argumentative discussion and attempts to gather all components into a whole. Literary silence, however, seems to slip in between, before and after any such conclusion. Literary silence has been approached as a movement that repeatedly jests with the analytical endeavour. It disrupts, destabilizes, and sets afloat those parameters that define the notion of a conclusion. But still, the book must reach its end. It must end, but cannot, it seems, be *concluded*. Is this the emergence of a last aporia? Is this the obligation to end, and the impossibility of concluding? Throughout the book the aporia has emerged as a topos of literary silence. And to read literary silence is to read from within this aporia, and not attempt to transcend it. Now the conclusion presents an aporia. And rather than attempt to overcome it, can we, perhaps, imagine that the aporia delineates a possible 'mode' or 'tone' for an ending? Is to conclude literary silence also to embrace, repeat, and be overcome by the aporetic mode—to revisit and roam, once more, the topos of the aporia?

In order to trace such an aporetic 'tone' for this conclusion, I suggest that we return briefly to Kierkegaard's *Repetition* and the quotation above. Constantin recognizes that repetition is impossible: 'There simply is no repetition'. This is his insignificant, yet *curious* discovery. And it is curious because this impossibility of repetition emerges as the result of a *repeated* manifestation of the impossibility. The impossibility of repetition is itself a repetition. The curiosity seems to be the indication that there is a possible repetition after all. Is this possible repetition the repetition of repetition's impossibility? The prospect is dizzying. And I do not pretend to be able to explain or disentangle this dizziness. Because this dizziness echoes the promise of the implosion, the reading of literary silence, as the movement that moves between text, reader, and silence, that moves the reader through the text, from topos to topos, from flux to reflux. And is it not therefore through such a vertiginous movement that there is a potential tone that can respond to the aporetic dynamic of literary silence? Based on Constantin's observation, the impossibility of concluding can perhaps be repeatedly concluded.

The conclusion, then, emerges as a *repetition* of the impossibility of concluding the exploration of literary silence. And as the movement of repetition, in the Kierkegaardian sense, the conclusion should point both backwards and forwards. And, ideally, it must be a moment of transition and of becoming, of the same that becomes different (see Chapter 3). In other words, the aim of this Conclusion is to introduce or delineate different aporetic nuances that can respond to and repeat the aporetic dynamic of literary silence. One such aporetic dynamic that I have so far not engaged with is the 'historical behaviour' of literary silence. In the Introduction I remarked that literary silence is not primarily a historical dynamic. Based on the exploration that I have now ventured, it is possible perhaps to further understand this statement. Literary silence might not be historical, but the structure of my study suggests some sort of historical development from Pascal to Beckett. Have I both dismissed and implied a historical understanding? What then is the role, if any, of history in this exploration? How is literary silence *not* a historical dynamic?

The exploration of literary silence ends with Beckett's trilogy as the last reading of literary silence according to chronology. However, it could be argued that the book should have started with Beckett and traced literary silence backwards through Rousseau and Pascal. This is because, in many ways, the exploration of literary silence has Beckett as its starting point: it is in the trilogy that literary silence emerges in its most intense, startling, and radical form. It is as a reader of Beckett that I read the *Pensées* and the *Rêveries*. Beckett's texts practise what Gadamer would call my most obvious *prejudice* (Gadamer 1994: 265–85). It is the historical situation that marks, directs, and colours my reading. Gadamer observes that 'historical research is carried along by the historical movement of life itself and cannot be understood teleologically in terms of the object into which it is inquiring' (Gadamer 1994: 284–5). Historical understanding, like all understanding, is also play, and 'Play fulfils its purpose only if the player loses himself in play' (ibid.: 102). That is, the movement of history, as play, is not under the control of the player (see Chapter 2). We are 'played' by history.

This hermeneutic view of history suggests that history is not a developing process that we can relate to from an 'outside'. Rather history is a playful movement that we are always already 'inside'. Our ability to recognize literary silence in Pascal's seventeenth-century apology is necessarily conditioned by the fact that we are readers of writers like Mallarmé, Blanchot, and Beckett. As indicated in the Interlude, the transition into modernism, as exemplified by Mallarmé's poetic practice, witnessed an increasing awareness regarding the dynamics of poetic language, and specifically of its relation to silence. So although my exploration has traced literary silence in earlier texts, it is none the less this later reflexive turn that frames, conditions, and 'plays' the readings. To read literary silence in the *Pensées* does therefore not mean that this marks the beginning of literary silence as a historical phenomenon. Rather, to recognize the prejudice is to question whether literary silence can ever be perceived as an evolving, literary dynamic *in itself*. We discern the possibility that literary silence is a dynamic that arises as my historical context approaches other historical contexts, as my prejudice meets both acceptance and resistance, both echoes and dismissals, in earlier texts. Again it seems that it is a *relationship*, a restless meeting of back-and-forth, that decides my readings and the corresponding historical nature of literary silence.

A historical framework clearly echoes throughout the first, more theoretical part of this book. Here I have delineated what one might call a modern and post-structuralist frame of associations. Notions like play, force, slips, *in-between*, repetition, and aporia provide pointers and indicators that describe the dynamic of literary silence. The underlying, historical *prejudice* is thereby put into play. Literary silence is explored from within this 'vocabulary'. On a more general level, this vocabulary can be summed up as the attempt to map and trace dynamics of the *milieu*, dynamics that move throughout the text, and that can be recognized by their resistance to analytical definition. This indicates a willingness to expand a certain theoretical 'imagination' towards a conceptualization of the 'unheard' of. The notion of literary silence arises in the wake of this expansion exactly as an attempt to describe that which makes it possible for texts to say the unsayable. The indication is that the exploration of literary silence emerges through a historical situation that has witnessed an increasing theoretical focus on that which is ungraspable, that which remains, in many ways, unsayable. The concepts, words, and theoretical language within which I read change or 'open' my reading, and let me address the texts differently. My historical situation has the strange ability to 'renew' and even change the earlier texts because my reading is the result of the relationship between my prejudice, my vocabulary, and the text. This indicates what we might call the 'role' of history in my book. As stated in the Introduction, history is not a teleological progression that can explain the emergence of a phenomenon called literary silence. It is rather a historical moment, a vertical cut, that opens and expands towards the past and the future and permits the possible rediscovery, the possible recollection of the past as it is coloured by my historical *milieu*.

The historical setting of literary silence has given rise to a certain paradoxical dynamic. As mentioned above, a concern has been to venture and invent a vocabulary that stretches towards different textual dynamics. Importantly these often emerge as dynamics that resist linear explanation. This, in turn, permits an alternative view of history. History, one might say, is no longer restricted to the teleological, but has shifted towards the topological. It can be thought of as various different topoi in relation to each other. In other words, the historical context of this book is one that, paradoxically, witnesses a possible move towards a repeated interruption of history as a metaphysical, linear explanation. Literary silence can be viewed as the performance of this repeated interruption and displacement of its own temporal, and perhaps also historical, origin. The implosion, because it is the momentary release from reflection, is also a momentary release from the awareness of a historical setting. In this sense, literary silence can be approached as a radical break with historical awareness. The voice in *L'Innommable* speaks from a place-less, time-less and 'I'-less impossible origin. Its historical setting is reduced to the arrival of the instant, *pan, paf, pan, paf.* No span or duration is conceivable as there is no meta-view available. Similarly the voice of the *monstre incompréhensible* and the voice that pronounces 'je meurs' can exist only in the instant, the collapse of reflection and of linear duration. Literary silence speaks from an origin that has no awareness of its prejudice. This signals a potential limitation of Gadamer's historical hermeneutics as far as the historical exploration of literary silence is concerned. The dynamic of literary silence as the implosion stages a repeated collapse of my reflective ability to relate to my historical context as a historical context. This aspect of literary silence cannot be further understood within Gadamer's hermeneutics. Again there is need for new or different metaphors that can supplement Gadamer's thought.

One possible description of literary silence that might embrace and evoke this paradoxical historical dynamic is the notion of a repeated *apocalypse* that happens in every instant. Derrida, who is of course central in my historical context, discusses the apocalyptic dynamic in the essay *D'un ton apocalyptique adopté naguère en philosophie* (1983). Derrida describes the dynamic of the apocalypse as an end that exactly does not and cannot end: *l'apocalypse sans apocalypse*. He suggests that this apocalyptic dynamic arises as a principle inherent in the literary voice: 'dès qu'on ne sait qui parle ou qui écrit, le texte devient apocalyptique' (Derrida 1983: 77). Further along he asks: 'l'apocalyptique ne serait il pas une condition transcendentale de tout discours . . . de toute marque ou de toute trace?' (ibid.: 77–8). James Berger, in his book *After the End: Representations of Post-Apocalypse*, links this apocalyptic dynamic to the movement of *différance*, claiming that '*Différance* is an ongoing apocalypse, a continual revelatory destruction built into the structure of language' (Berger 1999: 112). In Chapter 2 I recognized Derrida's descriptions of *différance* as a potential springboard for an initial understanding of literary silence. Again a description of *différance* can nuance the understanding of literary silence. Literary silence is the repetitive performance, repetitive release of the apocalyptic aspect of language. It stages an end that cannot end, an ongoing destruction of linear time, and an implosion of its own historical awareness or belonging. As the apocalypse, literary silence is a historical event or practice that also undermines its own relationship to the history it is part of. It is important to underline that the apocalypse, as a figure of literary silence, does not interrupt or implode the historical progression from the *outside*. The apocalypse figures a historical event that stages the momentary end, or at least suspension, of its own history. And literary silence writes itself out of the time that it is part of, not by transcending linear progression, but by introducing the instant to interrupt linear progression from the inside. Historically, literary silence emerges as a repetitive undoing of itself as a historical object, and a repeated staging of itself as an almost self-destructive or self-imploding historical topos, again, and again, and again.

It is possible to trace, in the three texts, a repetition of this apocalyptic dynamic. The texts, in different manners, stage linearity only to undermine it. They all practise a repeated disruption or reversal of a built-in narrative move towards an end. The *Pensées* present themselves as fragments that interrupt, or at least render problematic, any sense of progress towards a final resolution. Whatever the intention behind the various *liasses*, the text confronts us with scattered fragments. The *Rêveries*, as mentioned in Chapter 5, presents the walks in an order that openly goes against the original order in which they took place. Furthermore, it is relevant that Rousseau's description of the original state, the state of nature, is not only pre-linguistic, but also non-historical. It does not fit into any historical time-line, but is an invented original state. The reverie is perhaps the state which, more than any other, approaches or reproduces this original state. And the trilogy is, as shown in Chapter 6, the repeated collapse and implosion of any linear time. It moves towards a timeless experience of time that is always only in the moment. So the texts in which I have explored literary silence are in turn topoi of a certain playful, yet forceful, undoing of linear time. The temporality of these texts is congruent with a view of time that permits a topological view of history, which in turn permits a conceptualization of literary silence as apocalyptic implosions of the awareness of linear time.

It is now possible to indicate an understanding, or at least an impossible understanding, of how literary silence behaves as a historical dynamic. To read literary silence is to be involved in a relationship to one's own historical context that simultaneously suspends any belonging to this context. Literary silence invites an alternative experience of history as a series of topoi through which it is possible to move. Staging itself as a historical dynamic, it immediately dissolves itself as a fixed historical point. A new aporia emerges. Gadamer's historical hermeneutics have revealed how literary silence emerges as a historically determined dynamic. Yet, as an imploding, apocalyptic dynamic, it repeatedly collapses any attempt to think of it as a historically determined dynamic. And with the emergence of this aporia, we are, it seems, indirectly repeating the impossibility of ending, and the parallel obligation to end. The historical perspective, by producing and revealing yet another aporia, responds to literary silence, repeats its possible impossibility, speaks, somehow, from inside the obligation to end and the impossibility of concluding. To end the exploration of literary silence from the historical perspective is therefore to move along with the aporia that emerged through the conclusion of literary silence. This, I suggest, provides the best possible mode for concluding. Resisting the temptation to summarize, I have attempted rather to adopt a perspective that could both repeat the aporetic dizziness and add different associations, different nuances to the aporetic mode of literary silence, and thereby, paradoxically, also provide an overall appreciation of the dynamic.

And again literary silence has revealed itself as an invitation into the movements of the aporia. Whether we are reading, describing, or concluding literary silence, we are involved in this movement which escapes and challenges our analytical apparatus. Accepting the invitation, we are summoned to abandon our ability to reflect while reflecting, to sacrifice our ability to read while reading. Or we are invited to reflect in the limits of reflection, and to read in the limits of the readable. Through reading we can relate to states of consciousness that challenge expression because they escape reflection. We can listen to voices that could not speak in everyday language, the voices of the *monstre incompréhensible*, of the repeated *je meurs*, of the unnameable voice. And it is as such that the texts emerge as witnesses of the unsayable, and that we become readers of this strange silence that stages what we cannot think. And reading this silence we are also exploring the possibility that we might be *moved* and changed in manners irreducible to rhetoric, irreducible even to conscious effort, irreducible to explicative dialogue. This, it seems, emerges as the risk and gain of reading literary silence. If we want to explore further how and if the reading of literature, as an immediate, silent, and solitary experience of art, can change us, it is in these radical aporias, these unresolved, forceful, and weak dynamics, these *milieux*, and these topoi that we must search, and re-search, for everything that is no thing.

BIBLIOGRAPHY

ACHESON, JAMES 1997. *Samuel Beckett's Artistic Theory and Practice: Criticism, Drama and early Fiction*. Basingstoke: Macmillan.

ALEXANDRESCU, VLAD 1997. *Le Paradoxe chez Blaise Pascal*. Berne, Frankfurt/M, and New York: Peter Lang.

Anonymous 1978. *The Cloud of Unknowing and Other Works*. Harmondsworth: Penguin Books.

ARENDT, HANNAH 1963. *On Revolution*. London: Faber and Faber.

AUGUSTIN, A. 1991. *Confessions*, trans. and notes by Henry Chadwick. Oxford: Oxford University Press.

BACHELARD, GASTON 1960. *La Poétique de la rêverie*. Paris: PUF.

BALDWIN, HÉLÈNE L. 1981. *Samuel Beckett's Real Silence*. London and University Park: Pennsylvania State University Press.

BARCOS, MARTIN DE 1956. *Correspondance de Martin de Barcos*, ed. by Lucien Goldmann. Paris: PUF.

BATAILLE, GEORGES 1943/1954. *L'Expérience intérieure*. Paris: Éditions Gallimard.

—— 1973. *Théorie de la religion*, Collection Idées, 306, Philosophie. Paris: Éditions Gallimard.

BAUDELAIRE, CHARLES 1972/1998. *Le Spleen de Paris*. Paris: Librairie Générale Française.

BEAUJOUR, MICHEL 1980. *Miroirs d'encre*. Paris: Éditions du Seuil.

BECKETT, SAMUEL 1951a. *Molloy*. Paris: Éditions de Minuit.

—— 1951b. *Malone meurt*. Paris: Éditions de Minuit.

—— 1953. *L'Innommable*. Paris: Éditions de Minuit.

—— 1965. *Proust and 'Three Dialogues' (with Georges Duthuit)*. London: John Calder.

BEGAM, RICHARD 1996. *Samuel Beckett and the End of Modernity*. Stanford, CA: Stanford University Press.

BERGER, JAMES 1999. *After the End: Representations of Post-Apocalypse*. Minneapolis and London: University of Minnesota Press.

BERNAL, OLGA 1969. *Langage et fiction dans le roman de Beckett*. Paris: Éditions Gallimard.

BLANCHOT, MAURICE 1949. *La Part du feu*. Paris: Éditions Gallimard.

—— 1955. *L'Espace littéraire*. Paris: Éditions Gallimard.

—— 1959. *Le Livre à venir*. Paris: Éditions Gallimard.

BLONDEL, ÉRIC 1997. 'La Vérité et le moi dans *Les Rêveries du promeneur solitaire*', in J.-J. Rousseau, *Les Rêveries du promeneur solitaire*, ed. by Jean Louis Tritter. Paris: Ellipses, 20–6.

BOLD, ALAN ed. 1984. *Harold Pinter: You never Heard such Silence*. London: Vision.

BORD, ANDRÉ 1987. *Pascal et Jean de la Croix*. Paris: Beauchesne.

Bowie, Andrew 1997. *From Romanticism to Critical Theory*. London and New York: Routledge.

Brunel, Pierre, Bellenger, Yvonne, Couty, Daniel, Sellier, Philippe, Truffet, Michel, and Gourdeau, Jean-Pierre eds. 1972. *Histoire de la littérature française du moyen âge au XVIIIe siècle* (vol. 1), *Histoire de la littérature française, XIXe et XXe siècles* (vol. 2). Paris: Bordas.

Butler, Lance St John 1964. *Samuel Beckett and the Meaning of Being*. London: Macmillan.

Cage, John 1999. *Silence, Lectures and Writings*. London: Marion Boyars.

Caputo, John D. 1989. 'Mysticism and Transgression: Derrida and Meister Eckhart', in *Derrida and Deconstruction*, ed. by Hugh Silverman. London and New York: Routledge: 24–39.

Carnero-Gonzáles, José 1993. 'Silence in Beckett: *The Unnamable*—A Hinge Work'. *Samuel Beckett Today/Aujourd'hui: An annual bilingual review/Revue annuelle bilingue*, 2: 205–11.

Chambers, Ross 1965. 'Beckett's Brinkmanship', in *Samuel Beckett*, ed. by Martin Esslin. Englewood Cliffs, NJ: Prentice-Hall: 152–68.

—— 1971. 'Déstruction des catégories du temps', in *Les Critiques de notre temps et Beckett*, ed. by Dominique Nores. Paris: Éditions Garnier Frères: 91–106.

Chomsky, Noam 1966. *Cartesian Linguistics: A Chapter in the History of Rationalist Thought*. New York: Harper and Row.

Coe, Richard 1964. *Beckett*. London and Edinburgh: Oliver & Boyd.

Cohn, Ruby 1973. *Back to Beckett*. Princeton: Princeton University Press.

Compagnon, Antoine 1998. *Le Démon de la théorie: littérature et sens commun*. Paris: Éditions du Seuil.

Congar, Y. 1963. 'La Mystique rhénane', in *La Mystique rhénane, colloque de Strasbourg du 16–19. mai 1961*. Paris: PUF: 21.

Connor, Steven 1988. *Samuel Beckett: Repetition, Theory and Text*. Oxford: Basil Blackwell.

Courcelles, Dominique 1994. *Le Sang de Port-Royal*. Paris: Éditions de l'Herne.

Coz, Michel, and Jacob, François 1997. 'Introduction', in *Rêveries sans fin*, ed. by Michel Coz and François Jacob. Orléans: Paradigme: 29–47.

Critchley, Simon 1997. *Very Little . . . Almost Nothing: Death, Philosophy, Literature*. London and New York: Routledge.

Culler, Jonathan 2000. 'The Literary in Theory', in *What's Left of Theory? New Work on the Politcs of Literary Theory*, ed. by Judith Butler, John Guillory, and Kendall Thomas. London and New York: Routledge: 273–91.

Daniels, May 1953. *The French Drama of the Unspoken*, Edinburgh University Publications, Language and Literature, 3. Edinburgh: Edinburgh University Press.

Dauenhauer, Bernard P. 1980. *Silence: The Phenomenon and its Ontological Significance*. Bloomington: Indiana University Press.

DE MAN, PAUL 1979a. 'Autobiograhy as De-facement'. *Modern Language Notes*, 94: 919–30.

—— 1979b. *Allegories of Reading*. New Haven: Yale University Press.

DEARLOVE, J. E. 1982. *Accommodating the Chaos: Samuel Beckett's Nonrelational Art*. Durham, NC: Duke University Press.

DELEUZE, GILLES 1992. 'L'Épuisé', in Samuel Beckett, *Quad, et Trio de fantôme, . . . que nuages . . . , Nacht und Träume*, trans. from English by Edith Fournier. Paris: Éditions de Minuit.

—— and GUATTARI, FÉLIX 1980. *Capitalisme et schizophrénie*, vol. 2: *Mille plateaux*. Paris: Éditions de Minuit.

DERRIDA, JACQUES 1967a. 'Force et signification', in *L'Écriture et la différence*. Paris: Éditions du Seuil.

—— 1967b. *De la grammatologie*. Paris: Éditions de Minuit.

—— 1972. 'La Différance', in *Marges de la philosophie*. Paris: Éditions de Minuit: 1–29.

—— 1974. 'Mallarmé', in *Tableau de la littérature de Mme de Staël à Rimbaud*. Paris: Éditions Gallimard: 368–79.

—— 1983. *D'un ton apocalyptique adopté naguère en philosophie*. Paris: Éditions Galilée.

—— 1992. ' "This Strange Institution Called Literature": An Interview with Jacques Derrida', in *Acts of Literature*, ed. by D. Attridge. London and New York: Routledge.

—— 1999. *Donner la mort*. Paris: Éditions Galilée.

DESCARTES, RENÉ 1969. *Œuvres de Descartes, correspondance I*, ed. by Charles Adam and Paul Tannery. Paris: Librairie Philosophique J. Vrin.

DOUBROVSKY, SERGE 1988. *Autobiographiques: de Corneille à Sartre*. Paris: PUF.

DUCROT, OSWALD 1972. *Dire et ne pas dire: principes de sémantique linguistique*. Paris: Hermann.

ERNST, POL 1996. *Les 'Pensées' de Pascal: géologie et stratigraphie*. Paris and Oxford: Universitas and the Voltaire Foundation.

ESSLIN, MARTIN 1980. *The Theatre of the Absurd*, 3rd edn. Harmondsworth and London: Penguin Books, Eyre and Spottiswoode.

—— 1993. 'What Beckett Teaches Me: His Minimalist Approach to Ethics'. *Samuel Beckett Today/Aujourd'hui: An annual bilingual review/Revue annuelle bilingue*, 2: 13–20.

FIUMARA, GEMMA 1990. *The Other Side of Language: A Philosophy of Listening*. London and New York: Routledge.

FORCE, PIERRE 1988. 'Itus et reditus, de l'impossible édition d'un zigzag'. *Romantic Review*, 79/3: 412–21.

—— 1989. *Le Problème herméneutique chez Pascal*. Paris: Lib. Philosophique J. Vrin.

FOUCAULT, MICHEL, 1966a. 'La Pensée du dehors'. *Critique*, 229/22, June: 523–46.

—— 1966*b*. *Les Mots et les choses: une archéologie des sciences humaines.* Paris: Éditions Gallimard.

GADAMER, HANS GEORG 1976. *Philosophical Hermeneutics*, trans. and ed. by David E. Linge. London, Berkeley, and Los Angeles: University of California Press.

—— 1986. *The Relevance of the Beautiful and Other Essays*, trans. by Nicholas Walker, ed. by Robert Bernasconi. Cambridge: Cambridge University Press.

—— 1993. *Reason in the Age of Science*, trans. by Frederick G. Lawrence, Contemporary German Social Thought, 2. Cambridge, MA.: MIT Press.

—— 1994. *Truth and Method*, trans. and revised by Joel Weinsheimer and Donald G. Marshall, 2nd edn. New York: Continuum.

GENETTI, STEFANO 1992. *Les Figures du temps dans l'œuvre de Samuel Beckett*, Tesi della Facoltà di lingue e letterature straniere (Università degli Studi di Verona), 1. Fasano: Schena Editore.

GIBSON, ANDREW 1996. *Towards a Postmodern Theory of Narrative.* Edinburgh: Edinburgh University Press.

GILBERT, SANDRA, and GUBAR, SUSAN 1980. *The Madwoman in the Attic: 19th Century Literature.* New Haven: Yale University Press.

GOLDBERG, MYRNA 1990. 'Different Horrors, Same Hell: Women Remembering the Holocaust', in *Thinking the Unthinkable: Meanings of the Holocaust*, ed. by Roger S. Gottlieb. New York: Paulist Press: 150–66.

GOLDMANN, LUCIEN 1956. 'Introduction' to *Correspondance de Martin de Barcos*, ed. by Lucien Goldmann. Paris: PUF.

—— 1959. *Le Dieu caché: étude sur la vision tragique dans les 'Pensées' de Pascal et dans le théâtre de Racine.* Paris: Éditions Gallimard.

GOTTLIEB, ROGER S. ed. 1990. *Thinking the Unthinkable: Meanings of the Holocaust.* New York: Paulist Press.

GOUHIER, HENRI 1956. 'Le Mémorial est-il un texte mystique?' in *Blaise Pascal, l'homme et l'œuvre*, Cahiers de Royamont, Philosophie, 1. Paris: Éditions de Minuit.

—— 1966. *Blaise Pascal, commentaires.* Paris: Librairie Philosophique J. Vrin.

—— 1970. *Les Méditations métaphysiques de Jean-Jacques Rousseau.* Paris: Librairie Philosophique J. Vrin.

GRANT, PATRICK ed. 1985. *A Dazzling Darkness: An Anthology of Western Mysticism.* London: Collins, Fount Paperbacks.

GROSCLAUDE, PIERRE 1961. 'Le Moi, l'instant présent et le sentiment de l'existence chez Jean-Jacques Rousseau'. *Europe*, 391/392: 52–6.

GROSRICHARD, ALAIN 1997. 'Où suis-je? Que suis-je?', in *Rêveries sans fin*, ed. by Michel Coz and François Jacob. Orléans: Paradigme: 29–47.

GUSDORF, GEORGES 1991*a*. *Auto-bio-graphie.* Paris: Éditions Odile Jacob.

—— 1991*b*. *Les Écritures du moi.* Paris: Éditions Odile Jacob.

HAMMOND, NICHOLAS 1994. *Playing with Truth: Language and the Human Condition in Pascal's 'Pensées'.* Oxford: Clarendon Press.

HAPPOLD, F .C. ed. 1970. *Mysticism: A Study and an Anthology*. Harmondsworth: Penguin Books.

HARTLE, ANN 1983. *The Modern Self in Rousseau's Confessions: A Reply to St. Augustine*. Notre Dame, IN: University Press of Notre Dame.

HEDGES, ELAINE, and FISHER FISHKIN, SHELLEY eds. 1994. *Listening to Silences: New Essays in Feminist Criticism*. Oxford: Oxford University Press.

HEGEL, G. W. F. 1979. *Phenomenology of Spirit*, trans. by A.V. Miller, analysis and foreword by J. N. Findlay. Oxford: Oxford University Press.

HEIDEGGER, MARTIN 1993. 'The Origin of the Work of Art', *Basic Writings from 'Being and Time' (1927) to 'The Task of Thinking' (1964)*, ed. by David Farell Krell, rev. and expanded edn. London and New York: Routledge: 143–206.

HEINEMANN, MARLENE E. 1986. *Gender and Destiny: Women Writers and the Holocaust*. New York: Greenwood Press.

HESLA, DAVID 1971. *The Shape of Chaos*. Minneapolis: University of Minnesota Press.

HILL, LESLIE 1990. *Beckett's Fiction: In Different Words*. Cambridge: Cambridge University Press.

HIRSCH, E. D. 1967. *Validity in Interpretation*. New Haven: Yale University Press.

——1976. *The Aims of Interpretation*. Chicago: University of Chicago Press.

IDT, GENEVIÈVE, JULIEN, ANNE-YVONNE, MAUREL, ANNE, and ROBIER, MARTINE eds. 1996. *L'Écriture de soi: un thème, trois œuvres*. Paris: Belin.

JAKOBSON, ROMAN 1977. 'Fragments de "la nouvelle poésie russe" ', *Huit questions de poétique*, ed. by Tzvetan Todorov. Paris: Éditions du Seuil: 11–29.

JANKÉLÉVITCH, VLADIMIR 1961. *La Musique et l'ineffable*. Paris: Librairie Armand Colin.

KANE, LESLIE 1984. *The Language of Silence: On the Unspoken and the Unspeakable in Modern Drama*. Rutherford, NJ: Fairleigh Dickinson University Press, Associated University Press.

KENNER, HUGH 1961. *Samuel Beckett: A Critical Study*. New York: Grove Press.

KIERKEGAARD, SØREN 1983a. *Repetition*, ed. and trans. by Howard and Edna Hong, Kierkegaard's Writings, 6. Princeton: Princeton University Press.

——1983b. *Fear and Trembling*, ed. and trans. by Howard and Edna Hong, Kierkegaard's Writings, 6. Princeton, NJ: Princeton University Press.

——1997. *Gentagelsen*. (Danish original version of *Repetition*). Copenhagen: Det Lille Forlag.

KINGSLAND, WILLIAM ed. 1927. *An Anthology of Mysticism and Mystical Philosophy*. London: Methuen.

KOCH, EREC 1997. *Pascal and Rhetoric: Figural and Persuasive Language in the Scientific Treatises, the 'Provinicales' and the 'Pensées'*. Charlottesville, VA: Rockwood Press.

KÖGLER, HANS HERBERT 1996. *The Power of Dialogue: Critical Hermeneutics after Gadamer and Foucault*, trans. by Paul Hendrickson. Cambridge, MA: MIT Press.

KOONZ, CLAUDIA 1987. *Mothers in the Fatherland: Women, the Family and Nazi Politics*. New York: St. Martin's Press.

LACAN, JACQUES 1966. *Écrits I*. Paris: Éditions du Seuil.

LACOUE-LABARTHE, PHILLIPE, and NANCY, JEAN-LUC 1978. *L'Absolu littéraire*. Paris: Éditions du Seuil.

LAGARDE, FRANÇOIS 1993. 'Le Différement de Pascal'. *Papers on French Seventeenth Century Literature*, 20/38: 181–92.

LAPORTE, JEAN 1950. *Le Cœur et la raison selon Pascal*, Bibliothèque philosophique (Elzévir), 1. Paris: Elzévir.

LAURENCE, PATRICIA 1994. 'Women's Silence as Ritual of Truth: A Study of Literary Expressions in Austen, Brontë, and Wolf', in *Listening to Silences: New Essays in Feminist Criticism*, ed. by Elaine Hedges and Shelley Fisher Fishkin. Oxford: Oxford University Press: 156–67.

LE GUERN, MICHEL 2000. 'Introduction' to B. Pascal, *Pensées*, Bibliothèque de la Pléiade, 1, ed. by Michel Le Guern. Paris: Éditions Gallimard.

LEFKOWITZ, DEBORAH 1999. 'On Silence and Other Disruptions', in *Feminism and Documentary*, ed. by Diane Waldman and Janet Walker. London and Minneapolis: University of Minnesota Press: 244–66.

LEJEUNE, PHILIPPE 1975. *Le Pacte autobiographique*. Paris: Éditions du Seuil.

LINDEN, R. RUTH 1993. *Making Stories, Making Selves: Feminist Reflections on the Holocaust*. Columbus: Ohio State University Press.

MACHEREY, PIERRE 1966. *Pour une théorie de la production littéraire*. Paris: Librairie François Maspero.

MADISON, GARY B. 1991. 'Beyond Seriousness and Frivolity: A Gadamerian Response to Deconstruction', in *Gadamer and Hermeneutics*, ed. by Hugh J. Silverman. London and New York: Routledge: 119–35.

MALLARMÉ, STÉPHANE 1945. *Œuvres complètes*, Bibliothèque de la Pléiade, ed. by H. Mondor and G. Jean-Aubry. Paris: Éditions Gallimard.

——1990. *Divagations*, commented by Robert Greer Cohn. Berne, Frankfurt/M, and New York: Peter Lang.

——1995. *Correspondance: lettres sur la poésie*. Paris: Éditions Gallimard.

MARIN, LOUIS 1975. ' "Pascal": Text, Author, Discourse . . .'. *Yale French Studies*, 52: 129–51.

——1976. 'La Critique de la représentation classique: la traduction de la Bible à Port-Royal', in *Pascal et Port-Royal*, ed. by Alain Cantillon and Daniel Arasse. Paris: PUF.

——1990. 'Voix et énonciation mystique: sur deux textes d'Augustin et de Pascal'. *La Voix au XVIIe siècle* (special issue), ed. by Patrick Dandrey, Littératures Classiques, 12, January: 166–83.

MARINER, FRANK 1993. 'The Order of Disorder: The Problem of the Fragment in Pascal's *Pensées*'. *Papers on French Seventeenth Century Literature*, 20/38: 171–81.

MARTINEAU, EMMANUEL 1992. *Discours sur la religion et sur quelques autres sujets qui ont été trouvés après sa mort parmi ses papiers*, edition of Pascal's *Pensées*. Paris: Fayard-A. Colin.

MAY, GEORGES 1979. *L'Autobiographie*. Paris: PUF.

MELBERG, ARNE 1995. *Theories of Mimesis*. Cambridge: Cambridge University Press.

MELZER, SARA 1986. *Discourses of the Fall: A Study of Pascal's 'Pensées'*. London, Berkeley, and Los Angeles: University of California Press.

MESCHONNIC, HENRI 1985. 'Mallarmé au-delà du silence', in Stéphane Mallarmé, *Écrits sur le livre (choix de textes)*, ed. by Henri Meschonnic. Paris: Éditions de l'Éclat.

MESNARD, JEAN 1977–9. 'Martin de Barcos et les disputes internes de Port-Royal'. *Chroniques de Port-Royal*, 26–8: 73–94.

—— 1993. *Les Pensées de Pascal*. Paris: CDU/SEDES.

MICHON, HÉLÈNE 1992. 'Deus Absconditus'. *XVIIe siècle*, 177, Oct.–Dec.: 495–506.

—— 1996. *L'Ordre du cœur: philosophie, théologie et mystique dans les 'Pensées' de Pascal*. Paris: Honoré Champion.

MIEL, JAN 1969a. *Pascal and Theology*. Baltimore: Johns Hopkins University Press.

—— 1969b. 'Pascal, Port-Royal and Cartesian Linguistics'. *Journal of the History of Ideas*, 30: 261–71.

MOORJANI, ANGELA 1990. 'Beckett's Devious Deictics', in *Rethinking Beckett: A Collection of Critical Essays*, ed. by Lance St John Butler and Robert Davis. London: Macmillan: 20–30.

MORRISSEY, ROBERT J. 1984. *La Rêverie jusqu'à Rousseau: recherches sur un topos littéraire*, Lexington, KY: French Forum Publishers.

NADEAU, MAURICE 1971. 'De la parole au silence', in *Les Critiques de notre temps et Beckett*, ed. by Dominique Nores. Paris: Éditions Garnier Frères: 152–61.

NEHER, ANDRÉ 1970. *L'Exil de la parole: du silence biblique au silence d'Auschwitz*. Paris: Éditions du Seuil.

NÉTILLARD, CLAIRE 1997. 'Rousseau et le langage', in *Les Rêveries du promeneur solitaire*, ed. by Jean Louis Tritter. Paris: Ellipses: 35–48.

NIETZSCHE, FRIEDRICH 1967. *The Will to Power*, trans. by Walter Kaufmann and R. J. Hollingdale, ed. by Walter Kaufmann. New York: Random House.

NORMAN, BUFORD 1988. *Portraits of Thought, Knowledge, Methods and Styles in Pascal*. Columbus: Ohio State University Press.

PARAIN, BRICE 1969. *Petite Métaphysique de la parole*. Paris: Éditions Gallimard.

PARISH, RICHARD 1986. 'Mais qui parle? Voice and Persona in the *Pensées*'. *17th Century French Studies*, 8: 23–40.

PASCAL, BLAISE 1991. *Pensées*, ed. by Philippe Sellier. Paris: Bordas.

PICARD, MAX 1952. *The World of Silence*. Chicago: Gateway Books.

PINGAU, BERNARD 1971. 'Le Langage iréel', in *Les Critiques de notre temps et Beckett*, ed. by Dominique Nores. Paris: Éditions Garnier Frères: 161–4.

POULET, GEORGES 1978. 'Le Sentiment de l'existence chez Rousseau et ses prédécesseurs'. *Studi Franscesi*, 22/64–6: 36–50.

PROUST, MARCEL 1947. *Pastiches et mélanges*. Paris: Éditions Gallimard.

RANCIÈRE, JACQUES 1998. *La Parole muette: essai sur les contradictions de la littérature*. Paris: Hachette.

RASSAM, JOSEPH 1980. *Le Silence comme introduction à la métaphysique*. Toulouse: Association des publications de l'Universié de Toulouse-le-Mirail.

RAYMOND, MARCEL 1962. *Jean-Jacques Rousseau: la quête de soi et la rêverie*. Paris: Librairie José Corti.

RICATTE, ROBERT 1960. *Réflexions sur les 'Rêveries'*. Paris: Librairie José Corti.

RICH, ADRIENNE 1979. *On Lies, Secrets, and Silence*. New York: W. W. Norton and Company.

RINGELHEIM, JOAN 1990. 'Thoughts about Women and the Holocaust', in *Thinking the Unthinkable: Meanings of the Holocaust*, ed. by Roger S. Gottlieb. New York: Paulist Press: 141–9.

RITTNER, CAROL, and ROTH, JOHN K. eds. 1993. *Different Voices: Women and the Holocaust*. New York: Paragon House.

RIVKIN, JULIE, and RYAN, MICHAEL 1998. 'Introduction: The Class of 1968—Post-Structuralism *par lui-même*', in *Literary Theory: An Anthology*, ed. by Julie Rivkin and Michael Ryan. Oxford: Blackwell Publishers: 333–61.

ROBINSON, MICHAEL 1969. *The Long Sonata of the Dead: A Study of Samuel Beckett*. London: Rupert Hart-Davis.

RODDIER, HENRI 1960. 'Introduction' to J.-J. Rousseau, *Rêveries du promeneur solitaire*. Paris: Classiques Garnier.

RODIER, JACQUES 1981. *L'Ordre du cœur*. Paris: Librairie Philosophique J. Vrin.

ROSSO, STEFANO 1990. 'Postmodern Italy', in *Exploring Postmodernism*, ed. by Matei Calinescu and Douwe Fokkema, Utrecht Publications in General and Comparative Literature, 23. Amsterdam and Philadelphia: John Benjamins Publishing Company: 79–92.

ROUSSEAU, JEAN-JACQUES 1959a. *Les Rêveries du promeneur solitaire*, Bibliothèque de la Pléiade, I, ed. by Bernard Gagnebin and Marcel Raymond. Paris: Éditions Gallimard.

—— 1959b. *Les Confessions*, Bibliothèque de la Pléiade, I, ed. by Bernard Gagnebin and Marcel Raymond. Paris: Éditions Gallimard.

—— 1964. *Discours sur les sciences et les arts*, Bibliothèque de la Pléiade, III, ed. by Bernard Gagnebin and Marcel Raymond. Paris: Éditions Gallimard.

ROUSSET, JEAN 1962. *Forme et signification: essais sur les structures littéraires de Corneille à Claudel*. Paris: Corti.

RUSSIER, JEANNE 1949. *La Foi selon Pascal*. Paris: PUF.

RYAN, THOMAS E. 1988. *Hölderlin's Silence*, Studies in Modern German Literature, 17. Berne, Frankfurt/M, and New York: Peter Lang.

RYKNER, ARNAUD 1996. *L'Envers du théâtre*. Paris: Librairie José Corti.

ST JOHN OF THE CROSS 1974. *Spiritual Sentences and Maxims*, in *The Complete Works of St John of the Cross*. Wheathampstead: Anthony and Clarke Books: 211–40.

SCHIBBYE, A. L. 1993. 'The Role of "Recognition" in the Resolution of a Specific Interpersonal Dilemma'. *Journal of Phenomenological Psychology*, 24/2: 175–89.

SCHLANT, ERNESTINE 1999. *The Language of Silence: West German Literature and the Holocaust*. London and New York: Routledge.

SELLIER, PHILIPPE 1991. 'Introduction' to B. Pascal, *Pensées*, ed. by Philippe Sellier. Paris: Bordas.

—— 1995. *Pascal et Saint Augustin*. Paris: Albin Michel.

SERRES, MICHEL 1968. *Le Système de Leibniz et ses modèles mathématiques*. Paris: PUF.

SIBELMAN, SIMON P. 1995. *Silence in the Novels of Elie Wiesel*. New York: St Martin's Press.

SMITH, BRENDAN 1998. *The Silence of Divine Love*. London: Darton, Longman, and Todd.

SONTAG, SUSAN 1983. 'The Aesthetics of Silence', in *A Susan Sontag Reader*. Harmondsworth: Penguin Books: 181–204.

STAROBINSKI, JEAN 1970. *L'Œil vivant II: la relation critique*. Paris: Éditions Gallimard.

—— 1971. *Jean-Jacques Rousseau: la transparence et l'obstacle*. Paris: Éditions Gallimard.

STEINER, GEORGE 1985. *Language and Silence: Essays 1958–1966*. London and Boston: Faber and Faber.

TAYLOR, CHARLES 1989. *Sources of the Self: The Making of Modern Identity*. Cambridge: Cambridge University Press.

TERESA OF AVILA 1974. *Interior Castle*, trans. by E. Allison Peers. London: Sheed and Ward.

TOPLISS, PATRICIA 1966. *The Rhetoric of Pascal: A Study of his Art of Persuasion in the 'Provinciales' and the 'Pensées'*. Leicester: Leicester University Press.

TREZISE, THOMAS 1990. *Into the Breach: Samuel Beckett and the Ends of Literature*. Princeton: Princeton University Press.

TRIELOFF, BARBARA 1990. ' "Babel of Silence": Beckett's Post-Trilogy Prose Articulated', in *Rethinking Beckett: A Collection of Critical Essays*, ed. by Lance St John Butler and Robert Davis. London: Macmillan: 89–104.

TRIPET, ARNAUD 1979. *La Rêverie littéraire: essai sur Rousseau*. Geneva: Librairie Droz.

UHLMANN, ANTHONY 1999. *Beckett and Poststructuralism*. Cambridge: Cambridge University Press.

VANCE, EUGÈNE 1973. 'Le Moi comme langage: saint Augustin et l'autobiographie'. *Poétique* 14: 163–77.

VAN DEN HEUVEL, PIERRE 1985. *Parole, mot, silence*. Paris: Librairie José Corti.

VATTIMO, GIANNI 1988. *The End of Modernity: Nihilism and Hermeneutics in Post-Modern Culture*, trans. by Jon R. Snyder. Cambridge: Polity Press.

—— 1993. *The Adventure of Difference: Philosophy after Nietzsche and Heidegger*, trans. by Cyprian Blamires and Thomas Harrison. Cambridge: Polity Press.

—— 1997. *Beyond Interpretation: The Meaning of Hermeneutics for Philosophy*, trans. by David Webb. Cambridge: Polity Press.

—— and ROVATTI, PIER ALDO eds. 1983. *Il pensiero debole*. Milan: Garzanti.

VOISINE, JACQUES 1964. 'Introduction' to J.-J. Rousseau, *Rêveries du promeneur solitaire*. Paris: Garnier- Flammarion.

WETSEL, DAVID 1981. *L'Écriture et le reste*. Columbus: Ohio State University Press.

—— 1993. 'Pascal's *Pensées* and Recent Critical Theory: Illumination or Deformation of the Text?' *Papers on French Seventeenth Century Literature*, 20/38: 117–22.

WINKEL HOLM, ISAK 1998. *Tanken i billedet, Søren Kierkegaard's poetik*. Copenhagen: Gyldendal.

WOLOSKY, SHIRA 1995. *Language Mysticism: The Negative Way of Language in Eliot, Beckett and Celan*. Stanford, CA : Stanford University Press.

WULFSBERG, MARIUS 2002. *Det litterære rommet, En studie i Stéphane Mallarmés og Maurice Blanchots forfatterskap*. Oslo: Unipub.

INDEX